George B. Hill

A NEST

ON LIFANDOY

For Cousin Richard

George B. Hill

Acknowledgement and cover images:

The image, included in the cover illustration, of (probably) a Boeing C-17 Globemaster III USAF transport aircraft was derived from a photograph kindly made available on Flickr under Creative Commons (attribution license) by ©Moon Photography by Mel.

The background scene is of Beinn Sgùrabhal from the dunes of Tràigh Eais on the island of Barra in the Scottish Outer Hebrides.

A Nest on Lifandoy

Tim Corn, a nature warden on the beautiful little island of Lifandoy, is at war! His ideological foe, a ruthless farmer, is his devious Uncle Wilfred.

When chance places the island's wildlife under his sole care, Tim and his girlfriend Jessica struggle to find and protect the nest of a pair of rare birds. But unknown to Timothy, Uncle Wilfred is himself searching, with the aid of US Air Force agents, for a very different sort of 'NEST'!

In this comic story of wildlife and conscience, Tim also has to deal with Jessica's scheming young sisters Alice and Rosalind and other colourful island character as well as criminal egg-collectors and an invasion of rare bird 'twitchers'.

Uncle Wilfred is known throughout the island as a helpful but dangerous eccentric and is also, to Tim's irritation, a determined Christian. But Tim finds in both his uncle and in Jessica, who is an atheist like Tim himself, depths he did not expect. What deep memory has Jessica buried? And could Uncle Wilfred himself ever change? Can Tim's problems ever be untangled? What crazy or violent result might ensue? And where *are* those rare birds nesting, after all?

The author

George B. Hill is a retired research chemist. He has three grown-up children and lives with his wife in Sandbach, Cheshire, UK, where they attend a Baptist church. He began writing more seriously in 2012 and writes Christian fiction and on science and faith.

Books self-published by George B. Hill

(on Kindle, other e-books and in print):

Legend Sci-fi:
The Song of Rockall   (Kindle, 2013; others & print, 2014)

Lifandoy stories:
A Nest On Lifandoy   (Kindle, 2013; others & print, 2014)
An Orchid On Lifandoy   (Kindle, 2013; others & print, 2014)
Falcons Over Lifandoy   (Kindle, 2013; others & print, 2014)
Then...
Night Birds Off Lifandoy   (in writing)

See the author's website at www.hillintheway.co.uk for more details including his other writing.

There is one story for each… this one is for Pete

Table of Contents

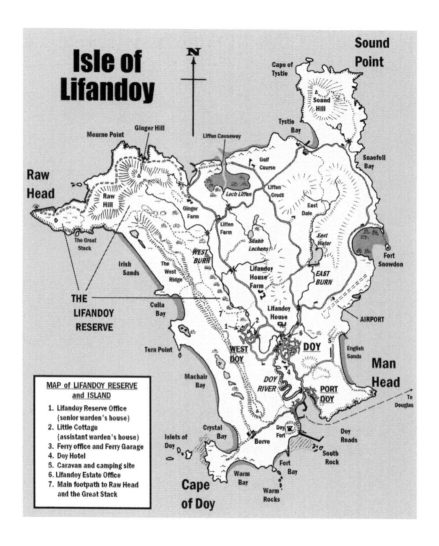

Map: A colour version of the above map appears on the back cover.
A large printable colour copy may be downloaded free from the '*My Maps*'
page of the author's '*My Writing*' website, at www.hillintheway.co.uk

*Lifandoy lies in the Irish Sea south-west of the Isle of Man. However, it is
not a real place! - although it is a composite of a several real islands. The
author invented Lifandoy and began writing stories about it around 1990.*

1 - A Grin and Two Letters

It became the most embarrassing ten days of my life; and it began with a strange delivery.

'A *letter* from my boss? What - genuine, handwritten snail mail? From *Keith*? For whom?'

'For *you*, Timothy.'

I stared at the envelope being held out to me in the large hand of its deliverer. The owner of the hand, my Uncle Wilfred, grinned broadly at me. I flinched and jumped aside. I always take evasive action when Uncle Wilfred grins at me - especially when he has just flung open my rickety gate and stridden up my path with a grin as wide as a maniac's, all the way from one curly white sideburn to the other.

Uncle Wilfred rarely grins about his own downfall. This is not because he cannot find humour in his own misfortune, for he can. In fact, he stands on his own dignity less than any person I know. But Wilfred - it embarrasses me to call him Uncle, he doesn't act like a real uncle, he doesn't have the air of seniority to be *anyone's* uncle - Wilfred Corn has a grin to be feared. The whole island of Lifandoy is full of people who dodge when they see him grinning in their direction.

Particularly feared are Uncle Wilfred's famous good deeds, which he does without hesitation to every apparently needy soul he meets. Always preceded by a grin, his acts of warm-heartedness regularly lead their beneficiary to fall into a pit. For Wilfred is one of the most naturally dangerous people of whom I know.

It's not that he generates bad luck. In my opinion, he is neither a jinx nor a lunatic, although many treat him as one or both. What Wilfred does generate is humiliation. He always manages to be on hand to assist in disaster and, even worse, to *enjoy* it. He appreciates hapless bad luck, sometimes his own but, much more often, everyone else's. I'm still not sure I've forgiven him for roaring with laughter that time when I... No, I must keep to my story. If I start listing my uncle's minor misdemeanours, I shall never finish what I mean to do, which is to record in warning, as a classic example of the Wilfred Effect, the special disaster which began for me with that one particular view of Uncle Wilfred's teeth.

∎ ∎ ∎ ∎

Thus, when my first glance outside that Monday had revealed no less a peril than Uncle Wilfred's grin approaching my door, my hackles had already begun to rise.

'So what are you grinning for?'

My tone dismayed him. The grin faded to a hurt look. 'What's up, Timothy lad? Can't I greet the new day with a smile?'

'It wasn't a smile, it was a *grin.*'

Wilfred affected a puzzled expression. 'What does that matter?'

'It matters because it tells me you're up to your tricks again. What's the trick this time?'

He sighed, and then re-adopted the pained look. He was good at it, from long practice. 'I think you must have got out of bed on the wrong side this morning, dear boy. As it happens, I came to your gate purely on an errand of kindness.'

He put on such a saintly air that I could not think of anything else suspicious to say. I felt quite ashamed of myself. I gave him a helpless look, the sort a rabbit gives to a dancing stoat.

'Oh? What errand?'

He grinned again. 'Speaking of your gate, I'd be delighted to give you a hand replacing those rotten gateposts of yours. Have you thought of looking out for a couple of stout bits of scrap to make into new posts? But as I said, I've brought your *mail.*'

'My letters? But what are you doing with them?'

'The postman left them at Big Cottage by mistake. Don't you want them?'

He proffered the envelope again, and like a conjuror produced several more items. I stared at the top one suspiciously, still bemused and wishing Wilfred had not appeared until my first coffee of the day was inside me.

'But whatever would my boss write me a real paper letter for? I might just possibly expect a holiday postcard from him, but nothing more than that. Keith writes no more personal letters than I do!' I frowned at him, then again at the flimsy thing, which Wilfred was holding just out of my reach. I should have glared much more fiercely, had I known the woe its contents would later bring me; and I would have torn it to shreds, had I realized the shame that would cover me before its secrets were explained. In the circumstances, however, I merely continued to splutter my doubt.

'You must be mistaken, Wilfred. I know what Keith is like on holiday. Once he gets out of sight of West Doy village, he forgets me entirely. He wouldn't even send me a one line e-mail or text, let alone a handwritten epistle. I mean, really! Snail post from Senior Warden Potts? I should be no more surprised to receive a parcel from the Moon! Anyhow, why does he not phone me, if he wants me urgently?'

Wilfred shrugged. As I reached out to take the first envelope, he pulled it away suddenly, then placed it at the bottom of the sheaf of paper in his other hand. Then he went through the pile, holding each item infuriatingly just beyond my grasp until he had produced a running commentary on it.

'*Here's* some tickets you ordered for a concert in Douglas - that will be for Jessica's birthday, I suppose? *Here's* your invitation to the Lifandoy island Summer Dance - mine came yesterday.

'*Here's* a leaflet about the choir concert a week on Thursday - the postman didn't bring that one, I slipped it in myself.' Wilfred's main hobby, apart from doing disastrous good deeds for other people, is coaching the squeaky choir at the local chapel. The choir's eccentric music is perfection to his prejudiced ears. Wilfred calls himself a committed Christian. I don't know if committed refers to a lunatic asylum of which he is an alumni, or to one he is destined for. As for Christian, he possesses a heart of gold, but has with it the brain variously either of a cabbage, or of a female black widow spider preparing to eat its mate, depending on whether he is refusing to listen, or insisting on speaking.

As he passed me my mail piece by piece, he continued. 'Here's the new ferry timetable. Here's next month's copy of *Bird-watching Magazine.* How can they send you the June edition less than half way through May? And the last is the letter from your boss.'

I snorted with irritation as I reached for the letter that was puzzling me. 'You're serious, then?' I grasped it firmly. 'Thank *you.* And you know what you can do with your squawking choir. But how do you know who *this* is from? Not that it's any of your business, mind you!'

Wilfred snatched the envelope back and flipped it over before returning it. 'Says it on the back,' he snapped. 'Couldn't help seeing it.'

'Hmm.' I scowled and peered at the inky mess. At the top of the envelope was printed neatly the legend: LIFANDOY ESTATE OFFICE, PROPERTY OF. The Estate Office controlled the affairs of our usually absent landlord, the Earl of Lifandoy, who owned most of Lifandoy island. Stamped smudgily across this title was the formidable statement: LIFANDOY RESERVE: STRICTLY FOR WARDEN'S BUSINESS COMMUNICATIONS ONLY!

Underneath this was printed the name K. K. Potts.

'But why write me a letter?' I frowned and turned it over. The address was plain enough:

Timothy Corn,
Assistant Nature Reserve Warden,
Little Cottage,
West Doy,
Isle of Lifandoy.

The nature reserve it referred to is the Lifandoy Reserve, generally known to the islanders just as 'The Reserve'. This is the gloriously wildlife-rich stretch of coast and countryside which forms the western slice of Lifandoy island. At the moment the Reserve was my sole source of employment and, more importantly, of cash.

I frowned again. 'Keith hasn't written me a letter.'

Wilfred sniffed at this dismissal of his detective powers. 'How can you say that?'

'It's not his writing. Keith's writing is like a spiders' get-together, as you can see from his signature. This is his mother's hand, I should think.'

'What's she writing Keith's letters for?'

'I shall find out in my own good time.' I sniffed and stuck the sheaf of envelopes in my pocket. 'Thank you for bringing my post, even if you did put it under the microscope before you gave it me. Oh, and while you're here–'

'Yes?'

I smirked. 'Here's *yours*. One pair of theatre tickets for you and Martha. One ferry leaflet. One invitation to the Lifandoy House Garden Party; I got mine yesterday. One invitation to the branch meeting of the *Sink the Whalers Fund*; the postman didn't bring that, I slipped it in myself–'

Wilfred fulminated. 'What? I'll get that postman transferred if he delivers our letters here again. And as far as your anarchist *Fund* is concerned, it's about time you remembered that two wrongs don't make a right.'

'Quite correct - the Right Whale is one of the endangered species. Where was I? Yes - here's next month's copy of *Tractors and Trailers*. And here's a letter from *your* boss.'

'Mine?' Wilfred wrinkled his brows as I turned the last envelope over. I paused, glancing down and savouring the moment. Again, had I known the whimpering fury the contents of this epistle would later reduce me to, I should have scorched the paper to ashes with my eyes alone. The first inscription was the same as on my own envelope. The second read: LIFANDOY HOUSE ESTATE FARM, STRICTLY FOR FARM MANAGER'S BUSINESS COMMUNICATIONS ONLY. The third was the handwritten name G. G. Fytts. On the other side the address read:

Wilfred Corn,
Assistant Farm Manager,
Big Cottage,
West Doy,
Isle of Lifandoy.

As it happened, Uncle Wilfred worked at the Lifandoy Estate's large and ruthlessly efficient home farm, whose land adjoined that of the nature reserve. The farm was regarded by the nature reserve wardens as the headquarters of their deadly ideological enemies.

Wilfred grabbed the envelope from me and ripped it open. 'That's not my boss's writing either,' he observed. 'What's going on around here?'

He scanned his letter rapidly, then read the last page again slowly. There was a gleam in his eyes when he looked up. It reminded me of the one the surgeon gave me an hour before I had my appendix out.

'Good news?' I asked politely.

'Er - not really.' Uncle Wilfred seemed to have some difficulty in answering. He swallowed. 'It seems that our poor farm manager has had an accident. He was having a few days holiday when he tried to pick up three suitcases at the same time. He has a badly slipped disc and will be scarcely able to move for a few weeks.'

I sighed. 'Poor fellow. Still, you'll be stepping into his shoes, I presume? At last you can run the estate farm the way you want it, for a while.'

'Yes I can, can't I.' Wilfred paused. His tone of voice had been odd, and when I glanced at him, the corners of his mouth appeared to be turning up into a grin. 'Ah - Timothy?'

'Yes?'

'On another subject, when you are on your nature patrols in the countryside, do you ever come across any abandoned - er - no, forget it.' He changed his mind about what he had planned to say, and glanced back down at his letter.

He looked up again, caught my stare and straightened his expression rapidly. He gestured. 'Don't forget *your* letters.'

'I won't.' I pulled out the one from my boss and opened it casually. I scanned the first part, then laughed. 'Would you believe it? Keith was having a fortnight's holiday in the Lake District when he tried to pick up two pairs of binoculars, two telescopes and four pairs of boots all at once. He collapsed and is in hospital for an emergency hernia operation. He will be laid up for at least four weeks. What a coincidence! I'm going to be running the nature reserve while you run the farm! And he also says...'

My voice tailed away as I scanned the final part of the letter. It read:

> '...so I'm sure, Timothy, that you'll cope with the routine work until I get out of hospital. If my mother can keep writing this letter for me for a little longer there is, however, one CRUCIAL thing I must tell you. And it is a secret you absolutely must keep - ESPECIALLY from that scoundrel of an uncle of yours next door.

'As you know, the nesting season is now underway for the birds on the Lifandoy Reserve. What you will not know, however, is that this season may prove to be rather an exciting one. Just before I left the island, I did a last quick survey of the birds that had already arrived. In a certain peaceful spot I came across A VERY RARE PAIR OF BIRDS INDEED.

'They are so rare that I dare not say where I saw them, or even what they are. I know that rascally Uncle Wilfred of yours occasionally gets your mail by mistake, and he of all people mustn't find out! I'm sure you'll guess what the birds were if I mention the name FETLAR. As for where I saw them, it was in a hollow near the West Burn where the stream separates the Reserve from the Lifandoy House Farm fields. I cannot say more than that. You'll recognize the spot easily if I emphasize how YELLOW the place is.

'I'm sure the birds are about to nest - you'll realize instantly how exciting that is. Whatever you do, DON'T let your pesky uncle find out about them. The Lifandoy House Farm people are always trying find excuses to stir up trouble for us. As you know, Fytts, the farm manager, is keen to persuade the Lifandoy Estate Office that our "weeds" spread onto the House Farm's fields and that less of the island should be kept as a nature reserve. If Fytts knew about the birds he would immediately let the local press know and laugh at the result.

'Some bad publicity for us might be all it takes to tip the balance! It's not only poachers or criminals like egg collectors that worry me on the Reserve. If the valley was flooded with silly birdwatchers from the mainland, some of them would be bound to stray onto the farm. One or two fools trampling crops or stampeding prize dairy cows would suit Fytts down to the ground. He could go straight to the Estate Office and destroy the years of work I've put in persuading them how valuable the Reserve is to the tourist trade. "Never

mind the tourists, a field of flat wheat is real money lost!" I can hear him saying it now.

'Remember - we have enough of a running battle with the farm manager as it is. If the Estate Office got upset they could give half our land to the farm and let Wilfred and his cronies plough it all up! FIND THAT NEST and put it under top secret surveillance, as soon as you can.

Yours hopefully,
Mrs. Agnes Potts
pp. Keith Potts.'

'What does he say?' inquired Uncle Wilfred casually.

'Ah, just a lot of boring details.' I gave an airy wave. Then I fixed Wilfred with a cold look. 'You didn't open any of my letters by any chance, did you?'

He was genuinely aggrieved. 'I wouldn't put that sort of behaviour past an anarchist conservationist!' he snapped.

'Sorry.' Uncle Wilfred has an eccentric outlook on life, but when he is serious he cannot be faulted. I apologized as handsomely as I thought I ought. 'I knew you wouldn't. Not deliberately, at least. But I'm not that violent either. Just concerned and green. We haven't actually sunk any whalers yet.'

'Concerned and green? Hah! That sounds like a disease to me.'

∎ · ∎ ·

With that, Wilfred stomped off before I could reply, banging my fragile garden gate again behind him. I was not anxious to talk. I had a lot to think about. I walked down to the road and watched him pass through his own gate, which was much more substantial than mine. Embarrassed by his offer of help with my gate, I rattled it thoughtfully. The gate survived the experience without harm, but its supporting posts sagged further: they were clearly the weak spots. Wilfred's suggestion of new posts had stuck in my mind. What could I use for the repair?

16

Measuring the old posts by eye, I calculated mentally the cost of new gateposts. Then I slouched back up my path, thinking gloomily of the tiny figure at the end of my last bank statement. As I neared the cottage, I kicked an old shoe off the path. Then I began to contemplate the many items of assorted junk lying around my porch.

When walking the nature trail, it was my habit to pick up any litter I found. If it looked at all useful, I would scavenge it and bring it home if I could. As I know all too well, the amount of rubbish that is transported onto the Reserve by both tourists and islanders is amazing; as is the variety of it. Despite warning notices, tourists regularly leave all sorts of paper litter; while the islanders are responsible for more substantial junk, such as rusting car wrecks, dead fishing boats, and stranger things.

Yesterday I had brought home several items. For example, atop the seabird cliffs of Raw Head, at the western tip of the island, I had picked up a metre-long piece of orange piping. It was covered in mud but a little had fallen off and revealed it to my gaze. Attracted by its brilliant hue beneath the slime, I had intended to toss it over the cliff. Yet, in my hand, although strong it was extraordinarily light, even though it was full of what appeared to be some sort of wiring. It would be just about the same size and shape as one of my rotting gateposts. Idly, I wondered where in my treasure trove I had finally stacked the strange thing.

I hesitated over my junk pile. Should I repair my gates now? Keith was away, so he would not know I had been wasting work time. But the rare birds he had described were important. Which task should I tackle first?

I walked back into my kitchen and made toast and coffee. Then I sat down and read Keith's letter carefully again.

'So what about these rare birds?' I murmured to myself. 'What were the clues?' I found the relevant part of the letter. 'They were in a *yellow* place. Where might that be? I don't see what Keith is getting at. Yellow could refer to a patch of flowers, say yellow iris or trefoil, or perhaps even a lump of that coloured limestone on Ginger Hill where the West Burn rises.

'And he mentions Fetlar! That's a famous place for birds. It's the best of the Shetland Islands, and every one of those is a naturalist's paradise. Yet, I wish Keith had been a bit more specific. The farm faces the Reserve across the Burn for most of the valley. And there's more than one bird for which Fetlar is famous. There were the snowy owls that used to nest there, of course; and there are also the red-necked phalaropes. Either species would be an exciting discovery here.

'It's not difficult to spot snowy owls - or their big, white eggs - but they would have to be somewhere I don't normally visit: probably at the head of the valley or even on Ginger Hill itself. But phalaropes are miniature birds. They could be elusive, tiny things paddling like clockwork toys on any little marshy pool...'

Thoughtfully, I picked up my coffee and walked out again, down to my gate. As I stood there, wondering what to replace my posts with, I saw Uncle Wilfred emerge from Big Cottage, carrying a parcel wrapped in a cloth under one arm. He jumped when he saw my head over the hedge. For some reason he seemed unhappy that I should be watching him. He hunched his head down between his shoulders, avoiding my eyes. I reflected that I would soon be trying not to see too much of him either. I would have to keep out of his way as much as possible, to make sure my movements were not observed.

Wilfred sidled out of his gate and started hesitantly down the lane away from me. This was strange, as his usual route to the farm was in the opposite direction. If he did not walk down past Little Cottage he would be on the road to the Reserve and would have wade the stream or to go round in a circle to get to the farm. I watched him curiously.

At that moment, chance took a hand, in the form of a low-flying plane. There was a thunderous noise as a small jet flew over. It was one of the American planes from the big air base over on the mainland. I hardly looked up: it was a regular occurrence, and very annoying.

Nevertheless, to Wilfred it seemed to cause alarm. He started like a rabbit, turned and walked back up the street past me. As he passed, he gave me a sort of sickly grin, meanwhile clutching his parcel tightly to the far side of his body. Then he headed off at a remarkably fast trot along the road away down through the village. Poking out of his jacket pocket as he retreated was a white envelope, doubtless his superior's letter. I wondered what on earth it could contain to make Uncle Wilfred act like that. How could I find out?

■ ■ ■ ■

To avoid later confusion, I think I ought at this point to reveal the contents of the letter Uncle Wilfred received, and which he finally showed me long afterward. I add here an extract from it, without comment…

To Tim's Uncle Wilfred from Wilfred's boss Graham Fytts - the end of the letter that Tim did not (until much later) see:

'…and I am sure, Wilfred, that you can manage the routine farm work for me until I recover. If Mrs. Fytts can put up with my dictation from my sick-bed for a little longer there is, however, one urgent matter I must mention.

'As you will be aware, all the summer crops are springing up fast in the valley fields. What you will not know, however, is that this summer is going to start off with something much more dramatic than watching them grow.

'Just before I had my accident, I had a visit from some VERY IMPORTANT PEOPLE. I can't tell you who they were. Suffice it to say that two of my visitors were hard-faced types who spent their time watching my every move. The third was an officer from the United States Air Force with a whole roll of gold braid encrusting his uniform; and the last was someone whom even YOU would recognize on television.

'You will have seen all those military planes that fly over the Isle of Lifandoy from the NATO air base on the mainland. Do you remember telling me about one which came over at night in the middle of last week? You said it was so low you thought it was in danger of a crash. It appears you were quite right. It nearly did come down: it was a top-secret American *warplane with only one engine left - and it only survived by jettisoning its cargo.*

'Unfortunately, the cargo it was forced to drop was a very special one. The main package went in the sea off Raw Head and was picked up by submarine. But two crucial pieces from it came loose and are still missing.

'It appears the Yanks have dropped something IMPORTANT on Lifandoy, something they want back both discreetly and badly! Apart from ourselves, only the Earl of Lifandoy himself has been told. My visitors weren't at all keen to tell me what they have lost, either, until I pointed out that we couldn't help them unless they told us what to look for.

'What they have lost is two sections of bright orange tubing, each about waist high. They don't look much, but they are in fact the core of a radiation sensing device that probably cost billions to develop. It's called a Nuclear Explosion Sensing Tube (N.E.S.T. for short) and it will detect a bomb going off - a covert nuclear explosion - half way around the world.

'The tubes are not dangerous, by the way. Apparently they are mildly radioactive themselves, but only enough for them to be located with exceedingly sensitive film detectors - especially if, as is quite possible, they buried themselves in the marsh or vegetation when they landed. That must be why an aerial search has not found them yet. Unless the world is to know they are there, the USAF will need the aid of discreet local aid to find them. And that is where YOU come in.

'Their best guess is that the two pieces of the NEST fell separately, on our side of the island. Unfortunately, at least one of them certainly landed on the nature reserve that that scoundrelly nephew of yours, Timothy, helps to look after. None of the crofters has reported anything, so it's probably up on the cliffs above Raw Head. I suggest that when the coast is

clear you sneak up there straight away and try to locate it. That thick scrub around Loch Liffen might also need a check. The other half probably fell somewhere along the western edge of our land, along the border between us and the Reserve. It is CRUCIAL that you find them both.

'You will realize, of course, that Timothy ABSOLUTELY MUST NOT hear of this! Those conservationist types are always trying to stir up trouble for us with the Lifandoy Estate Office, and this would be a perfect excuse for them! We already receive enough aggro from them over nitrate fertilizer draining into the West Burn, and over our sprays drifting across the Burn from our crop fields to kill their precious weeds in the marsh. If those knavish wardens found out about the NEST it could tip the balance against us. Even though we know there is no danger, a rumour that there was radioactive debris lying around in our fields would go a long way towards putting us out of business - and you, me and a lot of others out of a job. One whisper of "radioactive crops" or a similar wild exaggeration could close half the farm down and leave it for Timothy and his cronies to turn into a weedy wasteland.

'Your job may hang from two pieces of orange piping, Wilfred. FIND THAT N.E.S.T. and put it under top-secret cover, as soon as you can!

Yours anxiously,
Mrs. Nellie Fytts
pp. Graham Fytts.'

'PS. I forgot to mention that you will not be on your own. Apparently the US Air Force is also sending its own plainclothes search team. They will contact you but must not be seen talking to you. Look out for a black Volkswagen. The agents in it will be carrying some of their super-sensitive film sensors. They contain film which takes a day to expose and which can detect N.E.S.T.-type emissions from hundreds of metres away. The Americans have an odd sense of humour: in

order that the detectors can be left in the open while they are operating, they are disguised as large white eggs...'

2. - Reinforcements.

I watched Uncle Wilfred until he was lost to view. It was just possible that he might drop his mail. In which case, what could be more natural than that I should wander over to tidy up a bit of litter, and to check it to make sure it was not valuable? Perhaps I might have to read it to make sure...

But Wilfred and his mail both continued out of sight without incident. I stared after him, and then glanced back up the Street. As I did so, I observed that in his hurry my uncle had left his own gate unfastened. It swung smoothly to and fro on its hinges in the breeze, quite unlike my decrepit piece of carpentry. Annoyed, I kicked one of my gateposts; several splinters flew off as the rotting post sagged a fraction more. Then the whole gate slowly leaned over until it rested against the opposite post.

'Oh, no. I'll *have* to find something to reinforce it, now.'

I decided Keith's birds would have to wait for the half hour it would take me to hammer in at least one new gatepost. However, first I had to find a suitable piece of scrap. What might I use?

I trudged back to my porch and began to sort through the driftwood and pieces of old bicycle there. I began hopefully. But soon I realized that everything there was either too short or too insubstantial to bear a heavy gate. All the scrap I had assembled was evidently exactly that.

Then, I saw it. Where it stood in the shadows, long, strong, gleaming in a remarkable shade of bright orange, like a knight among villains, like a lord among commoners, it stood proudly above all the rubbish that surrounded it. Its appearance was so elegant and refined that it almost seemed to be pleading audibly for a few gentle taps from my sledgehammer. The orange pipe from Raw Head, smooth except for a couple of brackets almost perfectly positioned for my gate's hinges, stood ready to receive its destiny as my new gatepost.

I took my coffee mug back into the kitchen. Then I picked up the orange pipe and set to work.

Twenty minutes later my gate was vertical again, firmly hinged to a carefully inserted length of metal piping. The top of the tube was now filled in by a round piece of wood, which I had inserted to hide the messy wiring inside and to stop rain filling the post interior.

Only one problem occurred. While I was lovingly tapping the pipe one last time with my sledgehammer, a large piece of the orange paint flaked off. 'These modern paints don't stick properly,' I grumbled. 'Or maybe it's the metal. It's probably only of some poor alloy, like so many cheaply made things nowadays.'

Out of curiosity, I inspected the orange tube more closely than I had before. It bore no clue to its origin and no identifying mark, apart from some stencilled numbers, which meant nothing to me. But it fulfilled its new role almost perfectly. I stepped back and eyed it happily. Just one thing was still wrong. That orange colour... I went back into Little Cottage and hunted through a pile of nearly empty paint tins.

'Green? No, green looks tatty. Black is smarter. If it was good for Henry Ford it will do for me.'

With difficulty I found a brush which was not rock hard, then took the tin outside. Shortly I stepped back, paintbrush in hand. 'Although I say it myself, that's a work of genius. Waste not, want not, I always say.' I admired my gleaming black handiwork. 'All I need now is a similar pipe for the other post. I wonder if I might find a match for this one down at the Port Doy scrapyard.'

I made a mental note to keep a look out. Or perhaps I might find another orange pipe lying around on the nature reserve? I speculated aloud to myself on what the purpose of my find might formerly have been.

'It looks as though it was one of a set. But a set of what? It looks like some sort of cable piping, or a piece of something much longer. Hey - here's a thought. I don't suppose that some mobile phone company is starting to erect an aerial on Lifandoy at long last? It's far past time - Lifandoy is about the darkest electronic black spot in Europe. We've been waiting for a decent telecommunications mast for years. Mind you, if someone is building some sort of structure up by the lighthouse I must warn them not to disturb our birds!'

I shrugged. Probably Keith had forgotten to tell me about some project authorized by the Lifandoy Estate Office, which controlled most business affairs on the island. Such things had happened before.

More importantly for me, if one piece of radio aerial had been abandoned, there might be a good chance of me picking up a second. I would certainly keep a careful watch for one. And merely having made a start on the repair was a boost to my morale, in any case. Uncle Wilfred's humour at the state of my gate would not bother me much longer. He could even keep his little secret about his own mysterious letter; whatever his epistle contained, it could not equal the excitement of my own news, nor would it rob me of the satisfaction of having a respectable gate to show off to my uncle when he next passed it. Perhaps Uncle Wilfred's famous grin was not the prelude to disaster on this occasion that I had feared. Or was I wrong somewhere?

But now, real work called. I went to refill my coffee mug, then sat down to plan my search programme for the rare birds. 'The first thing I need here is reinforcements.'

I picked up my home phone and tapped a number. 'Bob? Is Jamie there, too? Good. Bob - something big has come up. Can the pair of you head round this way pronto? Er - yes, I suppose I can run to coffee.'

I sighed and replaced the receiver. Going to my bookshelf, I picked up a map that was at the top of an untidy pile. Sitting down, I spread the map across my kitchen table. It was a large map, for it covered the whole of Lifandoy island. I studied it thoughtfully.

■ ■ ■ ■

Lifandoy lies, of course, in the Irish Sea to the south-west of and not far from the Isle of Man. It has one harbour and port, one main town and one village, lots of fertile farmland and a strikingly scenic west coast. I studied the coast for a moment. Although I am native to Lifandoy and was brought up here, I never realized how beautiful it is until I returned to West Doy from the mainland. Years spent away, as a student and later as junior warden on several nature reserves, had opened my eyes. Lifandoy is a treasure trove of variety; and so, as it happens, are its inhabitants.

The island community is much smaller than that on the Isle of Man. We have no special language or parliament or anything like that. Due to the various economic booms and slumps that have affected the island, it has an extremely mixed community. There are Welsh sheep farmers, Irish fisherman, Scottish crofters and English dairy and arable farmers. All keep somewhat to themselves, preserving their accents and prejudices.

Visitors are amused when the islanders talk about their own island. The Irish pronounce it LIFandoy to compare with the River Liffey. The Welsh say liFANdoy to remind them of their legendary hero the Blessed Bran, although the latter is actually believed by some of the more rustic Celts on the island to be a specially favoured make of breakfast cereal. The Scots say lifanDOY to go with Rob Roy; while the English either emphasize all three syllables the same - to show that they are none of the other three - or else choose whichever style might most irritate their hearer.

Port Doy on the southern coast of the island is home to most islanders of Irish origin. To a visitor arriving there, the main geographical feature of the island is the valley of the Doy Burn, the island's only river. This descends to Port Doy from Lifandoy's main town, which on the map is simply marked Doy but to the inhabitants is universally known as Doytown.

The various races co-exist uneasily in Doytown. As if to keep the peace, the upper part of Doytown is overlooked both by the modern structure of the Lifandoy Estate Office and by the most impressive building in the valley, the opulent Victorian heap of Lifandoy House, the home of the usually absent Earl.

Above Doytown the Doy River is formed by the meeting of the East and West Burns, whose valleys comprise much of the broader northern part of the island. The East Burn is a pleasant trout stream flowing through a shallow limestone dale that contains the island reservoir.

The valley of the West Burn, which I know very well, holds the small village of West Doy, which is inhabited mostly by islanders of English extraction including Wilfred and myself. Above West Doy, the boggy course of the West Burn marks the dividing line between the sanitized, intensively cultivated fields of Lifandoy House Farm to the east and, grimly facing them, the wild, lovely marshes of the Lifandoy Reserve, of which more later.

Pensively, I traced the meandering line of the West Burn on my map. This blue squiggle, then, was the front line between the forces of exploitation, marshalled by Wilfred, and those of the green revolution, championed by me. Now it was to be the search area for a valuable prize, one for which I would have to play a game of real cunning. For there was nothing wrong with Uncle Wilfred's eyesight; and the House Farm overlooked nearly the entire valley.

■ ■ ■ ■

As my finger moved I realized with dismay that the search area was huge. The Reserve was bordered by the farm for nearly the entire length of the West Burn from Ginger Hill in the north to the marsh above West Doy village in the south, a distance of almost two miles all told. My reinforcements would obviously be needed.

At that moment there was a rattle of the gate and a knock at the door. 'Tim?'

'Come on in, Jamie. And you, Bob. Ah - coffee?'

I poured some weak coffee slowly into two mugs, stopping before they were full and hoping there would be no complaints. The newcomers were two bearded ruffians of about twenty-two who were Keith's - now my - right-hand men. Both students, they were on Lifandoy for the summer, funded by their university to spend part of their time carrying out their own research projects and part helping with the Lifandoy Reserve's normal work. Each morning they called around to see what maintenance, census work and the like I needed help with, while the afternoons were for their own research. I had already grown to like both them and their appetite for hard outdoor work.

'Thanks.' Both accepted. Bob Backley, a wiry Lancashireman with a red beard, looked at my own cup with interest.

'How long have you been here?'

'I haven't been out yet. Why?'

'I was a bit surprised when you rang. Jamie went for an early walk and he told me he thought he saw you going out as he was coming back, about fifteen minutes ago.'

'He thought? Weren't you sure, Jamie? Obviously you were right not to be.'

'I didn't actually recognize you; I just presumed it must be you because you were wearing binoculars.' Jamie MacLeod was tall, dark and beefy, with a huge beard and a soft Highland accent that became broader whenever he became angry. 'It's too early for any tourists and I couldn't think of anyone else who might be wearing bins around here.'

I shrugged. 'Where was he?'

'On the main Reserve track, Tim. He was just past the lowest little marsh and heading up in the direction of Raw Head. Thinking about it, I should have known the chap wasn't you, because he was shorter, although he had your build.'

'But you didn't recognize him?'

Jamie thought a moment, then laughed. 'I know it sounds silly but it could almost have been your Uncle Wilfred.'

I spluttered. *'Uncle Wilfred?'*

'It was hard to tell. He was wearing a hat pulled right down over his head. And he was acting strangely, too. He looked a bit dishevelled, as though he'd taken a short cut through someone's hedge. And I'm sure he deliberately walked behind some bushes when he saw me. Do you know something we don't know? Or does he?'

I stood up in alarm, spilling the last of my coffee. 'Drink up as fast as you can, and read this letter from Keith while you're drinking. Somewhere on the Lifandoy Reserve something very rare and precious is hiding, either on the hillside or in some little marshy hollow. I don't know what Wilfred knows about it. But one thing I am sure of is that we have to find out!'

3. - In the Bushes

Five minutes later, we were striding in file past Wilfred's cottage. As we did so there was a gentle call.

'Timothy? Are you going in the direction of the Reserve?'

It was Wilfred's wife, Martha. She was a doll-like lady, possessed of as much sensitivity as Wilfred was of alarming helpfulness. Adorned with a shock of white hair, Martha was a long retired schoolteacher, some ten years older than Wilfred, with no change left out of seventy. She was my favourite little old lady and I always had time for her.

'Yes, Martha? Do you have a message to be carried?'

She smiled. 'I was wondering if you could drop this dress in at Mrs. Bull's next to the chapel as you pass. It's her eldest daughter Jessica's: I've been mending it for her.' Martha was a skilled seamstress and always had plenty of customers around West Doy village. 'It's the cottage beyond the chapel, the one with the wooden fence overlooking the bottom marsh. You may not know Jessica well, she's a quiet girl, but I'm sure you've met her mother.'

'Yes, I have met them both.' As it happened I knew Jessica rather well, and I would not have described her as a quiet girl: not, at least, on the evidence of the hot embraces she had given me the previous evening. We had been cuddling amongst the flowers beyond the fence while her mother was at the chapel service. 'I'll drop it in right now.'

Behind me, Jamie muttered something.

'Pardon, Jamie?'

Bob hissed at me. 'I thought we were in a hurry?' He smiled at Martha. 'I'm surprised Wilfred couldn't have taken it for you, Martha?'

'Wilfred?' Martha was puzzled. 'Wilfred went off towards the farm as usual. He'd have to wade the West Burn to get to the farm if he went by way of Mrs. Bull's.'

'Ah. It must have been someone else Jamie saw, then.'

'Unless Wilfred's been keeping a secret from me,' Martha smiled again, and we all laughed politely while Jamie frowned at me in puzzlement when Martha was not looking. What *was* my uncle up to?

Mrs. Bull's was a modest stone's throw off our route, down the tiny lane on which the chapel stood. It was the only dwelling beyond the chapel, together with which it bordered the marsh at the start of the Reserve. The lane ended at the Bulls' cottage; the West Burn gurgled along one limit of its well-stocked garden and there was no bridge over the Burn.

Across the Burn a long slope clad with shoots of growing wheat and oil-seed rape, both undoubtedly heavily laced with nitrates and other chemicals, stretched up the hill toward the lawn and rear terraces of Lifandoy House. Between crops and lawn, two distant hedges marked the road that led up from the other end of the village - Wilfred's normal route - to the baronial seat and round it towards the farm. The chimneys of the latter were just visible where the road disappeared round the hill.

The three of us walked past the chapel and its notice boards to the cottage gate. As we did so we saw the Reserve, which was well seen from the chapel yard, disappear from view. Mrs. Bull was a fanatical gardener and she had erected a high wooden fence to protect her flowers from the vigorous island winds. I regarded the fence beyond the house with fondness, remembering my beloved Jessica's hot lips against mine in our secret nook beyond.

As it happened, the fence was a matter of amusement to us, because of Mrs. Bull's eccentric habit of repainting it frequently. It was a standing joke among the Reserve wardens and helpers that we would not know what colour it was going to be until we came in sight of it each evening on our way home. Mrs. Bull had repainted it yet again in a brilliant crimson hue only last Saturday, just after Keith Potts had left for his holiday. Jessica and I had been almost overpowered by the smell of paint as we snuggled behind it. It occurred to me that I had not the foggiest idea what colour it had been before. Possibly green, I thought.

Jamie and Bob waited at the gate while I went to deliver the sewing. To my annoyance, it was not my darling Jessica who opened the door, but her youngest sister, a sharp-eyed brat of about eleven called Alice.

Alice scowled at me from the threshold. 'Jessica's in bed with a chill. Mother thinks she got it from lying on something damp. She's to stay in bed all morning.'

I smiled innocently. 'Poor dear. Her hot water bottle must have leaked. I've brought her dress from Martha Corn.'

Alice stepped forward and snatched the dress. Then she grabbed me by the throat and forced her mouth to my ear.

'I saw you snogging behind the fence!' she hissed. 'I was watching you through a crack in the fence all the time Mother was at chapel. I know how Jessica got her chill, lying in the marsh grass. What will you give me to keep my mouth shut?'

'You sneaking little blackmailer!' I hissed back. 'I don't negotiate with spies. You tell your mother and I'll box your ears!'

'Bluff.' She let go of my throat and stuck her tongue out. 'I'll have an ice cream at the Summer Fair.'

I bared my teeth at her. She ignored me. 'Or I'll have a giant milk shake at the Garden Party, a strawberry one with one of those fancy straws. Now I'm shutting the door before Mother comes. Thank you for the dress.' Alice gave an angelic smile and kicked me on the ankle. I hopped back off the steps in anguish as the front door closed suddenly, narrowly missing my fingers.

At the gate, Bob and Jamie were wide-eyed. 'Who's that little Amazon?' asked Bob in admiration. I swung my binoculars at him in annoyance. He dodged and repeated the question.

'That's Alice. She controls the sisterhood around here. She runs the local protection racket.'

Bob laughed. 'It looks like you're the one needing protection.'

Furious, I swung my binoculars at him again. This was a mistake, as the strap broke. I gave a neigh of horror as my precious binoculars crashed through Mrs. Bull's conifer hedge into the dense rose border beyond.

We poked around through the hedge with a stick. After a couple of minutes, Alice's voice spoke suddenly on the other side of the hedge.

'A quid,' she said definitively. 'I saw your stick moving. They're in the middle of a rose bush.'

'*A pound?* Not flippin' likely,' I replied, mindful of my amused audience. I'll give you ten pence.'

'Through those thorns? No chance. You can crawl through yourself.' Her footsteps receded disdainfully across the lawn. *'Ten pence,* I ask you.'

Muttering imprecations, I wormed through a space under the conifer branches to find myself in a cage of flesh-ripping barbs. It cost what felt like half a pint of blood to retrieve my precious binoculars; then I found it was impossible to retreat. My only escape was to crawl through a tunnel of thorns parallel to the hedge, unable to choose any other direction. Lost in a jungle of rose bushes, I had a vague idea I was heading towards the chapel next door. I kept going manfully until I burst through a last, deadly barrier.

I was free! Crawling onto the gravel chapel yard, I gave a shout of triumph and lifted my head. The result of this was that I hit my head hard on something wooden which had been obviously been positioned with great care ready for me. I collapsed moaning on the gravel surface.

I opened my eyes to the sound of wild laughter. I was prone in the yard and Bob and Jamie were leaning over the wall close by, showing no sympathy at my pitiful state. Bob pointed upwards, and my nose followed his gaze. Above me was a wooden notice board, knocked slightly askew in its attack upon me. The board bore a hand-drawn poster - to add insult to injury I thought I recognized Uncle Wilfred's vigorous if erratic artwork - with the large words: JESUS LOVES THE FALLEN SINNER. I staggered out of the chapel yard and followed hastily after my chortling assistants back to the lane that led down to the marsh.

Before long, we were well along the Reserve track past the marsh and within sight of the main eastern expanse of the Lifandoy Reserve. The first priority was obviously to find out whether it was really Wilfred who had passed that way. From here, we could see parts of the track a mile or two ahead: but the landscape was empty. Wilfred, assuming it was he, had vanished into the stony island earth. My assistants strode along eagerly, scanning everything that moved. I limped behind, bleeding from many wounds and wishing I could go back to bed for a week.

I cheered up after a while. The Lifandoy Reserve is too beautiful a place on a sunny mid-May morning for even a bleeding cripple to stay wholly miserable. The West Burn valley alone is to a naturalist an absorbing place. Fed by lime-rich water draining into a wonderful mix of marsh, fen and swamp, it is a pot-pourri of flowers and birds both colourful and rare. All across the lower valley, swathes of the year's last early purple and a few green-winged orchids were in bloom on the edge of the drier grassland. In the damp meadows and marsh a whole spectrum of different marsh orchids were starting to lift their elegant spikes. Above us, the sky was all but filled with the song of invisible skylarks. Small birds flew shrilling from our path, while to both sides larger ones wheeled protesting at our passing. Hovering redshank yelped over the wetter meadow while on all sides black-and-white lapwing wailed down around us like avian fireworks.

Jamie was in the lead. He strode along, disturbing a few cattle from behind a fence. They were not sleek Friesian stock, such as were to be seen at the House Farm, but a hardy tribe of long-horned beef animals from one of the little nearby crofts to whom we rented parts of the grazing from November to May. Careful management of the grazing marsh was necessary each year to keep the marsh in the correct state for nesting birds. Careful fencing was also necessary to keep the herd from wandering into the lush but treacherous swampy areas.

Jamie paused on a slight rise and gazed to his right. 'If it's marshy pools you're looking for, you have any awful lot of them to choose from, Tim. The whole of the valley bottom along the Burn is a patchwork of little pools.' We surveyed the colourful tangle of vegetation solemnly.

I nodded. 'Fytts and Wilfred couldn't grow wheat on this land without spending a fortune on drainage first. But that doesn't stop them wanting to try.'

Bob surveyed the uniform crop-fields across the valley beyond the West Burn. 'And wouldn't these birds appreciate a bit more wildflower meadow instead of that chemical-soaked crop desert over there!'

'Absolutely,' Jamie agreed. 'But speaking of lakes, I see a neat little bird paddling round in circles on that little pool over there, the one with the big patch of yellow marsh marigold by it.'

'Yipe!' My heart pounding, I leapt to his side with binoculars at the ready. 'What pool?'

Jamie laughed as I lowered my bins with a scowl. 'You blackguard of a Gael,' I snapped. 'Don't you know a duck when you see one?'

'Of course I do, dear boy. And not just any old duck, either. That little beauty is the husband of one of my most valued tenants.' He pored over a map. 'Breeding pair of teal, reference number TX2... present and correct.' He scribbled in a notebook. 'Mrs. Teal will be sitting on her eggs right over there, on that dry hummock with all the greenery on it.'

Bob grinned. 'Much more faithful than human birds, aren't they Jamie? Much to be preferred. And that reminds me: how are you getting on with the gorgeous Jessica at the moment, Tim?'

I had the grace to blush. Fortunately, I had no need to answer, for at that moment a distant movement caught my eye.

It was undoubtedly Wilfred. Previously hidden by the contours of the land, he had emerged a long way ahead of us on a short visible section of the path where it sloped up westward out of the lower valley. We focused our binoculars on him.

'You were right, Jamie. It *is* Wilfred. My apology.'

'Accepted, Tim. We'll have to move fast to catch him.'

'He's not going that fast. He could have been a lot further on. And he's going uphill at the moment.'

Bob was puzzled. 'Why has he left the valley track?'

'I don't know,' I said. 'But the track gets very muddy higher up the valley. Wilfred will know that much. Even if you were heading up to the top of the valley it's more pleasant to follow the ridge path.'

'That should take him some time. Can we overtake him?'

I grimaced. 'If we don't mind being covered with mud up to the eyeballs, yes. I shall try, anyway. If there's anything like a pair of snowy owls up there I must divert him at all costs. If I belt up through the marsh, I should have ten minutes to spot them and shoo them off before Wilfred comes down off the ridge into view.'

Jamie raised an eyebrow. 'Shoo off a pair of nesting snowy owls? What's after that? Pushing a few swans off their eggs? Wrestling with sharks off Port Doy breakwater? Snowies are big birds! I've seen a snowy owl on Fetlar face up to a whole squadron of dive-bombing great skuas.'

'Yes, but skuas are simply other birds. Any nesting bird will make themselves scarce if a human disturbs them.'

'Hmm.' Jamie was unconvinced.

Bob was eager. 'We could wait for Wilfred where the ridge path comes down to that patch of heathland between Ginger Hill and the sea. There's lots of cover there.'

'Brilliant. If we give him a surprise then, perhaps he'll give up whatever nefarious plot he has in mind.'

The posse set off. We jogged along as Wilfred's small figure crept up onto the ridge that lay between the West Burn valley and the coast. Shortly he disappeared onto the crest of the ridge.

The track was as muddy as I had expected and our progress slowed badly. But we were nearly unscathed as the end of the mire approached. I gave a faint cheer as we negotiated the last mud-hole. Then I slipped and rolled with a mighty splash back into the swamp.

As I struggled, Bob and Jamie collapsed in laughter for the second time that morning. They were giving it their utmost when something large and white flew past behind them. It was within my view only for a moment but I was galvanized to action.

'Did you see it?' I clapped my binoculars urgently to my eyes.

'What, Tim? A mud plover, was it?'

The bins were coated with slime and useless. I shouted in fury and let them fall to my chest. The other two howled. 'Tim, you've got muddy rings all around your eyes!' Jamie got out his notebook. 'Mud plover in full summer plumage,' he declaimed. 'Identified by its large brown eye rings.'

'Silence, you morons. It flew right behind you. Big and white.'

They took the point abruptly and grabbed their own binoculars. 'Big enough for a snowy owl?' inquired Bob hopefully.

'Or for a big gull?' added Jamie discouragingly.

But the landscape was empty, the bird having vanished over a rise in the ground ahead of us. We raced up the small rise to a viewpoint. From it the head of the valley, a half-mile-wide bowl below the bulk and bare limestone terraces of Ginger Hill, was empty of white birds. We scanned every inch of it until we were sick of looking.

'Have we time to go further?'

'No, we're late for our ambush!'

We jogged off again. As we came in sight of the heath and of the final descent from the ridge there was no-one yet in view on the downward slope. At the foot of the hill, the path passed through a steep natural cutting and then forked. One fork was the one by which we were approaching. The other, more well-trodden one, led seawards across the uneven heath to the coast and the start of the dramatic Raw Head cliff walk, a must for most tourists.

'We're in luck,' gasped Bob. 'He must still be on the way down. Where do you want us, Tim?'

'You two disappear into the bracken at the bottom in case he tries to make a break when he sees me. I'll hide in the bushes above the cutting and slide down that gravel slope right in front of him.'

We were only just in position when the sound of boots was heard. I risked enough of a glance to see a short, grey-haired figure cautiously descending the last of the hill.

Choosing my moment, I rose silently and stepped onto the top of the gravel bank. I took another step and started to slide down.

'Fancy meeting you here!'

The grey-haired figure glanced up at me in shock. Leering down at it, I suddenly lost my nerve. I stumbled. One of my feet flew outwards and I landed heavily. Gravity took over, and I descended the slope on my side, rear end first, in a shower of dust and pebbles.

When I halted, I became aware that a completely strange face, not dissimilar to Wilfred's but with a goatee beard and glasses and no sideburns, was staring thunderstruck down at mine. The stranger's gaze travelled over my bloodstained, mud-spattered, dust-coated form. Then he returned to my face.

'Your eyes, man! What's happened to your *eyes?*'

I remembered the mud rings. Reaching up hastily, I rubbed at them, merely converting them into war paint. 'I... I... you're not Wilfred,' I commented feebly.

His gaze concurred silently with the obvious.

I tried again. 'Are you a tourist?'

He ignored the question. 'I was told I might find the Lifandoy Reserve warden somewhere along this path.'

I knew it was a mistake as soon as I said it. 'Er - I'm the warden.'

The stranger closed his eyes for a moment in horror. When he opened them, he recoiled at the sight of two more figures that were rising out of the undergrowth.

Bob and Jamie acted with shaken nonchalance. 'Why, it's Tim!' said Jamie in wonder.

'Hello, Tim!' said Bob. 'Fancy meeting you here.'

'Fancy.' It was the only word I could think of.

There was a strained silence. It was broken by the sound of more approaching boots. When I looked up, I saw Wilfred's stocky form coming down the ridge path. When he observed us all, his eyebrows slowly ascended his forehead. Then he began to grin.

4. - Sir Charles

Uncle Wilfred regarded the bearded stranger with surprising warmth.

'Sir Charles,' he said. 'Welcome back to Lifandoy. I didn't expect you to return to us so soon...'

The other took the proffered hand, peering. 'I remember the face. Did I meet you on my last visit?'

'Wilfred Corn.'

'Ah, yes.' Still hesitant - the name clearly did not open all doors of memory.

'And this is my nephew, Timothy.'

Sir Charles nodded grimly. 'We *have* met. I am informed that your nephew is the Lifandoy Reserve warden.' He gave me the sort of appalled stare I once elicited from my bank manager when mistakenly ushered into his office in place of his best customer.

I opened my mouth, but Wilfred forestalled me. 'Actually, Timothy is only the *assistant* warden.'

Sir Charles relaxed visibly. He turned with relief to view Wilfred, who was resplendent in shining binoculars and his little-used and spotless walking gear.

'Aaah. Then you must be—'

'Lifandoy House Farm is at your service, Sir Charles.'

'Oh!' Sir Charles was taken aback. 'Oh - then you're not - yes, I remember you now. You were with Graham Fytts, the farm manager. And you expounded your views to me in a very long letter afterwards. But you don't appear to... I mean... the clash between conservation and profitable agriculture...'

Wilfred was positively purring. 'Whatever you may have been told by others, Sir Charles, you may rest assured that Lifandoy House Farm takes its environmental responsibilities in the *broadest* way. Conservation is an essential part of farming to us! All the land available to us will always be farmed in a sympathetic manner. In fact I believe that there are strong arguments for enlarging our area of operations and turning over to serious cultivation some of the presently neglected...'

This was too much. 'Wilfred,' I interrupted. 'Stop talking through your hat! A field of your wheat, with all the chemicals you put on it, is an ecological desert. And you have about as much interest in wildlife as the average London property developer!'

Sir Charles protested mildly. 'Should we not listen to both sides...?'

'Not when one of them is Wilfred Corn,' I snapped.

By now I had assessed the newcomer to my satisfaction. From time to time odd serious naturalist bods appeared on the Reserve without warning. They were mostly of two types, either stubble-chinned bird rarity hunters - the notorious 'twitchers' - or else myopic eggheads from the Wild Flower Trust. Sir Charles corresponded perfectly to the latter variety. As such, he should be a respectable botanist who ought easily to be able to rubbish the claims of a smooth-talking super-farmer like Uncle Wilfred.

I drove the point home. 'Only a fool would listen to that rubbish. In all my life I've never known Wilfred spend two minutes together in studying wildlife!'

'Then what is he doing *here?*' Suddenly Sir Charles's voice had an edge to it that startled me. As we both stared at Wilfred with his gleaming binoculars, I was briefly flummoxed. Wilfred, who was beaming, chose this moment to drop his bombshell.

'Timothy my boy, I think I ought to introduce our visitor properly. Meet Sir Charles Hamilstone-ffrench, an old school friend of Lord Lifandoy and one of the most respected agricultural land agents in the country.' Wilfred continued blithely as I froze in horror. 'Sir Charles has agreed, as a special favour to the Earl, to survey the estate and decide whether any more of it could be profitably converted to intensive crop farming. I shall be briefing him on *our* opinions: he may or may not choose to show an interest in your point of view.'

Wilfred stepped softly past me, giving Sir Charles one of his broadest smiles as he did so.

I did not watch Wilfred depart. Through the mist of my own stupidity, all I could see was a long line of tractors and ploughs rolling over the lovely Reserve marshes, destroying all that irreplaceable wildlife. I did not dare to think what Keith Potts would do to me when he found out about my bungling.

By the time I recovered, the land agent was saying something intense about 'yields per hectare'. Seeing Sir Charles standing alone, I swung round in surprise. Uncle Wilfred's squat figure was marching firmly away, not towards Ginger Hill and the 'snowy owl zone' - as I already thought of it - but in the direction of the faraway towering cliffs of Raw Head.

At least he appeared to be out of the way for the moment. But I couldn't take it for granted: Uncle Wilfred was as canny as a fox with radar. I waited impatiently until Sir Charles paused for breath, then smiled as warmly as my petrified facial muscles would allow.

'Sir *Charles*. I am entirely at your disposal. I shall be delighted to answer any question you may care to ask. We are always eager to assist *all* visitors to the Reserve. But perhaps I could take just a moment to instruct my assistants.'

Bob and Jamie were still standing helplessly waist-deep in bracken. I addressed them in strained tones. 'Gentlemen, dear Uncle Wilfred is obviously keen to learn. Might I suggest that you escort him personally around the Reserve?'

If Sir Charles had not been standing at my side I would have added 'and *off* it!', but I didn't dare. I was already as deep in his bad books as I cared to go. I gave Bob and Jamie a piercing gaze and hoped that they would understand that Wilfred was to be guided as firmly as a kleptomaniac at the British Museum.

They grinned, saluted ironically and loped off, leaving me with my waiting guest.

∎　∎　∎　∎

There followed one of the most uncomfortable days I can remember. Sir Charles took me at my word. As he towed me around all the muddiest and most featureless parts of the valley, he showered me with salvoes of precise and penetrating questions.

Every tussock and ditch came under his gimlet eye. Every rough ley and the shaggy cows on it became the subject of an intense inquiry as to why this particular pasture should not be 'changed in use'. Each swamp pool had to be pointed out by me for its natural wealth - even if it had none. Every quaking fen had to be defended to him for its key value to wildlife - even the ones which were just foul-smelling sloughs even to me.

As I made each reply, I watched as it was noted down precisely by the agent on a page marked 'NO' in a pocketbook he carried. I caught one glimpse of the previous page, which was headed 'YES'. What else was written on it, I dearly longed to know.

In one thing, at least, I struck gold. The wildlife itself could scarcely have performed better if it had been rehearsing all week. Wherever I pointed, I had the Midas touch. If I claimed that redshank nested in *this* pasture, up one flew, piping above its running, ball-of-fluff chicks. If I announced a corn bunting territory in *that* dry meadow, one would fly to a post to start its jangle-of-keys song. If I pointed to a reed bed, the expected warbler would start its scratchy song from its depths; if I said there were snipe in the fen, one would rocket up to perform its crazy display flight, drumming its tail feathers in a rhythm that throbbed across the sky.

Painstakingly, we examined the whole valley of the West Burn. We descended through the swamps and fen near to the course of the Burn, and then returned back up the dale through the damp marshland. The only areas I avoided were the little marsh below Mrs. Bull's fence - I had an unreasoning desire to come no further under Alice's ever-present scrutiny - and, to Sir Charles's annoyance, the 'snowy owl zone'. As we approached the head of the valley on our return trip, Sir Charles set his step firmly in the unwanted direction.

'I don't see why we haven't examined the head of the valley yet,' he grumbled. 'We should have done that area first.'

In alarm, I thought fast. Sir Charles must not know our secret. He was an acquaintance of both Wilfred and Graham Fytts. I *must* divert him. Perhaps I could distract him with a lecture while I led us elsewhere.

I racked my brains for a theme on which to waffle. Sir Charles had shown a firm grasp of natural history: blinding him with words would be hard. But in my time as a warden I had listened to the scientific gibberish of many boffins, as I guided them around the Reserve. Their discourses, on obscure topics from bug- to fossil-hunting, were ingrained into my grey cells. Such a lecture, making Sir Charles forget his purpose, might do the trick. Going through the possibilities, I chose geology as the subject on which Sir Charles might know least.

'Of course, the Ginger Hill complex is not really a part of the Reserve proper,' I rattled off as fast as I could, 'because of its geology! You will probably not know that Ginger Hill is made of *boring* limestone. In fact, it is notable only for the obscure and even *more* boring feature known as the - er - Lifandoy Nonconformity.'

'Ah - Nonconformity...?' Sir Charles tried to interrupt; I waved him to silence, speeding my flow further.

'The Lifandoy Nonconformity is actually invisible, since it is only the meeting of the Upper-Estuarine-Jurassic-Series with deposits-of-a-subzone-of-the-Lower-Inferior-Oolite!'

'Eh? But–'

'But sadly that means it has *no* part in our present survey! What we must do now is to turn leave the valley and go west, straight to the coast.'

I had no idea how much of my waffle made sense. Fortunately, from the stunned expression on his face Sir Charles probably did not know either. He made only a feeble attempt to stem my flow.

'But I say... lime-rich grassland is particularly fertile and suitable for–'

'Exactly my point!' I beamed. 'So let us walk straight round to see the Lifandoy Reserve's particularly fine example of *coastal* lime-rich grassland!'

'But... but... the Lifandoy Nonconformity–'

'Will have to wait for another day!'

Stunned into submission, Sir Charles followed in my footsteps. Without more ado, I marched him past the scene of our first meeting and on to what is, on a fine day, my favourite part of the Reserve.

Apart from sandstone Raw Head, the west coast of Lifandoy is made of granite. At least, I think it is granite... The granite extends out westwards into the sea in a series of jagged tongues, each pair of which encloses a beach of pure white sand. The sand, like that of the Scottish Outer Hebrides, is derived largely from powdered shells, which accounts for its colour. Inland, the peat covering the granite is buried by a layer of wind-blown shell-sand. This in turn bears a flower-rich grassland of the sort which here, as in the Hebridean islands, is called the *machair*.

The *machair* was solid with colour, to the extent that it was almost hard to remember that plants were supposed to be green. Grazed areas held daisies, dog violets and the blue stars of spring squill by the million. Nearby, more miniature forests of orchids fringed water-logged areas below the West Ridge where some late golden kingcups surrounded iris beds, from one of which came the machine-like call of a corncrake.

Sir Charles was astounded by the *machair*. 'I've never seen so *many* flowers in my life. How do they survive the grazing?' Several shaggy beef cattle scarcely raised their eyes from the rich sward as he paused to inspect them.

'The cattle are grazed from November to May. They'll soon be moved up onto the *sliabh* - the inland peat marsh - for the summer. It's a long established rotation.'

'But wasteful! Are you telling me that all this pasture is left to grow into hay all summer?'

'You can't graze cattle on the *machair* all year,' I said. 'They need the peat grazing for a balanced diet.'

'We'll soon see about that.' Sir Charles had a gleam in his eye. 'Lots of inorganic fertilizer; and sheep to graze much more closely and turn this floral abandon into rich turf; all I need is a soil sample for analysis. We can soon add what is necessary.'

He bent down and began to scrape with a pocket trowel at the turf. Then he stopped. 'What on earth?'

I gave a pitying smile. 'Unfortunately, that's what the *machair* doesn't have.'

He stood up, staring at a scoop full of white grains. 'But there's virtually no soil under these plants! They're growing in sand!'

I smiled again. 'Standard farming methods are useless here.'

'And these flowers. They're primroses. In sand. Thousands of primroses!'

'That's right.'

'But primroses grow on sheltered hedge banks.' He looked around hopefully. The land was flat. Not a hedge, not a bush was in sight. I made no reply. He poked at the greenery again in disbelief. 'And I was told that some of the crofters grew barley?'

'That's right. This is the grazing *machair,* but further south where the crofts are it is arable farmed. The soil - or sand - is just the same there.'

Sir Charles held out a trembling trowel. 'But... barley in this?'

'Or even without it. One or two of the old crofters still grow it without even the sand.'

'Don't be ridiculous, man.

'They spread the tangle - the seaweed that the winter storms leave - on the stones at the tops of the beaches. Then they sow their seed directly on the weed. When the weed rots it sinks into the gravel and the barley grows up through the stones.'

Sir Charles made a curious noise in his throat. 'I'm wasting my time here,' he said angrily. 'Which is the shortest way back to Doy?'

'Doy? Oh, you mean Doytown. I'd better guide you back.'

■　■　■　■

To my disappointment, the agent did not even want to have a look at any of the beaches on the way. We walked quickly, in silence. Sir Charles had nothing to say; and I was going over the things I had said to him and indulging in too many recriminations to care. I put my energy into walking, reasoning that I would soon be free to release Bob and Jamie from their surveillance duties. I had not seen anyone else all day, so they must still be up on Raw Head. I could not imagine what Wilfred could want to be doing up there for a whole day.

Sir Charles made no move to dismiss me before we reached West Doy. I led him round the little marsh and up past the chapel; then we came to a halt outside Little Cottage. At that moment one of the House Farm Land Rovers appeared, driving up the road into the village and coming to a halt a short distance away. Three familiar figures emerged. As their vehicle reversed direction, they saw us and approached, walking stiffly.

Sir Charles greeted the foremost with surprise. 'Good day, Mr. Corn. Do you normally do your bird-watching from a Land Rover?'

Uncle Wilfred eyed him sourly. Bob and Jamie, behind him, looked to be in excellent spirits. I stared curiously at them. 'You two go in and make me a coffee,' I said. 'I'll join you in a few minutes.'

They nodded and headed through the swinging gate and up the garden path.

Wilfred looked suspiciously at me and then at the agent. 'Have you had a good day?'

Sir Charles stepped back and examined the pair of us as though we were two mischievous children.

'I dare say.' He smiled thinly. 'In your turn both of you have been extremely helpful. Each of you has views which are firmly and conscientiously held. I have already learnt a great deal about Lifandoy, for which I am much obliged.'

We looked at him, neither of us willing to depart without a hint as to his conclusions.

'I have not yet taken any clear decision,' he said. 'However, one thing at least has become clear to me about the evidence of you both.'

Wilfred cleared his throat. 'Which is?'

Sir Charles looked firmly down his nose. 'Both of you are clearly prone to so much prejudice and exaggeration that much of your evidence will have to be dismissed as virtual balderdash!'

'What?' we gasped together.

'You heard me. In particular' - I didn't at all like the way Sir Charles was looking at me - 'I have never heard such geological drivel in my whole life. For your information, young man, the term for a meeting of rock surfaces representing a break in the geological record is an *unconformity. Nonconformity* is, I believe, a religious expression!'

Sir Charles turned on his heel and strode away. At my side, Wilfred dissolved into giggles. 'A religious expression?' he spluttered. 'Dear Timothy, a religious expression!'

Wilfred had the air of someone who was laughing at the first joke he had heard in a long, hard day. I gave him a look that should have turned him into Lower Inferior Oolitic limestone and retreated to Little Cottage.

■　■　■　■

In the cottage, Bob and Jamie were grinning like a brace of successful thieves. They started pouring out their story before I had sat down with my coffee.

'You should have seen their faces,' chortled Bob. 'They took every word we sold them! Talk about being one up!'

'Half a minute,' I interrupted. 'Who's *they?* I left you only with Wilfred! And how come you arrived back in a farm Land Rover?'

'Wilfred must have arranged for his men to drive up the old lighthouse track to meet him on Raw Head,' explained Jamie. 'We got a lift back with them. And we had them as an audience all day.'

'An audience?'

'We found them gazing all around the cliffs,' said Jamie, 'Wilfred and three of his men, all with shining new binoculars. They seemed to be looking for something - we don't know what. When we jumped them, they had the gall to claim they wanted to learn about seabirds. So we announced we would give them a lesson.'

Bob wiped his tears from his eyes. 'Jamie spent a whole hour explaining to them how to tell a female guillemot from a male guillemot.'

I relaxed and grinned. Maybe it had not been such a bad day after all. Whatever plot Wilfred had been cooking, I was fairly sure it had been hard-boiled. His day had evidently been as bad as had mine.

I closed my eyes and sank back into my armchair, letting the coffee warm me from within. Then a thought occurred to me. I opened one eye curiously.

'Just a minute, you two. How do you tell a female guillemot from a male guillemot? I thought they both looked the same?'

'They do.'

'Then how...'

Jamie winked. 'Simple. You just wait until one of them lays an egg!' My assistants collapsed as usual in hysterical chortling. For once, however, their humour was not at my expense. Or so I thought.

5. - Port Doy

After a while, I felt pleased enough to reach for another coffee.

'All gone,' mumbled Jamie.

'Where's the jar? I'll make some more.'

'You're out of luck,' said Bob. 'Jamie likes it strong. He's emptied the bottle.'

'*What?*' This struck me as a tragedy. 'You've run me out of coffee? How will I survive?'

Bob looked at his watch. 'Four o'clock. You've plenty of time to get to the Co-op in Doytown. Can we have a lift?'

Jamie and Bob were always happy for me to chauffeur them around the steep island lanes in my battered Ford. I scowled. 'You planned this. Are you sure that coffee jar is really empty?'

Bob held it upside down. 'Every last granule.'

'Doytown it will have to be, then,' I grumbled. 'But if I break down you can push me all the way back to Little Cottage.'

I was just revving up the spluttering engine when there was a sound of soft footsteps and an angelic voice entranced my ears. It was my darling Jessica.

'Sweet Timothy,' she cooed through the car window, 'We've missed the bus and it's *ages* before the next is due. Mummy said that with my chill I wasn't to get cold waiting at the bus stop. You wouldn't by any chance be on your way to Port Doy?' The car filled with perfume and a few strands of long, blonde hair fell against my cheek.

'What a coincidence!' I beamed. 'Out of that front seat, Jamie. Make way for a lady!'

Jamie uncoiled his massive frame in astonishment. 'I thought we were going to Doytown?'

I grinned. 'You and Bob can get out at Doytown. But you'll have to walk back up the hill yourself. I'm going down to Port Doy with Jessica.'

'And Alice!' At Jessica's side a horrible visage appeared. Alice gave me a scowl which changed to a simpering smile as her big sister looked down indulgently.

'You won't mind, will you, Timothy dear? I promised to take Alice down after school to see the ferry coming in. She's *so* looking forward to it.'

I tried to snarl and smile at the same time: the result must have been frightening, because Alice jumped back as though she expected a bite.

Jessica took my expression to be one of approval. 'Oh, thank you. Alice, hop in with the nice men in the back seat and don't hold Timothy up, please.'

There was a churning of bodies in the back as Jamie and Bob squeezed up to let Alice in. The lads were seated at either side while in the middle was a heap of cagoules and old magazines. Somehow Alice managed to find her way in between the men where she fastened her seat-belt and gazed from on high like a waiting predator, staring straight at me in the driving mirror.

As I started off, the reflection of Alice's eyes glared at me. I stared back, willing her to blink. She blinked no more than a statue. Unnerved - although it came as no surprise as I had always believed there was reptilian blood in her makeup - I temporarily forgot how to drive. The poor car hiccoughed and started to kangaroo.

Jessica gasped. Behind us, Bob and especially Jamie were wedged tight. But in the mirror I had a vision of Alice's head being thumped hard against the car roof several times.

This made me feel better than I had all day. When the car stalled I sat behind the wheel trying so hard not to laugh that tears ran down my face. Jessica was deeply solicitous. 'Oh, you poor lamb! What happened, Timothy? Are you in pain?'

In the back seat, Alice's voice replied indistinctly. 'Not yet, he isn't!' In the mirror, I observed with interest that her face was now purple.

'No, I'm all right.' I gave Jessica one of my especially warm smiles. 'But thank you for asking.'

She sighed in relief. 'I wouldn't want you suffering, darling.'

'I would,' muttered Alice, a little more clearly now.

I felt eight feet tall. I started off again, smoothly this time. 'Men aren't easily hurt, you know.'

Alice started to speak. 'Except when you…'

There was a gurgling sound from behind me. I glanced in the mirror to find that Jamie had clamped a judicious large hand over Alice's mouth.

'Nice little girls don't need their mouths washing out with soap and water,' he murmured. I accelerated hard as we drove out of West Doy village, staying in low gear to raise the engine noise and distract Jessica's attention from what was about to come.

Alice bit Jamie's hand hard. He gave a yell and pulled it away. Alice kicked him somewhere; from painful experience, I guessed it was on his ankle. Bob came to his aid by grabbing her foot. She stamped on his fingers. He gasped and recoiled. His elbow thumped my seat hard from behind, making a dent somewhere near my kidneys. I gritted my teeth and screamed round a bend, just missing an oncoming tractor and halting hostilities briefly by compressing the combatants into a solid mass in the back.

Jessica gazed gently around. 'I do like all the sweet young animals in spring. Aren't the little calves funny with their mothers?' She pointed into a briefly seen field as we whizzed by.

'Not half as funny as I ought to be with you,' hissed Bob at Alice as he pushed her off him. She made no reply, partly because she had just been flattened under Jamie's sliding bulk.

I realized that I was approaching the Doytown river bridge at a considerable speed. Alarmed, I slammed on the anchors. Jessica gave an excited 'Oooh!' while in the back there was another gasp from a flattened Alice.

We bounced over the bridge, crashed the crossroads and screeched to a halt right at the door of the Doytown Co-op, scattering three boys and a dozen starlings. The boys - whom I recognized as from West Doy and members of Wilfred's chapel choir - watched in awe as two large men and a squashed small girl fell out of the back seat.

I was sorely tempted to drive away without Alice, and was restrained only by the thought of what my darling Jessica might say. We waited until Alice, her face now a shade of green, had resumed in silence her former perch. Then I drove all the way down the river valley to Port Doy without daring to look at the baleful eyes in the mirror.

■ ■ ■ ■

On a small island like ours, the arrival of the thrice-weekly ferry is an event that always commands notice. Almost everyone has some interest in its safe coming. A few essential supplies and the mail come via Lifandoy's small airstrip. But most goods still arrive from Heysham on the mainland, or occasionally from the Isle of Man if the ferry has called there, on the ship that is the island's lifeline.

At least, they are supposed to arrive. The ferry captains can be a slapdash lot, sometimes in a hurry or now and then downright careless. The captain of the ferry company's flagship, the old S.S. *Bagpipe,* always had a jolly attitude to life. A couple of months back he found it exceptionally funny when he left the container with the island's greengroceries for the week behind, on Heysham quay - until they sent him straight back for it. Then before that was the time he was edging the *Bagpipe* slowly round to Port Doy's old jetty when he rang Full Ahead instead of Full Astern on the engine room telegraph. He split the wooden pier right down its middle.

However, such dramatic arrivals are rare. Mostly the mooring, especially on a fine summer evening, is a merely pretty spectacle of sunshine on red and white paint and blue water, deft dockers, admiring passengers and tourists, and a queue of impatient shoppers waiting outside the harbour shops for the newly arrived magazines and newspapers.

Although Jessica might not know it, I had a feeling Alice's purpose in coming was not to admire the expertise of the merchant marine. Probably she hoped to obtain the latest copy of the *Teenyboppers' Express* just an hour before all the rest of her envious circle back in West Doy. My guess was proved right when she totally ignored the hive of activity on the pier to station herself first in the queue outside the harbour newsagent's shop.

■ ■ ■ ■

Jessica and I strolled along the quay as the *Bagpipe* sailed into the port, sparkling in her colourful paint.

'Is that the new ship?' asked Jessica in surprise. 'I thought the old *Bagpipe* was staying in service until next month.'

'Oh, didn't you hear? The captain went drinking with the chief engineer in the engine room one night last week at Heysham. Between them they managed to knock open one of the engine-room taps. After they went home the old *Bagpipe* sank at the quay in the night.'

Jessica roared. 'Ha - ha - *hee'*. Although I had been going out with Jess for several weeks, I'd never heard more than a restrained chuckle from her before. Her laugh was suggestive and raucous, and completely upset my mental impression of her.

'Will he get the sack?'

I was off balance. 'Who?'

'The captain.'

'Oh, I should think so.'

We mingled with the crowd at the foot of the gangplank, enjoying the bustle and evocative sounds and smells. Foot passengers flooded past and the slow release of cars and vans from the sardine-packed car deck began as the vehicles edged back and forward in turn until a way of escape presented itself to each.

Jessica was impressed. 'It's a lot faster unloading than the old boat, isn't it?'

'Safer too, I should think. We've needed a new ferry for years.'

A voice spoke challengingly from the bridge deck above us. 'There was nothing wrong with the old *Bagpipe!* Did we ever drop a car in the dock?'

We looked up. 'Not to my knowledge, Angus Donald,' I laughed.

'Nor mine! But what are you two doing arm in arm? This is a development my spies haven't informed me of, to be sure.'

The speaker was a shortish, muscular barrel of a man in a seaman's jersey with a twinkle in two deep brown eyes and a soft accent that sounded sometimes Scottish and sometimes Irish. He bounded down the gangplank like a big cat and stood with arms akimbo.

'Timothy Corn canoodling with Jessica Bull, eh? I'll drink to that, or would if my doctor hadn't banished me to a desert of prohibition!'

I gave a smirk. 'Has he indeed? Then you'll be able to see where you're steering the ferry for the time being, will you Angus?'

Angus Donald was the second mate and regular helmsman on the ferry and, like most of the crew, was well known to islanders. He was even better known than most, being both Lifandoy born and a one-time Port Doy ship-chandler and lifeboat-man.

Angus had been a friend of mine since my student days. We had met one day on the old ferry shortly after he had taken up his new job. During an apprenticeship working on bird reserves in England and Wales, it had become second nature for me to have some sort of optics to hand. This was good news on the *Bagpipe,* since Angus was a keen birdwatcher and immediately befriended any binocular wearers he saw on board. He had pointed out a couple of storm petrels to me, the first I had seen. Thereafter I had cultivated his friendship assiduously, later often going walking with him. I would now always let him know about any rarities that turned up on the Reserve, in exchange for the chance to receive his hospitality and share the unparallelled view from the ferry's bridge whenever I took passage.

He snorted. 'Even with a hangover I could spot a storm petrel while you were still looking for a herd of swans in the harbour, Timothy boy.'

'Less of the boy and a bit more of respect for a professional, if you please,' I grinned.

'Sorry, Mr. Assistant Warden!' Angus got down on his knees and started saluting in mock servility. He bounced up again. 'And how's your boss doing at the moment? I was looking to be having a word with him if he were around.'

'You're out of luck until nearly midsummer, Angus.'

'Oh? Why's that?'

'Keith is under doctor's orders too, with a hernia. He won't be back on Lifandoy for quite a while.'

Jessica looked at me in surprise. 'Oh, the poor man.'

Angus looked interested. 'Really? Who's in charge up at the Reserve, then? Not you, surely?'

I drew myself up to my full height. 'Who else?'

Angus exploded in laughter. Observing my hurt look, he gave me a solid slap on the back. 'Sorry, Mr. *Acting* Warden! A pretty companion, and promotion to boot! You *are* coming up in the world.'

'Thank you.'

'Mind you, I suppose you've a long way to come.'

Jessica chuckled. I frowned at her. Angus put a mollifying arm around me. 'Never mind, you've got friends to help you. While you're here, though, I'll need to have a word with you unless you're in a great hurry.'

Angus was suddenly in a more serious mood. Jessica gently disengaged her arm from mine and smiled at us. 'I'd better track Alice down. You men can talk business on your own.'

As she walked away, both of us watched her appreciatively. Angus nodded. 'You've made a fine choice there, Tim. Don't underestimate her, either. I've known Jessica Bull since her father was coxswain of the Port Doy lifeboat and there's a lot more to her than meets the eye. She isn't just the pretty face she makes out to be. That's a mask for her real feelings.'

'That sounds alarming! Thanks. Well, what's up?'

Angus lowered his voice. 'I've a warning for you.'

'A warning? From whom?'

'The grapevine.'

'Sounds mysterious. About what?'

Angus's face gained a dusky hue. 'You may be about to receive some unwanted visitors. *Egg collectors.*'

I scowled. 'What? Are you sure?'

'Keith Potts and I have an understanding. He has well-informed contacts at your Nature Reserves Society's headquarters who supply a list of suspect cars and licence plates. I circulate them round the ferry crews. One of the egg-collectors' cars - a black Volkswagen - has been seen on the Isle of Man ferry. That means they could turn up here.'

I rubbed my nose. 'That's awkward.'

'Unfortunate. But why awkward?'

I hesitated. Then I reached into my pocket. 'This letter from Keith came this morning.'

Angus read it with growing interest. There was a gleam in his eye when he had finished. 'Fetlar, eh?'

''Yes.

He licked his lips. 'Snowy owls, perhaps? Or red-necked phalaropes?'

'I wish I knew. At the moment, I'm guessing the owls. I saw something white this morning. Something that didn't look like a gull. But Wilfred is prowling round.'

'Your Uncle Wilfred? What on earth is he after?'

'Not eggs, anyway. He's devious but not a criminal. But he's the last person I want on the Reserve at the moment.'

'Oh? Why?'

I told Angus about Sir Charles and his survey. He sympathized. 'It's a fine pot of soup you have in the stirring, Tim. Well, I can't help you on the Reserve. I have no time off until the middle of next week. But I'll watch every car that arrives.'

I nodded. 'Thanks. I'd appreciate that. Ring me at Little Cottage if anything happens. Now I'd better be getting back to Jessica.'

■ ■ ■ ■

The trolley carrying the newsagent's delivery was trundling along the pier. I followed it, thinking up plots and plans. As the trolley clattered over a trailing hawser, its rearmost parcel of magazines toppled off with a soft thud. A passing docker lofted it back into place with one muscular arm. As it landed, a small piece of card fluttered out of the parcel and fell at my feet.

Instinctively, I picked it up. After all my litter-collecting on the Reserve it was second nature to thrust it into a pocket for later disposal. I had no idea what it was.

I caught up with Jessica a little way before the newsagents. She was chatting to a small, plump man standing outside a grand-looking building that had clearly come down in the world from its original use since it bore only a grimy signboard, 'FERRY GARAGE'.

Jessica looked up as I approached. 'Timothy, isn't it a shame! Dear Mr. Dooley has been telling me he's lost his pet, Cocky!'

The smell of assembled livestock emanated from the garage. I vaguely remembered that old Jack Dooley, an eccentric self-employed mechanic and the island scrap dealer, was the owner amongst a large collection of other pets of a small and ill-favoured cocker spaniel. Its name had not registered in my memory, but no doubt this was the missing Cocky. The memory was not so vague that I could not remember getting a nip on the ankle a couple of times from the bad-tempered creature. 'Oh, I do hope you find him,' I said, lying through my teeth.

We moved on to the shop. The parcels had been ripped open and the contents spread on the shop counter. The proprietor, a choleric shrimp of a figure, leafed through them unhappily.

'There's quite a lot missing this week,' he said. 'There's a strike on, you know. Only a single copy of the *Teenyboppers Express.* You're a lucky lassie, Miss Alice.'

Alice seized it from him and threw coins on the counter. 'I had better be! This is the special edition with the signed picture of Simon Splutter in it. And less of the lassie and the Miss, too. I'm neither a baby nor a servant.'

'Oooh, sorry I'm sure.' The newsagent ceased to smile and turned to the next customer. *'Racing Times* is it, Mr. O'Shaughnessy?'

Jessica and I were turning away when there was a scream of horror from behind us. 'There isn't one! You've lost it. Find it, *find* it will you!'

The little newsagent gave Alice a grim stare, eye to eye. 'Are you addressing me, *Miss* Alice?'

'The picture of Simon Splutter! It's missing! Look, this is where it was stuck onto the cover.'

'Simon Splutter? Would that be a real person?'

Alice went white. I reflected that there were not many colours left for her to go. 'Simon Splutter is the greatest rock guitarist alive today,' she pronounced. 'Only musical philistines haven't heard of him!'

The shopkeeper was unimpressed. 'Well, you may call me Goliath, then. But your picture isn't here. You can see for yourself.'

'Tell me where it is, then!'

He had no more time for her. I didn't blame him. 'Back in England? Now, Mr. O'Shaughnessy…'

Alice stormed out of the shop. As she stomped off along the quay in a fury, with Jessica following, something occurred to me. I paused and pulled the piece of litter out of my pocket. The picture on the card was appalling, and the signature was nearly illegible. But the name printed at the bottom was clearly that of a certain Mr Splutter.

I started to call out. Then my better nature was overcome by a wave of swift mental calculation. A bargaining chip with Alice could be a very useful thing. Anyway, she deserved a bit of punishment for being so rude in the shop. I placed a sympathetic smile on my face and folded the picture carefully inside Keith's letter as I walked on after the sisters. Alice would get her picture… eventually. It was turning into a good day after all. I wondered what excitement tomorrow would bring.

6. - A Meeting with the Snowy Bird

I felt obliged to give Bob and Jamie the next morning off after their day of tailing Wilfred and his men. So I was on my own as I strode up the village street after breakfast. I gazed longingly up the lane to the Bulls' as I passed the chapel. Wilfred's poster on the chapel notice board caught my eye and I gave it a scowl, feeling the lump on my head gingerly with my fingers. I walked on rapidly round the little marsh and on up the long Reserve track, which was empty. There was no sign of Wilfred or Sir Charles, and the Reserve seemed dead after the excitement of the previous day; until, that was, I reached the foot of Ginger Hill.

Ginger Hill is a curious, roughly cone-shaped eminence with a flattened apex, which forms a distinctive feature on the Lifandoy skyline. Strewn with huge boulders and rock terraces, it has no distinctive features apart from, on the east side, one stunted wood of ash trees. As I had told Sir Charles, truthfully as it happens, Ginger Hill is made of limestone. This is a rock otherwise scarce on the west side of the island. Apparently, the meeting of it with the sandstone of Raw Head and the granite of the west coast is geologically odd. It draws quite a few amateur geologists and from them I have picked up just enough long words to be able to impress fools with - unfortunately not including Sir Charles.

The day was also a contrast. Gone was the clear air of Monday. The swiftly changing island climate had brought low cloud and a patchy mist to the valley, into which Ginger Hill and the other high ground disappeared frequently from view. The landmark of my interest began to vanish again for the umpteenth time as I came toward a full view of its foot.

The bare, bowl-shaped, raised vale below Ginger Hill which holds the headwaters of the West Burn is hidden from a distance by a rather earthwork-like encircling bank, cut only by the channel of the Burn itself. On entering the bowl's half-mile-across circumference the whole comes in a moment into view. Had Sir Charles, on our tour, taken twenty strides more then the valley head - and its contents - would have been revealed at once.

I knew to a pace where to stop and crouch to the ground while sidling to a convenient tiny knoll on the bank. The knoll was, in fact, the same one I had stood on with Bob and Jamie the morning before. My heart was beating hard in hope as I pressed aside a few sprigs of heather and raised my glasses.

Several pairs of wings were flickering around the valley: but to my disappointment, none were pure white. Most were the chequered wings of displaying lapwing, whose cries assailed each other constantly. Near the burn a curlew was displaying, while somewhere in the fen where fen sedge grew thickly I could hear the reeling song of a grasshopper warbler. Nearer on my left, I could hear the sad piping of a golden plover.

I scanned the drier parts of the valley carefully. But every owlish-looking grey-white rock remained a rock, however many times I willed it to open a sleepy eye, or turn a head.

Retreating a little way, I began to circumnavigate the bowl below the top of the bank, remaining always just below the horizon to its occupants. After a hundred paces, I crawled to another viewpoint. The golden plover saw me and half-ran, half-flew to a safer spot from which to whistle at me with great interest. The valley was still empty of white owls and the plover's plangent calls began to get on my nerves.

I stood up. Within seconds, a long-winged, pale bird flew from close by and began to move away silently over the blue moor-grass. Stifling a cry, I dropped again. But even as I did so, my eyes had already pointed out the mistake. It was a false alarm: the bird was pale brown, not white.

'Short-eared owl,' I muttered. 'Probably there's a pair of them in the valley, too. But I don't want a pale brown owl, I want a white or a grey one. Female snowies have a few dark markings, males are pure white. Either would do me. Preferably both!'

The mist started coming down again, and it started to drizzle. Depressed, I pulled my hood over my head, tucked my bins inside my jacket and zipped up tightly, leaving a minimum of exposed flesh. I walked on, slowly, to the foot of Ginger Hill.

The first of the rounded limestone terraces rose abruptly from the peaty vegetation below. The change of the vegetation at this point on a sunny day can be delightful, from the dark green of the fen to the verdant limestone grassland starred with yellow rock-rose and blood-red cranesbill. At close quarters the rock itself, when not encrusted with lichen, also has the honey-warm hue of Cotswold limestone. But in the fog the land simply went from flat sodden to steeply sloping sodden. I was about to give up when something prompted me to one last effort.

I ascended the first few yards of the slope, looking for a vantage point to overlook the valley. Near the base of the hill was a small spur with a small white-surfaced stone at its foot. I made for the spur, which was narrow, and cautiously stepped out onto the rock promontory.

The white stone was below and to one side of me. Gazing anxiously outwards, I was just disentangling my bins from the depths of my waterproofs when from the corner of my eye I saw the stone open broad, startlingly white wings and vanish around the spur.

With an amazed cry, I turned to follow it. Instantly I lost my balance and was forced to save myself by leaping down from the rock onto the peat a couple of metres below. I sank into the boggy ground. But this was a minor discomfort. Far more painful was losing sight of the bobbing white shape, which was already flickering ghostlily far away through the fog.

Somewhere on the hillside the bird settled and vanished from view. Then it lifted again. I clambered back onto rock and tried the binoculars. But the bird was already approaching the limit of visibility, and it faded into the greyness in a moment.

I scrambled up Ginger Hill as fast as the wet rocks would allow me to. I had to know - and besides, my blood was up. A drenching would be worthwhile if I could just see the bird clearly just once - and be certain what it was.

The white bird could have been training all year for this exercise in outwitting me. On the whole climb up Ginger Hill, I never got in sight of the bird for more than half a second at a time. Most of the hillside was strewn with knobs of limestone, peppered with ghostly hawthorn scrub. The bird - whatever it was - kept disappearing into the hawthorns, a pale blur buried among leaves and white blossom. Time and again I crept to a vantage point only to discover that it was the wrong one or that a receding white flicker in the mist was my poor reward.

I did not in any case want to approach the bird too closely. Apart from the possibility of disturbing a nest, there was also the nature of the bird itself. Owls of all species are to be taken seriously. At least one well-known bird photographer famously lost an eye to the attack of a mother tawny owl. And snowies were an order of magnitude bigger than tawnies.

I stopped to think out loud again. 'What a lumbering fool I am! I should have had a clear view four or five times. As it is, all I can say so far is that it's white and of reasonable size. Not very big, mind you - although it's hard to tell in the fog. But this can't be the female. It's too small and white for that - obviously it's *Mr.* Snowy if it's a snowy at all.

'But I haven't even proved it's an owl yet. It's not a gull - those wings are as white as a swan's. If it wasn't a snowy it would have to be something even rarer, a gyr falcon from Greenland perhaps.

'But I can't claim anything on the basis of what I've seen so far. Not on my second day as acting warden! I'd be a laughing stock if some rare bird twitchers turned up and proved me wrong!'

As I reached the summit of Ginger Hill, the drizzle thickened into a downpour. Being well used to Lifandoy's extremes of weather, I was clad to face it. But my cladding was thick enough for the climb to have left me as soaked within as without. Feeling like a walking puddle, I plodded on miserably, scanning the hillside every minute or so through dripping binoculars.

Suddenly, I saw it! Banks of mist were still drifting across the hillside, but as a bank drifted away leaving a clear view, I glimpsed my quarry. The bird had settled far down the further slope of the hill, where it was almost concealed within a small ash tree. The tree, the first of the little wood on the further face of the hill, was no more than a dense shrub clinging to the brow of a low cliff. All I could see was a splash of white plumage through the twigs.

There were no paths to follow. This was an area of the Reserve little visited by wardens. I studied the landscape. There was no way I could approach from above without being spotted. Keeping one eye on the white speck in the distant tree, I took a wide detour around and down the face of the hill. When I was well below the cliff, I dropped out of sight and sidled along the base of a convenient terrace towards a carefully calculated point. Feeling my way with my feet, I shortly found them halted by the edge of an abrupt drop. Still not looking down, I inched up over the limestone and raised my head.

My stalking had been immaculate, for the tree was exactly where I had planned, on the skyline. But it was empty. I cursed.

Then it happened. From my right there came a blur of movement. Before I could react, there came a buffeting of fast wings. Something struck a glancing blow on the side of my head - a white tornado. I felt a sharp pain just in front of my ear as the tornado passed on.

Balanced at the top of the unseen bank, I found the blow light but disastrous. All at the same time I tried to duck in alarm, to fend off the white thing and to determine its departing course. For a fraction of a second, I saw something large and flapping close to me, of unfamiliar shape and with apparently a hint of yellow somewhere in its white make-up. Then my time ran out.

One ankle went crooked beneath me. I rolled yelling downhill. What lay at the foot of the slope I wot not. All I could remember at that moment was the sloping but high limestone cliff somewhere not far away, where the north foot of Ginger Hill sloped hundreds of feet to the sea. There was a despair in me that lent me hidden strength as I reached out to grab whatever solid object might come first to hand.

There was a roar in my ears - the waves below? - as the bank levelled out onto some sort of gravel ledge. Half-blinded by dirt, and scrabbling for a hold before the next drop, I heard a screech as from some savage bird - with my luck, it was probably waiting for the carrion that was slithering down the cliff towards it. There followed a painful and breath-removing impact. Still half-blinded, I reached out and clamped like a starfish onto something round and wet.

There was a pause. Then above the thunder of the rain came the sound of moving objects on the gravel. I clung tighter, willing the round thing not to dislodge.

The voice of Uncle Wilfred entered my consciousness slowly.

'Why,' it enquired, with a note of wonder in it, 'are you clinging to my front nearside wheel?'

I opened my eyes and mouth wide, blinking and spitting away mud. The gravel surface was no dangerous cliff ledge. It was the narrow strip of the track to Raw Head lighthouse, down an embankment of which I had rolled. The existence of the snaking, potholed track, the one break in the downward slope of the hill, had slipped completely from my memory. To my chagrin, I found myself embracing no rock but a muddy tyre of the farm Land Rover that Wilfred had screeched to a stop on seeing my descent.

I ceased my imitation of a goldfish. 'Er - that's none of your business.'

He scratched his head. 'Well, I can't drive very far with you like that, Timothy. Wouldn't you prefer to ride inside?'

I released the tyre hastily. 'No, thank you. I can make my own way.' I started to get up.

'Oh, you're most welcome to a lift. I'm always ready to do a good turn. We're all here to help each other.'

The idea of being helped by Wilfred was so alarming that it took my breath away.

'No... no, thank you,' I gasped. 'I'm quite sure I don't need any - *Yeeoww!'*

Wilfred watched as I collapsed, then grinned down at me.

'You're not making your way anywhere with a sprained ankle,' he observed correctly. 'And that's a nasty cut by your ear, too.'

I was reminded of the bird. I looked at him worriedly. 'Did you see anything else when I fell?'

'Couldn't see a thing in this weather. You were lucky I saw you before you went under my wheels.'

I relaxed. I was drenched, crippled, and my secret was safe.

'All right,' I scowled ungraciously, 'I give in.'

■　■　■　■

With no word of rebuke, Uncle Wilfred helped me into the vehicle, as carefully as if I were his baby. He reversed the vehicle smartly and set off at a cautious pace back down the now heavily foggy track.

The warmth revived my brain. I eyed Wilfred suspiciously. 'What were you doing up here, anyhow? This is a long way from the Home Farm!'

He gave me a sideways stare. 'I could ask the same of you. The track is open for anyone to drive. But not everyone would think of rolling down Ginger Hill in the rain.'

This was true. 'I slipped. Is that a crime?'

Wilfred surveyed my bleeding temple. 'You look more like the victim of one to me, Timothy.'

I changed the subject back again. 'You still haven't told me why you were driving up to Raw Head in the fog. Don't tell me you were there for the view?'

'Why should you care?'

I grinned mischievously. 'We're still on the Reserve. It's the duty of the Reserve warden to investigate all visitors. And it's their duty to answer his questions.'

Wilfred looked distinctly uncomfortable. Being a Christian, he could not lie. I had him where I wanted him. I waited in an expectant pose.

He hesitated. 'I was looking for something lost.'

'Something lost? Did you lose it yesterday?'

He muttered something unintelligible. His face was colouring slowly. The Land Rover accelerated down the track.

'Pardon?'

'I said, I didn't lose it.'

'Oh. Who did? One of your men?'

'No.' His face was now bright pink.

'Then who? You have to tell me.'

Wilfred had a coughing fit. I waited until it subsided. 'I beg your pardon, Wilfred?'

There was a pregnant pause. Without warning, the twisting track crossed a wooden bridge that loomed darkly from the mist. Then it sloped upwards. Dim buildings shot by, then a tarmac road appeared. Wilfred turned right and accelerated enthusiastically on the smooth surface.

'We're off the Reserve now,' he observed. He sounded immensely relieved. He shut his mouth with an audible snap.

I sulked. The injury to my ankle had done nothing for my state of mind and, worse, I had become the object of charity from one of my ideological enemies. I stared sourly ahead, hardly noticing that the hill-fog had gone now that we bad left the high ground.

As the valley road unreeled before us, I glared at the featureless fields that lined our route. Compared with the rich patchwork of the landscape of the distant Reserve across the valley, the estate farmland was as wearying as plain wallpaper. It glided smoothly past as Wilfred's home farm Land Rover purred powerfully on.

'I suppose this sleek vehicle was paid for by some of that fortune that you make out of intensive farming?' I waved an arm angrily at the dull scenery. 'Wilfred, you make money from floral desertification! Your wheat-fields are like wildernesses. Have you killed off *every* wild flower on this side of the valley?'

'Yes,' said my uncle, proudly. 'It's as clean as a whistle. When I was young, these fields were full of weeds - everything from cornflowers to poppies grew here. We've eradicated them all.'

'And you truly don't miss them? Not even around the edges, say?' I felt sick.

'Miss them?' He gave me a puzzled glance. 'What for?'

'For the sake of preserving biodiversity; or to encourage the local birds and insects; or even for simple old colour and beauty…'

'Beauty?' The concept appeared to startle him. My uncle shook his head firmly. 'You're being irresponsible, Timothy. Weeds harbour pests and diseases. Up to one third of all world crops are lost to those three causes each year! And why should we grow weeds where we could grow valuable crops?'

'Oh, you can't sell all the weeds, of course. Sorry, I forgot. Money comes first.'

Wilfred shook his head again. 'I'm not a farmer for money. Graham Fytts thinks only of profit. But I'm doing my little bit to keep the world moving.'

'Oh, come on,' I protested. 'Don't come the good Christian! You're feeding the farm bank account first. And you're feeding your own; you don't earn coppers as assistant farm manager. The farm coins money and so do you. You must have a good-sized pot of gold buried away by now.'

Wilfred eyed me strangely. 'Do you really believe that?'

'Eh? Well, I know you give a lot away, but you must have savings–'

'For a rainy day? And to provide us with a reasonable pension? Of course. But I don't believe in burying treasure. Martha and I have no children, now, to help on in life. So we keep only–'

'The essentials? Then you must dispose of a lot.'

Wilfred frowned. 'That's my business, but I certainly believe the only useful thing one can do with money is to use it,' he said.

'Use it to get more, I presume?' I nodded. 'Of course, you're a God believer. Like those evangelists on the telly, I suppose - give so that you get given, 'cos God is there to make you prosperous. That's how Christians think nowadays, isn't it?'

'Most definitely not,' said my uncle sharply, 'any more than they did in the past, such as when you learnt from me about giving, in Sunday School when you were small. You know very well that is not worshipping Christ, it's worshipping prosperity.'

'Is that so? Don't a lot of religious people do both?'

'I believe there are those who try very hard to prove they can worship both God and money. But anyone truly following in the footsteps of the Crucified One does not. It's impossible.'

'Why?'

'It's a question of what you value, Timothy. Everything that you do and are is determined by your order of values. Worshipping, or worth-shipping, as the word originally was, simply means devoting yourself to what you value most. And not just devoting yourself. Whatever you value most - whatever you worship - you will come to resemble!'

'Resemble?'

'Putting your faith in Jesus in order to get earthly prosperity and riches from Him - as if you could! - is worshipping your appetite, not God. If you try to do that you merely become ugly, bloated and hungrier than ever.'

'Huh.' I lost interest. 'Well, my ambition is to become bloated and rich.'

He glared at me. 'Nephew, the love of money does nothing for your life. Prosperity adds nothing real to you! You do understand me, don't you? Repeat after me - "I understand you perfectly, Wilfred."'

'I understand you perfectly, Wilfred.'

'Hmm.' Yes, I'm not convinced.' He snorted. 'Listen, Timothy - it's not your business, but do you think I would be a better person with a life of luxury?'

'Well, no. You certainly don't try very hard for one, anyway. You're not famous for taking lots of holidays in the Greek isles. Your car is as old as mine. And that antique you call a television is not far behind it. But you've always earned the maximum from your job.'

'Naturally. I use all my skills and earn all I can. And I'm not perverse or ascetic: I wouldn't refuse a promotion I deserved, or anything like that. But I am content with what I keep.'

'Don't you want to gain just a little more?'

'No. I don't accept raffle tickets, if you're about to try and sell me one. And I would not know top from bottom of one of those national lottery tickets you fill in so *religiously* every Saturday.'

'But surely you're not really content? Just think of all the extra good you could do! Anyone would think you don't want your God to make you rich.'

He glanced at me, then stared at the road ahead. 'That's His decision, of course. But I have prayed many times that I might never be given riches. It is certainly not my ambition to become rich, now or ever.'

'You're mad, Wilfred! Stark, staring mad!' Astonished, I sank back into my seat, trying to find a comfortable position for my ankle.

As he drove down into the valley, Wilfred's spirits rose and he began to sing a hymn. This made me feel ill as well as uncomfortable. I counted off the minutes impatiently until the road rose up the further side of the valley to the village of West Doy. I was anticipating an embarrassing reception.

7. - Hopping Mad

To my relief there were no onlookers in the village street to watch my ignominious return. Just as I thought the coast was clear, however, the door of Little Cottage opened and Bob Backley emerged down my garden path with a steaming mug in his hand.

I scowled at him as I hopped out of the Land Rover. 'Who said you could drink my coffee?'

Bob had not the grace to look even a little embarrassed. 'The door was unlocked. I guessed you hadn't gone far in the rain and that you'd want a drink when you got back.'

'I always leave my door unlocked. Who locks their door on Lifandoy?' He looked suitably surprised.

Wilfred got out and started round the vehicle to assist me. Hastily, I hopped past him and lunged for my garden gate, determined to evade his helping hand.

Bob and Wilfred both were there just in time to stop me going headlong over my own gate. I hung onto Wilfred reluctantly as he pushed it open.

Bob sniffed on seeing me limp. 'Hmph. I see you've been listening to the weather forecast. A couple of days with your feet up while it rains, I suppose, while your minions slog round in the mud.'

Uncle Wilfred swung my gate to and fro with interest. 'I see you've fastened up that rotten old gatepost. About time, too.' He peered closely at my handiwork. 'Your gate was becoming a disgrace to the good name of the Corn family. And that's a solid lump of metal you've acquired for the job. Where did you come across that?'

I was in no mood for chitchat. 'It was lying in my porch.'

'And before that?'

Wilfred was not associated with any mobile phone company to my knowledge, but I was not about to tell him the probable origin of my post.

'It didn't come from the farm, if that's what you're wondering.'

He laughed. 'Never thought it for a moment, nephew. You could do with another support for the other side, that's all.'

'I know. Do you have one to offer?'

'You could try Jack Dooley down at Ferry Garage. He had a few posts in his yard when I was down there on Saturday.'

'At Ferry Garage? What were you doing there? I thought Jack had threatened you with blue murder if you ever set foot in there again?'

Wilfred gave me a wide-eyed look. 'What, because of that good turn I did for him when his boiler leaked? No, Jack saw the light about that long ago. We're good friends again now.'

'That's the most surprising thing I've heard all day. Did you ever hear that story, Bob?'

All at once Wilfred was in a hurry. 'Right, off I go, then. I'll drop in later to see if the patient is still alive. Cheerio, lads!'

He leapt into the Land Rover and vanished at speed. Bob stared after him in astonishment.

I took the mug from Bob's unresisting hand. 'Want to hear about the real Uncle Wilfred, Bob? Give me a shoulder up the path and I might even let you have a small coffee while I tell you about it.'

■　■　■　■

The famous affair of Jack Dooley's boiler had begun a year the previous November. As a classic example of the 'Wilfred effect', it had already passed into Lifandoy folklore. Bob and I settled into armchairs, my ankle resting m a bowl of cold water and a cold cloth pressed to my head, as I regaled him with it.

Jack's little repair and scrap business at Ferry Garage occupied what had once been the steamship booking office, a Victorian edifice on the quay with a heating system of large iron radiators and four inch pipes. The heating system was never overhauled and rarely used: Jack was too thrifty to use fuel on behalf of himself or his sole employee except in freezing weather. Consequently, he always delayed heating up the geriatric boiler until the first frosty morning of the winter. The battered boiler leaked like a sieve: the starting up process thus invariably involved hasty addition to the boiler contents of several raw eggs or whatever other leak remedy Jack had to hand to gum up the cracks in the venerable vessel.

About the middle of that November, when the weather forecast predicted frost, Jack was complaining to his crony Uncle Wilfred about the price of eggs. Wilfred mentioned helpfully to Jack that a farmer friend of his cured boiler leaks with the aid of a cupful or two of fresh cow manure. Wilfred grinned ominously as he said it, but unfortunately Jack, being rather short-sighted, failed to notice.

Next day, Wilfred brought down to Jack's half a bucketful of the necessary. Jack and he became rather carried away with the medicine, and in the end the whole half bucketful went, cup by cup, into the boiler. It was a great success: the boiler for once leaked not a single drop. That following year Wilfred was an honoured guest at Ferry Garage whenever he happened by the harbour - until the cold weather came again.

At the start of the recent winter, Jack was in his usual hurry to get the heat on. At his telephoned appeal, Wilfred shortly appeared with the required pail of malodorous filth. Full of optimism after their former success, Jack tipped the contents in wholesale as soon as he had lit the boiler.

Half an hour later, the cold engineer was still poking around with bits of old bamboo at the sludge in the bottom of his clogged vessel. The reason for the contretemps was plain. The dose of the previous year had set solid during the summer, crystallizing like concrete in the piping; the fresh treatment had merely added insult to thrombosis.

Wilfred remained unabashed. 'Heat it up, lad,' he said, grinning enthusiastically. 'Give it a bit of what for!'

Jack obeyed. When he and the boiler were both steaming Wilfred started wandering round, opening and shutting radiator taps and banging the piping with a block of wood.

Eventually the clot moved. As Wilfred banged, the boiler gurgled ominously up at Jack. Water surged into the system, rattling the radiators loudly.

There was a growing sound of much bubbling. Then came a belch that would have impressed the mother of a colicky baby hippopotamus. The piping released a mighty volume of air. In an eruption of increasing force the boiler coughed and retched, building up to a climax. Then with a malevolence that repaid in full Jack's long misuse of it, the vessel exploded with vomit, throwing much of its foul contents over its owner as a steaming brown wave.

The first the outside world knew of the disaster was when Jack emitted a yell that must have been nearly audible on the Isle of Man. Two or three burly Lifandoy dockhands came running in curiosity along the quayside. They were confronted by Uncle Wilfred, who emerged from the garage preceded by a terrified stampede of Jack's cats, dogs and other lodgers and dragging Jack himself. The unfortunate garage owner was covered from head to foot with hot, stinking muck. Wilfred gave the dockhands a broad grin, at which they flinched and prudently drew back. Then he planted a large foot securely in Jack's ample spare parts and propelled the scalded engineer in a headlong dive into the harbour.

At the nearby ferry terminal a group of passengers were waiting solemnly to board the newly arrived ferry to the mainland. On seeing the hapless Jack's leap, they presumed it to be a stunt for charity. They accepted their release from boredom with joy, threw their boarding passes into the air and cheered wildly.

Heartened by their applause, Wilfred bounded down the quay steps into a dinghy and rowed out to retrieve a severely chilled Jack with the aid of a well-placed oar. The subsequent transfer of the patient to a swaddled situation in front of a bottle of whisky in the bar of the Harbour Inn was slowed purely by Wilfred's tendency repeatedly to drop the oars and to collapse, grinning and giggling hysterically, in the bottom of the dinghy.

■　■　■　■

When he heard the end of my story, Bob roared. 'Hoo - hah - hoo! I must tell Jamie this one. But wasn't he badly hurt?'

'Jack? Not too badly. Mind you, it didn't seem to impress him that Uncle Wilfred quite possibly saved his life by pushing him into the harbour. I didn't know until just now that they had exchanged a word with each other since.'

'Did Jack never thank him?'

'Not that I heard. The only thing Jack appreciated about it was all the whisky Wilfred poured into him. Wilfred is nearly teetotal and it was the first time Jack had ever known Wilfred to treat him to spirits!'

Bob raised his cup and drained it, then looked hopefully at the dregs. I took no notice.

'Wilfred seems to make a habit of rescues,' he observed.

I frowned. 'Another way to put it is that he's always there at the wrong moment.'

'You don't sound very grateful. What did happen to your ankle, then? Was it the same thing as happened to your head?'

'No.' I related to Bob my adventures on Ginger Hill, omitting any mention of Wilfred's tyre. He was excited.

'It definitely wasn't a big gull?'

'With claws?' I removed the cloth from my temple, looked at it ruefully, and replaced it. 'No way. It was pure white. Except that I had that brief impression of something yellow somewhere about it.'

'Is there any yellow on snowy owls?'

'Not that I can remember. But we'd better check. Where's my field guide?'

We pored over a book. 'Their eyes are yellow,' we chorused. I thought hard.

'It could have been its eye I saw, I suppose. Certainly it was somewhere around the head area.'

'You sound confident. I thought you were in mid-air at the time?'

'More or less.'

'You did well to see that, then. What about size and shape?'

'I couldn't say for certain. Shape, broad-winged, probably owl-like but I couldn't claim that for certain. Size, bigger than a barn owl, or even a short-eared owl - but nearer the length of a crow than a raven. That's a bit smaller than I'd expect, even for a male. Perhaps it was a youngish one. Anyway, you'll keep a sharp look out, Bob?'

'Jamie's more likely to be down in the valley than I am. He's the inland man. I'm working along the coast most of the time. Yes, I'll let him know.' Bob looked once more into his cup, then put it down reluctantly. 'Ah, well. Back to the grindstone. I've the contents of two hundred tern nests to check on along the shore by the end of the week.'

'You'll let me have your counts of them for the Reserve logbook, won't you?'

'Sure. Anything else you want me to do?'

'Er - well, yes. If you're passing the Bulls' cottage you could drop in and let Jessica know I'm looking for a friendly nurse.'

'Isn't she working today?'

'No, she's only at the office Wednesdays to Fridays.' Jessica had a part-time job in Doytown where she was a secretary at the Estate Office.

Bob paused uneasily. 'Will Alice be at home?'

'She should be at school today.'

'Oh, that's all right.' He brightened and made for the door.

The rest of the day, in the company of an attentive and adoring companion, was exceedingly pleasant but included no events of relevance to this story. The following days, Wednesday and Thursday, were equally unremarkable except that with sweet Jessica at work I sat in numbing boredom making small inroads into a huge mound of Reserve paperwork spread on small tables and stools about my propped-up faulty limb.

By Friday morning I was desperate for company. When Jamie and Bob came by, I virtually threw the coffee jar at them to make sure they stayed for a chat. They enquired pleasantly whether I was still playing truant.

'Would I be sitting here tearing my hair out strand by strand if I could be out on the Reserve?' I expostulated. 'Uncle Wilfred could be driving a plough across the *machair,* for all I can do about it!'

They inspected my ankle sympathetically. 'You could be back on your rounds slowly with a tight bandage round it by tomorrow,' thought Jamie.

'That's four days missed. Do you know how much work there is to be done at this time of year?'

'We've been doing the regular counts for you between us. And no visitors have been anywhere within half a mile of Ginger Hill while we've been around.'

'Really? Not even up the lighthouse track?'

'Couldn't be sure about that; we haven't been on the high ground enough to see that far. But I wouldn't have thought so. Anyway, what are you doing today?'

I grimaced. 'What can I do? I couldn't manage more than a five minute walk.'

Bob scratched his head. 'Can't you drive?'

'I wouldn't like to risk it.'

'Do you want us to drive you anywhere?'

The thought of my precious car being handled by my two ruffian colleagues was painful. But the sight of my pile of paperwork decided me.

'Give me a chance to get a bandage on. You can take me down to Ferry Garage for a new gatepost.'

As I had feared, I was forced to grit my teeth as Jamie screeched down the hill out of the village.

'Hey, *watch* this corner! Not so far out! Look *out*, there's a tractor coming...'

By the time we reached the harbour I was clutching my seat belt with white fingers. Jamie drove my Ford to within inches of the quay edge before stopping with a jerk.

The ferry had just arrived and the harbour was humming with activity as the last cars were unloaded. The quay was busy with people walking and talking. As I hobbled over to Ferry Garage, I saw Jack Dooley chatting to someone at his door. When we got closer, I was surprised to see it was none other than Angus Donald. Both of them raised an eyebrow as I limped up to address them.

'Good morning, Jack. Hi, Angus, what are you doing here? Haven't you got a big enough lump of scrap iron already?'

'Hello, Mister Acting Warden,' said Angus, 'Yes, but my bit of scrap iron floats, which is more than will be said for that rusting vehicle of yours if you've not left your handbrake full on. And even if I was looking for more iron, I'd leave Jack enough for him to make you a pair of crutches. Tell us what you've been doing with yourself, if you can do so politely!'

I grinned lopsidedly. 'Injured on active service is all I shall be telling you, you Gaelic raider. What's he after, Jack? If it's on the ferry company account, squeeze him for every penny you can get.'

Jack Dooley gave his usual doleful smile. 'Mr. Angus wasn't after buying anything, Mr. Timothy', he wheezed sadly. 'It was I who stopped him to ask if he might have seen anything of poor Cocky on his travels.'

'Still missing, is he?'

'Yes, I'm afraid he might get into trouble while he's out. He has a nasty streak about him with strangers, you see.'

My ankle throbbed at an old memory. 'I had noticed. I will keep a look-out.'

Angus cleared his throat. 'I'll keep a good watch too when I'm here, Jack. But if you'll excuse me I need to grab a word with these three gentlemen right now. Tim, as it happens I was on my way to phone you from the harbourmaster's office.'

Jack disappeared mournfully. Bob, Jamie and I walked to the edge of the water with Angus.

'You look serious again, Angus,' I said.

'I am that, lad. I am. See over there...' Angus levelled a steady finger across the harbour. We followed his gaze to the nearby pier along which the last cars from the ferry were cautiously rolling their way.

'*There*. That black car.'

'The little Volkswagen with three men in it?' asked Bob.

'Right. Do you recognize any of them?'

We peered intently as the approaching car halted in the queue. The men were hard-faced, solid-muscled characters, as like as peas in a pod.

'No,' said Bob. 'Should we?'

I looked at Angus expectantly. 'Are they egg-collectors?' We tensed *en masse* at the dreaded words. Angus surprised us.

'Yes and no,' he said.

We all looked the same question at him.

'What I mean,' he continued, 'is that they *ought* to be. A black VW with three men in it, that's the description that is going the rounds.'

'What about the registration number? Surely Keith gave you that?'

'Yes. That's why I was hesitating.' As the black car bumped off the pier onto the concrete quay, Angus held out to us a dog-eared list of car registration numbers. One was ringed in red.

We looked at the front registration plate of the car, then back at the list.

'It's different,' said Jamie.

'But only just,' I objected. 'Only the last letter is wrong.'

'The last letter is a G instead of a C,' agreed Bob, 'but that's hardly a big difference. Could the list be wrong?'

Angus rubbed his chin. 'Keith Potts told me everything on the list was supposed to have been checked. He didn't say how.'

The queue started to move. The car rolled past us, gaining speed. We looked at the rear registration plate; it was identical. I took a decision. 'It's them. It must be. Let's drive after them and see where they go.'

Jamie looked surprised. 'What about your gatepost?'

I grinned. 'Never mind about that! Not when I can say something I've always longed to say - *follow that car.'*

8. - Taken Down in Evidence

We piled in and raced off, leaving Angus gazing after us. Jamie overtook everything on the road, and burnt weeks of wear off my tyres around the first few bends out of Port Doy. Then he braked sharply as we came within sight of our quarry. The VW was proceeding sedately up the valley road, its occupants gazing around with interest. Jamie dropped back and kept the black car just within sight on the winding road ahead.

The car ambled to the edge of Doytown and stopped there outside the island's main hotel, a venerable building adjacent to the playing fields of the island school and overlooking the verdant valley of the Doy River. We knew the hotel as a Victorian establishment with an interior of panelled wood, oak doors and faded giant trout in glass cases. It contained a popular bar to which Reserve wardens were wont to resort not so much for alcoholic solace, which was cheaper elsewhere, as to pump the local farmers among the customers for information about corncrakes and other rare birds nesting on their land. The hotel was at its busiest in high summer and in the sea-trout season in September. At this time of year, it held fewer staying guests and its car park was nearly empty. The only vehicle there which looked like an off-island model was a smart blue Jaguar by the main door.

As the three passengers emerged from their vehicle, Jamie pulled the Ford off the road where it overlooked the hotel. Immediately, we examined the visitors minutely through the pairs of bins that, as birdwatchers of long standing, we each carried by habit.

'A suitcase apiece?' muttered Bob. 'They look like they're here for a while. Hey, isn't the Doy Hotel a bit up market for egg-collectors?'

'There's money in selling rare eggs.'

'If they hatch into peregrine falcons, yes, I know that.'

'And otherwise, evidently. And in any case,' I added, 'these chaps could be here a week or a day. If they suspect we're on to them they'll vanish like will-o'-the-wisps. What we want is to catch them in the act before they can do any damage.'

'That's if they are who we think they are,' said Jamie.

'We'll soon see. If they are collectors they'll go nowhere near the main Reserve footpaths - but we'll have to guard our sensitive areas day and night.'

Bob winked at Jamie. 'If you say so, Tim. Have you thought of a chastity belt?'

Jamie winked back. 'Who for? Tim or Jessica?'

The newcomers, who had disappeared into the hotel foyer with their luggage, reappeared before I could think up a furious retort.

'What, back for more luggage?' muttered Jamie.

'They'll have climbing equipment of some sort with them,' I commented. 'But they will leave that in the car out of sight.'

'Hey, that's not climbing equipment,' hissed Bob excitedly. 'What's in that big, square attaché case that they're carrying so gingerly?'

I lowered my binoculars slowly. 'Eggs?' I asked angrily.

. . . .

We drove on rapidly and parked the car in a street, then walked back a little way - past the school building - to within sight of the hotel. The playing fields of Lifandoy's only high school ran up to the hotel grounds on this side. On the slope between the school fields and the road above was a small terraced garden with a shady arbour looking across the field towards the hotel building and the river valley beyond. The arbour formed a perfect observation post for our espionage.

The morning was almost soundless: unusually for Lifandoy there was no wind. Once the ferry traffic had all ceased, virtually the only noise came from groups of children on the field below. These appeared to be a junior class following some sort of organized nature project around the school grounds, looking in trees and bushes and under stones and logs. I nudged Bob, and pointed.

'I hope they don't let that lot loose on the Reserve! Egg-collectors are bad enough - but thirty kids trampling down the orchids would be all we needed!'

He laughed. 'They're taking it seriously, aren't they? Look, there's one with a camera. And there's a group with a recorder and microphone. I guess they're trying to tape some bird song.'

'Hah. They won't get within range of a deaf robin with the disturbance they're creating.' We forgot the budding naturalists and returned our attention to the problem in hand.

'We know they're in there, but when will they come out?' I wondered aloud.

'Perhaps not until tomorrow.' Jamie was pessimistic.

'Surely not.' Bob was ready for the chase. 'If those fellows spend the rest of the day propping up the bar in there I'll eat my telescope. They've come to the island for a purpose, there's no doubt about that. They'll make a move soon.'

I studied the hotel windows through my binoculars. Someone tall appeared at an upstairs window to stare across at the town, and was joined a moment later by a second, slightly smaller figure. I focused on them intently.

'That's them! That must be their room - the window behind that huge yew tree.'

Bob had them too. 'I see it. The tree to the right of the *'Welcome to the Doy Hotel* sign.'

Jamie woke up. 'Wow, what I would give for a look into that room!'

A pensive silence descended as our exclamations ceased. There was only the rustle of some hidden creature in the undergrowth of bushes that lined the wire mesh fence of the school field just below our arbour. I turned to my companions and eyed them thoughtfully.

'So which of you is good at climbing trees?'

They looked worried as they saw the gleam in my eye. 'We can't break in broad daylight,' objected Bob.

'We're not going to break in. Just climb a tree.'

'That's nearly as bad.'

'Why? There's no law against climbing trees. It's perfect - and that tree is so bushy they'll never see someone buried in the branches.'

'We'd be seen climbing the tree.'

'No, you wouldn't.' I waved my arm expansively. 'That side of the hotel is invisible from the road. This arbour is the only spot that overlooks it: and that window is the only one near the tree. If you climb up with the trunk between you and the window they won't see you. All we have to do is wait for the school kids to be chained up back in their classrooms and there will be no-one to watch.'

'Unless another guest decides to take a walk.'

'We'll keep a watch out for that. Come on, let's toss a coin. Bob, you call!'

Bob lost. We watched until all the schoolchildren had disappeared. Then we sidled alongside the school fence until only a line of large shrubs lay between the hotel grounds and us.

We crept through the shrubbery. A few steps above us was the gravel path which ran alongside the hotel, between the building and the field. It was out of sight of the hotel frontage. We dusted the twigs out of our hair and stepped nonchalantly along the path - in my case, with a pronounced limp.

In the shade of the tree, we stopped.

'Jamie, give Bob a leg up, would you? I'll check the car park again and whistle if anyone appears.'

Bob had clearly misspent his childhood, for within half a minute he was safely in the dense foliage at the top of the tree. By that time I had checked that the car park was deserted, while Jamie was just returning from a similar errand to the rear of the building.

'OK, Bob,' I whispered. 'All clear - now's your chance.'

Nervously, he parted the branches.

'I can see them!' he hissed down. 'They're at the table, poring over a map. The attaché case is by the window. It's open, but it's facing just too far away from me to spot what's inside. I shall have to risk leaning right out.'

Bob stretched out cautiously along a large branch. He was just at full reach, outlined against the hotel wall, when a piercing voice spoke clearly from behind and below us.

'Smile, please. *Hold* it...'

We turned as one, in guilty shock.

CLICK.

'That's magnificent! Sergeant Farquhar at the police station will be delighted with that one. Well done, Rosalind.'

Behind us, a narrow strip of hotel lawn angled down to the bush-encrusted school fence. Directly below us was a gap in the bushes. Staring coldly through the holes in the mesh was the alarming face of Alice Bull. Together with here were three other little girls, one of whom, a larger edition of Alice herself, was firmly holding a camera.

I spluttered in unconvincing indignation. 'Hey! What do you think you're playing at...?'

Alice waved me to silence. She signalled at the girl on her left. 'Play it back. Cynthia.'

The latter, a miniature angel of a girl, suddenly produced a very small music player. She tapped the screen and to our lasting horror we heard our own voices.

'...Their room - the window behind that huge yew tree on the left.' 'I see it. The tree to the right of the *Welcome to the Doy Hotel* sign.' 'Wow, what I would give for a look into that room!' 'So which of you is good at climbing trees?'

Cynthia depressed the fast forward button for a moment.

'...We'd be seen climbing the tree.' 'No, you wouldn't.' 'If you climb up with the trunk between you and the window they won't see you. All we have to do is wait for the school kids to be chained up back in their classrooms and there will be no-one to watch.'

Alice sniffed. '"Chained up in their classrooms", eh? We'll see who will be in chains soon. I can see the local headlines: "The three rogues were recorded planning their burglary on both sound a vision by young girl heroines Alice and Rosalind Bull, Cynthia Fish and Patricia..."'

I found my voice at last. 'Hey, I didn't say that!'

Alice raised a languid eyebrow. 'Play it again, Cynth.'

'No, I mean I said more than that. I said we weren't going to break in, just climb a tree.'

Alice smiled innocently. 'Oh, no, you didn't. Cynthia will soon see to that. She's our electronic boffin, aren't you, Cynth?' The small girl grinned.

Jamie and I marched angrily down to the fence, while in the tree above Bob climbed back to the main trunk.

'Now look here,' I started. 'You give me that player and camera or I'll come over this fence and get them.'

Demurely, Alice held up the music player. But she threw it to a tall, leggy girl behind her. 'Run Patricia!' she said. 'He won't catch you, you're the best sprinter in the class. Give the player to teacher.'

'Hey, stop! I didn't mean it!' I cried. Patricia came to a reluctant halt just within earshot, still poised for a getaway.

Bob hissed down from the treetop. 'We're not burglars, girls.'

They gave us frankly disbelieving looks.

'Of course not,' I said with a forced laugh. 'Would we burgle the Doy Hotel in broad daylight?'

Alice looked puzzled. 'So what on earth were you doing, then?'

Jamie winked behind his hand at me. He leaned forward and spoke in a conspiratorial whisper. 'We're hunting *real* criminals, Alice.'

Some of the girls looked interested, but their leader was unconvinced.

'Real criminals don't come to Lifandoy,' she whispered back. 'What sort of crooks would come here?'

Jamie glared at her. *'Egg collectors...'* he hissed darkly.

There was a murmur of excitement. A light of interest kindled in Alice's eyes. 'How do you know?'

I nodded melodramatically. 'Angus Donald on the ferry saw their car. He has a list of registration numbers. He tipped us off this morning.'

Alice smiled slowly. 'So you thought you could see through their window from the tree? Wow, what a bunch of amateurs. Don't you know the first thing about espionage?'

We felt foolish. 'Why? Do you?'

'Of course. I've read all the books.' She preened herself. 'Rule number one - get inside assistance.'

We wrinkled our brows. 'Inside assistance? Where from?'

She looked over her shoulder. 'We must be getting back. Teacher will be looking for us. Go back to the garden where we recorded you. It's playtime in half an hour. I'll tell you what to do then. But mind, it'll cost you dearly.'

'What about the music player and camera?'

'We'll delete the picture before we give the camera back to Teacher. But we're keeping the recording as an insurance. We'll copy it before we give the player back to Teacher. Meanwhile, isn't it time you failed spies got your lackey down out of his tree?'

I walked back up to the yew tree. 'Bob, come down.'

'All right. I didn't see much, anyway.'

We stood at the foot of the tree, watching as Bob slid down in a shower of twigs. We were so engrossed in watching him that we failed to notice a walker approaching on the path with head low in thought.

Bob landed almost on top of the stranger. I turned to the man in surprise and dismay. Happily it was not one of our presumed egg-collectors. But I knew him well. My heart sank into my boots as I recognized Sir Charles Hamilstone-ffrench.

He looked up in wonder. 'What the - ? What are you doing, you men? Oh, it's *you,* Mr. Corn. Have you taken leave of your senses?'

My mind went into overdrive. I pointed desperately, and lifted my binoculars. 'There. *There!...* did you see it, Sir Charles?'

'See what?' he grumbled in curiosity.

'It's gone. You're too late.'

'What has gone?'

Boldly, I adopted a knowing stance. 'The lesser crested yew sparrow! We had a report that a rare bird had been seen in this tree. It must be a visitor on migration.'

'The lesser crested yew sparrow?' He was incredulous. 'I've never heard of such a bird.'

'It's the first record for Lifandoy,' I proclaimed. 'Perhaps the first for Britain!'

Sir Charles was impressed. To my relief he appeared to have swallowed my tale. 'The first for Britain? Where did it go? I'd like to see this for myself.' He beetled off with interest.

As he was receding, Bob muttered 'Now we know who that smart Jaguar in the car park belongs to.'

The three of us beat a hasty retreat before Sir Charles could reappear. As we emerged beyond the shrubbery there was a loud 'Tut, tut!' and a series of titters from the school fence nearby.

I turned. 'Haven't you gone?'

'We're going. But your conversations are always worth overhearing.' Alice was shaking her head in deprecation. '"Oh, what a tangled web we weave, when first we practice to deceive!"' It's a good job your Uncle Wilfred wasn't listening to all your fibs.'

I scowled. 'Uncle Wilfred? What have you to do with Uncle Wilfred?'

Alice gave me a disdainful look. 'Wilfred Corn has a high opinion of me,' she said. 'He thinks I sing beautifully.'

My jaw dropped. 'You've not joined the chapel choir?'

Her only reply was to blow a raspberry as all the little girls ran off shrieking with laughter. I sank to the ground in shock and looked around for a rock to bang my head on. 'Tell me it's not true,' I moaned. 'Alice in the choir? Someone tell me it's not true!'

Bob and Jamie helpfully carried me back to our reconnaissance post at the arbour. When I had recovered from hearing Alice's news, we quizzed Bob about his observations, to little effect.

'I couldn't see what was in the case,' he said disappointedly. 'All I managed to see clearly was the map they were studying. Raw Head had a ring round it. And the West Burn was marked heavily in black - all the way up to Ginger Hill.'

Jamie sat back. 'That's bad. What are you thinking, Tim?'

I looked at them both. 'I was wondering what Alice means by inside assistance.'

He nodded. 'I think we're about to find out.'

9. - In League

Shortly, a howling mob of children emerged from the school building. A small group detached themselves purposefully from the rest and sidled around the field edge to a gap in the hedge below us.

We inspected the arrivals dubiously. Alice had brought several more young delinquents with her.

'Hey, how do we know all these can be trusted?'

'If I've picked them you can trust them,' said Alice firmly. 'And besides, we need them.'

'What for?'

Alice indicated a rather overweight blonde girl with a large brace on her front teeth. 'Meet Carmen,' she said with satisfaction.

'Hello, Carmen,' we said dutifully.

'Carmen, tell the nice men where you live.'

Carmen stepped forward solemnly. 'My houth ith the Doy Hotel,' she announced, lisping through an ill-fitting dental brace. 'My Daddy ownth it. And I know where he keepth all hith keyth.'

'Ah.' Jamie and I went red. Bob developed an intense interest in a bush to the right of Carmen's head.

'He's the one who climbed the big yew tree,' said Alice, pointing. Carmen gazed at Bob in admiration.

'I've never climbed that tree. That'th a big tree, that ith.' Bob jumped, then smiled. Carmen stared at him. 'You mutht really hate egg-collectorth. What do egg-collectorth collect, anyway?'

'Eggth.' interrupted Alice impatiently. 'I mean - *eggs.*'

'Why?'

'*Ach!*' said Jamie suddenly, descending without warning into broad Scots. 'Huv ye no hearrrd of the wickedness of yon collectors?'

'Wickedneth? N-no.'

'Then let ma telt ye…' Jamie began a graphic description of the horrors of oology. His account was so colourful that all the girls were soon agog with wild indignation. By the time he had finished, he had made it plain that the arrival of egg-collectors among us was almost tantamount to the ruin of Lifandoy island. He was emotionally moving on to the perfidy of all Sassenachs and the tragedy of the Jacobite rebellions when I decided to stem his flow.

'Frae Glenfinnan tae Culloden Muir we wis betrrrayed–' he thundered.

'Yes, Jamie, but it wasn't actually your eggs that the English were after, was it?'

'They widnae hae got them–'

'And we're wasting precious time. Bob, tell the girls what you saw in the room, if you don't mind, please…'

Bob reported his observations of the map and the attaché case. All of the Cabal - the name by which Alice introduced her tittering band - agreed that the case obviously held a terrible secret, which must at all costs be discovered. We held an immediate council of war to find out who should do what.

Alice thought that the question of the hotel room was best left to the Cabal.

'You're needed on the Reserve,' she admitted generously. 'And we don't want you getting in the way again.'

'Oh yeah?' Bob was truculent. 'In the way of whom?'

'Of our team. First, Carmen can get the keys to the room. Second, meet Ailsa.'

'Hello, Ailsa.'

'Ailsa's Dad is Sergeant Farquhar at the police station.'

I grasped Bob's arm firmly as he groaned. 'Steady, lad,' I murmured.

'Yep,' said Ailsa. 'I know where he keeps *his* keys, the special ones that will open *anything.*'

'And third, my sister Rosalind. Rosalind is our photographic expert. She has her own camera. All she needs is a memory card.'

Rosalind, the middle of the Bull sisters, advanced to Alice's side. The pair of them together were a frightening sight. Rosalind held out her hand.

'Six quid, please.'

As we gagged, Alice smiled up at her sister. 'She's our treasurer, too. Don't try and fiddle us out of any of the ready while she's around: not if you know what's good for you. Well, come on then! Hand it over so that we can get going!'

'You're joking!'

Rosalind did not have a vestige of humour in her expression. She held out the other band. 'And the Cabal costs a tenner a week to hire, too. We'll have the first week now in advance.'

Seeing our expressions, Alice muttered in her sister's ear. Rosalind nodded her head. 'As a special discount, because it's a good cause, we'll make that five quid a week.'

Bob growled at me. 'They must be out of their tiny little minds!'

'Wait a minute, Bob. We *need* them. Let me negotiate.' I held up a hand. 'Alice, a parley. Just you and me.'

She nodded and gestured to another gap in the hedge. We met there, watched suspiciously from a distance by the respective factions.

'You can't expect us to fork out sums like that,' I stated.

'We need the memory card. No memory card, no evidence,' she said.

I sighed. 'All right, I'll see what I can do about that. But I'll want it back when you've finished with it. And you can't expect us to pay you for doing your moral duty.'

Alice stonewalled. 'No cash, no espionage.'

The argument continued for some minutes without me getting anywhere. To my alarm, she was on the point of throwing the whole thing in - and possibly reporting us to Sergeant Farquhar - when I had a stroke of genius.

'Of course,' I said slowly. 'Payment could be in kind. You know, you scratch my back, *et cetera.*'

She shook her head vigorously. 'There's nothing I want from *you.*'

I reached into my jacket pocket, unfolded Keith's letter and revealed a small photograph. Concealing it in my hand from the watching Cabal, I held it up against the fence in front of her nose. 'Not even this?'

Alice turned the colour of an overripe plum. *'Where* did you get *that?'* she fulminated, keeping her voice below a scream with difficulty. 'Give it here at once, you snake, you creep, you lizard, you *boa constrictor,* you...'

As she clutched the fence with both hands in apoplexy, I withdrew it from the reach of her fingers. I leaned against a tree and hummed happily.

'Lovely day, don't you think?'

'Foul. Where did you get it?'

'It fell out of the newspapers onto the pier when they arrived. I thought you were very rude to the newsagent. I think he deserves an apology. But I also think your Cabal doesn't need pocket money, right?'

'You won't tell them about the picture of Simon Splutter?'

'Not if you co-operate and give us the tape back eventually.'

Alice was in despair. 'But I can't pay them and the picture belongs to me. They need *something* to reward them.'

I took the point. 'I suppose so.' I gave a long, sad sigh. 'Perhaps we could run to an ice cream each.'

'At the Summer Fair next week?'

'Why then? All right, if you like.'

'OK, it's a deal.'

We shook hands - or at least as many fingers as Alice could squeeze through the mesh. I replaced Keith's letter in my jacket pocket. On reflection, I slipped the picture of Simon Splutter into my trouser pocket - it was less easily pick-able there. The others scowled nervously as we walked back to join them and reveal to our separate parties the details of the pact.

■　■　■　■

Across the fence, the Cabal was visibly disgruntled at Alice's news. But I saw them brighten as the words Summer Fair were repeated several times. I wondered briefly why a few tiny ice creams should create such excitement. Bob and Jamie thought I had done surprisingly well.

'We didn't think you had such a forceful personality,' said Bob admiringly. 'We thought that without some bargaining chip you would let Alice stonewall you and break you down.'

I blushed. To cover my discomfiture I took the offensive. 'Right. All I need now is two pounds from each of you for your shares of the memory card.'

'Eh? We didn't agree to that! That's real money!'

'I know it's real money. I'm as serious a capitalist as either of you. But we'll all be in the soup if Alice hands the recording in. Your voices are on it as well as mine.'

With very bad grace Bob produced two pound coins. Jamie whined and came up with one pound in small change. Since he was the biggest of us we decided not to strong-arm the rest out of him until later. I made up the total temporarily to six pounds by emptying every pocket I had.

Bob did some mental arithmetic. 'There are nine girls altogether. If you buy very small ice creams you should get three to a pound. That means your total outlay should be three plus two, that's a fiver.'

Glumly, I agreed. 'I'll try and wangle some of it back out of Keith - if there's enough in the Reserve's petty cash fund, that is. It was nearly empty the last time he let me see in the tin.'

We handed the money through the fence to Rosalind, who watched our every move and counted each coin three times before she was happy. To our astonishment, she produced an official receipt book and wrote one out - which made Bob wonder loudly who else the Cabal was in the habit of extorting cash from. As she finished writing, the school whistle sounded. The Cabal galloped off back to their classes and we watched them go. Then our attention swung urgently elsewhere.

'Uh-oh. Signs of action at the hotel!' exclaimed Jamie. 'You were right, Bob. It looks as if our crooks are on the move already.'

In the car park, our three suspects were getting into the Volkswagen. We inspected them closely. 'They've not got the attaché case with them,' said Bob.

'Hey,' Jamie leapt up, 'I'd better get the car started. Be ready as soon as you see them move.'

Within minutes, Bob was peering over my shoulder from the back seat as Jamie in the driving seat manoeuvred my car down into the centre of Doytown.

'Your turn to be right, Tim!' said Bob.

I nodded. 'They're not going straight to the Reserve. They've gone past the turn for West Doy. They might only be going shopping.'

Without warning, the VW stopped. One of the men got out and the vehicle started off again. The man was holding a mobile phone and frowning at it. He walked to a phone box and stepped inside.

'He has no phone signal, like nearly everyone else on Lifandoy. What do I do?' Jamie brought us to a halt at the roadside. 'Do I follow the car, Tim?'

I was about to say yes when Bob came out with a firm negative. 'No. Look - the car is just going round the block.'

'You're right, Bob. Stay here, Jamie. They just don't want to be seen parked. Hey, that's suspicious.'

'And why didn't they phone from the hotel too? I wish we could know who he is contacting.'

Exactly as the third man returned to the kerb the black car slid up smoothly and collected him without even coming to a halt.

'Wow! That was smooth. These egg-collectors are alarmingly well-organized.' I sat back thoughtfully. 'I thought eggers were generally a bunch of ruffians! Watch out, they're off again. Don't lose them, Jamie.'

We negotiated the twisting streets of Doytown. Our quarry was going even slower than before.

Jamie glanced across. 'They've gone past the turns for West Doy and for Raw Head,' he said in surprise. 'And now they've taken the road towards the airport. There's only one more fork that they have to pass. Which way do you think they'll go there, Tim?'

'They could head past the airport towards Snaefell Bay - though I don't see why they should do that as it takes them far away from the Reserve - or they could take the little road up the East Burn valley. If they did that, there's no other road for them to turn onto before Liffen Cross, the crossroads above Loch Liffen - you know, the one on the low knoll overlooking the lake. Perhaps they plan to do that, to approach the Reserve by the least obvious route.'

'Will they keep to roads?'

'That depends how good at map-reading they are. But if they don't, the only track off the East Burn road that goes anywhere is the one over the hill to Uncle Wilfred's farm.'

We held our breath as the road fork approached.

'Ah-hah. They've gone left: Loch Liffen here we come.'

On what was now a rural, single-track lane the black car stood out like a spider in grass. Jamie expressed the thought of all of us.

'I suppose they will have seen us by now.'

'Stay as far back as you can,' I ordered. 'There's no way we can lose them before Liffen Cross.'

The bends went by. Shortly, Bob gazed out of the side window. 'Is that the track from the House Farm, that faint line down the hillside?'

'Yes,' I said without looking. 'It's rarely used.'

'It's being used now. There's a Land Rover coming down it.'

'Really?' I squinted up the hillside curiously. 'So there is.'

We watched the descending vehicle. It was well down the track before I realized a potential problem.

'Jamie, could you speed up a bit, please? That Land Rover might get to the road between the VW and us. We wouldn't want to get stuck behind it on a road this narrow.'

Jamie obliged. As we accelerated, however, the Land Rover seemed to do the same. Ahead of us the Volkswagen ambled past the junction of track and road, apparently innocent of the race behind it. Jamie speeded up again. Again our movement was matched on the hillside above.

Suddenly, the competing vehicle careered forward in a cloud of dust. Jamie was taken by surprise. As if it had done so deliberately, the Land Rover roared round the last bend of its track and beat us to the junction by moments.

Immediately, it decelerated. The black car was travelling slowly: but our new arrival dropped its speed to near tortoise velocity.

I shouted angrily. 'What's he up to? What's that fool doing? Blow your horn, Jamie. Make him pull over. We've got to get past him!'

We had one last glimpse of the Volkswagen as it climbed up out of the East Burn valley and over the watershed out of sight. The vehicle in front of us refused to budge, proceeding at a testudine pace in the middle of the road and declining to pause in any of the passing places. Jamie weaved from side to side in frustration, then blew his horn several times, but in vain. For all we could tell, the driver of the Land Rover was stone deaf as well as daft.

'Who's in that crazy Rover?' I stormed. 'Where are my bins? Bob, can you make him out?'

'I can't see anything of him through his back window. But when he was coming down the hill I had my glasses on him for a moment. The only thing I could tell was that he had grey hair.'

'That would fit three or four of the farm workers.'

'Wilfred?' enquired Jamie.

'Unlikely,' I said. 'The House Farm has sheep in some of the fields on this side of the hill. But my dear uncle doesn't come over this side unless for some special reason. He usually sticks to crops and cows.'

At last the Land Rover turned up a field track, one which left the road at an angle that prevented any glimpse by us of the driver's face. We glared after our tormentor, then transferred our attention urgently to the road ahead.

It was only a short distance to the junction at Liffen Cross. The crossroads was on a slight hummock that commanded a fine view of the tidal expanse of Loch Liffen. The inlet, Lifandoy's only sea-loch, was an almost enclosed muddy bay. Surrounded by acres of sea buckthorn scrub, it held huge flocks of migrating wading birds in spring and autumn. In summer only a few terns remained. Although separate from the Lifandoy Reserve proper, it was looked after informally by the Reserve wardens for the simple reason that no one else, except for cockle diggers and an occasional shooting party led by the Earl, saw fit to bother with it.

Around the main Loch area, and especially to the north where they nearly separated it from the sea, were large areas of thorn-coated sand dunes peppered with damp, hidden dune slacks rich in strange flowers. As Jamie approached the crossroads he came to a halt within sight of the rolling dune-scape. We could see a long way down the road to our right: but to the left and ahead the little island roads soon disappeared from view among the dunes.

'Rats and mice!' I was livid. 'They've disappeared. Which way did they go?'

'We'd better choose quickly before we lose them,' added Bob unhelpfully. 'Do you think they're headed for the Reserve, Tim?'

'Straight ahead will only take us to the golf course. Left goes to the fork at Liffen Farm - they could walk right onto the Reserve from there.' I flung out an arm. *'Left, Jamie!'*

Our willing chauffeur screeched more rubber off my tyres as he obeyed. We were ten seconds down the road when Jamie glanced in his rear view mirror and slowed in astonishment.

'Wow!'

10. - Strange Happenings

'What's up?' enquired Bob.

'The Land Rover! It just went straight over the crossroads behind us.'

'So?'

'So it was going like the clappers!' Jamie gestured dramatically. 'It was almost in the air when it went through the junction! It must have been doing sixty at least.'

We looked round. The crossroads was just disappearing from view. It appeared a placid rural scene. The road to our left was entirely Land Rover free.

'Jamie, this rally car stuff is going to your head. You're seeing things. Slow down, before we all go into orbit.'

We were all on edge by now. Jamie was not pleased at our disbelief. He promptly lost his Scottish rag and started lambasting us as stupid Englishmen. I objected violently to this, on the grounds that Scotland became English property before Lifandoy did. This made him see tartan, and we were on the point of getting out of the car and coming to blows when Liffen Farm appeared before us.

There was no black car in sight. The only moving object was a shepherd leaning over a gate chewing something horrible. Bob lowered his car window hopefully.

'Have you seen a car?'

'Yes, boyo. Yours.' His accent could have come straight from the Rhondda.

'A black one, I mean.'

'There are plenty of black cars on LifANdoy, boyo. I've probably seen most of them at one time or another, you know.'

'Have you seen a black car *in the last five minutes?*'

'No. Nor all day.'

Bob stifled an agitated cry.

Jamie attempted to reverse smartly by backing the car into an open gateway. The theory was good but the gateway was a quagmire. It took five miry minutes for us to extricate ourselves, watched with amusement by the Cymric shepherd.

Along the road back to Liffen Cross, we bounced like peas in a barrel as Jamie gave his all to the cause. But when we got there he brought the car to an astonished halt. Parked neatly on the grass at the crossroads was an unmistakable black Volkswagen. It was empty.

'Oh, no!' We leapt out and stared vainly in all directions.

I was enraged. 'They've gone egging! Either they're in the dunes or else they've gone off round the Loch.'

'I can't see them from here.' Jamie was surveying the area carefully.

'But why have they come back to the crossroads?' bleated Bob.

'Never mind that!' I waved my arms angrily. 'Perhaps they were trying to mislead us. Get after them! Jamie, you take the path round the Loch. Bob can work through the dunes and down to the shore. I'll hide the car in those bushes over there and then hobble along the road between the pair of you. We can all meet on the beach.'

'What do I do if I find them?' asked Bob dubiously.

'Don't tackle them alone. Head for the road and tell me where they are. Then we'll approach them en masse.'

Jamie thumped the palm of his hand with his fist. 'That's when the fun starts.'

■   ■   ■   ■

In fact the fun never started. For two hours, we sneaked around the east side of the Loch. Covered with seemingly endless buckthorn, the wilderness would have taken a company of troops to search it effectively. I limped along the road, acknowledging the increasingly frustrated signals of Bob or Jamie whenever either found a viewpoint from which to semaphore.

Sheer exhaustion brought them back in the end. Both of them were covered in midge bites and had wounds acquired from many pointed arguments. We hobbled back to the crossroads leaning on each other like some demented three-legged race.

The black car was still sitting peacefully in the sunshine. We debated briefly whether to tow it away or whether to merely remove its wheels and throw them into the Loch. But we were so tired that even mindless vandalism was beyond us. In the end we dropped into our own vehicle in its place of concealment and, after agreeing to take turns on watch, promptly all fell asleep in the warm sun.

I was awakened by a buzzing sound. Thinking I was being attacked by an insect I slapped at it vengefully. The only result of this was that I banged my fingers painfully on the fascia.

This woke Jamie up. He and I were gazing blearily through the windscreen when the source of the noise rolled past.

'It's them! Follow them, Jamie, Bob, wake up. It's the eggers.'

Bob sat up reluctantly. As he did so, the suspects' car passed out of sight. Instantly, another vehicle came into view.

Bob rubbed his eyes in confusion. 'You've got your eyes crossed, Tim. That's a Land Rover. And this time it *is* your Uncle Wilfred driving.'

I groaned heavily. 'I don't believe it. Don't tell me it's him who is in our way now! Get after him!'

■　■　■　■

Both vehicles were heading back down the East Burn road. Wilfred appeared to be keeping up with the black car ahead of him. But when we appeared in his rear view mirror he slowed down, letting the Volkswagen move away.

Jamie blew the horn. The result was infuriating. Wilfred stopped, but not in a passing place. Instead he stopped dead on the road halfway round an ascending bend, blocking the way completely. His engine stopped; leaning out of the window I could hear his voice, addressing someone loudly and urgently in a monotone.

'That's odd. There must be someone lying down in the back of the Land Rover,' I muttered. 'There certainly wasn't anyone else sitting with him. Whatever lunatic trick is Wilfred playing this time?'

Jamie switched off. The voice fell silent. 'I can't imagine,' Jamie said. 'Stopping in the middle of the road, speaking to himself, there's clearly lunacy in the Corn family. Hold on, here he comes.'

Wilfred had emerged from his vehicle. As if he had all the time in the world, he dawdled down the road to us.

'Hello Timothy! Hello, lads! I didn't expect to meet you here. I might not have recognized you if you hadn't blown your horn. Did you want to speak to me?'

'No,' I said through clenched teeth. 'We simply wanted you to get out of our way!'

'Are you late for the shops? I thought they closed late on Fridays.'

'We're not going shopping, We're just in a hurry.'

'Righto! I'll move straight away. Mustn't hold the world up, must I? Hello, Bob, hello Jamie. Is Timothy keeping you busy?'

'Yes, Mr. Corn,' they chorused shortly, and looked at him.

Uncle Wilfred was about to say something else, but he saw from our faces that he was pushing his luck. He cleared his throat noisily and ambled back to his Rover bearing a pleased expression. He fiddled with his key, eased himself very slowly into the driving seat and eventually started the engine.

After ambling past the next two passing places Wilfred finally came to a stop in the third. He gave us a friendly wave as we cannoned past, released from the trap. We shook our fists at him and thundered off round the next bend - to find the road full of sheep.

Jamie just saved us from eating mutton for a month. As we came to a juddering halt, I recognized the milling woollies as bearing the mark of the House Farm. They were trotting around in confusion as though they had all just stampeded onto the road. A rustic-looking shepherd strolled into view through an open gateway. To our amazement, he was muttering into a large mobile phone with a long aerial.

'Shepherding with a mobile?' Jamie stared. 'Does he have an electronic sheepdog? And on Lifandoy - I thought most mobile phones don't work on the island?'

Bob pulled a battered old mobile out of an inner pocket, tapped a couple of buttons on it and stared at it ruefully. 'Mine certainly doesn't.'

'Ordinary mobiles are no good,' I confirmed. 'Only satellite phones work up here. But ordinary islanders don't carry them.'

Jamie scowled at the shepherd. 'He's got to be from the House Farm.'

I nodded. 'So that's where all their wheat and oilseed cash goes to! Trust Fytts and Uncle Wilfred to splash out on something like that. It's a pity they didn't spend more on mending field gates instead.'

The shepherd saw us, and gave us an odd look. He whistled loudly several times. A couple of sheepdogs appeared briefly, but the only noticeable change on their intervention was more sheep flooding around us, trapping us in a woolly, smelly sea.

'Get them out of the way!' I leaned out of the window and hollered at the yokel. 'Get off the road!' But there was no response.

I looked round to see if we could back out of the flock. Behind us, rolling up smoothly, was the Land Rover. Uncle Wilfred, the only occupant, was driving slowly and talking animatedly at the windscreen as if having a conversation with it. When he saw me, he abruptly shut his mouth, leaned down to touch some hidden control, then gazed out of his window as if he had not seen me.

'I - er - um...' My brain was refusing to make sensible connections. 'Lads, I don't understand...?'

Jamie drowned my witterings with a bellow of Scots descended from some Celtic war cry. 'ACHARANOO! Clear at last!' Through a tiny gap in the woollen dam he drove us like a guided missile. Sheep fled in all directions, some leaping right up onto drystone walls in their terror. The road stretched empty before us.

Empty was the word. The remaining tread on my tyres was probably close to being illegal by the time we had screeched hopefully around every bend on the road back to Doytown. Not a vehicle obstructed us, The Volkswagen had done another disappearing act.

We drove to the hotel: but its car park was empty. Wearily, Jamie turned my car round and turned its nose toward West Doy. When we got there the village presented its usual late weekday afternoon impression of a tourist postcard, undisturbed by cars, egg-collectors and all other modern influences.

■　■　■　■

Jamie stopped at my gate. Without a word, he and Bob got out and walked into Little Cottage. There was the distinct sound of a kettle being banged forcefully onto a stove, followed by loud creaks from two crushed armchairs.

I tried to move in pursuit. But my ankle had set as if rusted solid. I shouted angrily. After about five minutes the pair emerged and with bad grace condescended to drag me up the garden path and into my residence, where I was dumped like a sack onto the sofa.

It took an hour and a week's supply of instant coffee to return our behaviour to a reasonably human manner. By that time we had made our peace and were listening half-heartedly to a soporific cricket commentary on the radio when there came an imperious thump on the front door.

'It's open!'

There was no response to my yell, so Jamie shambled over and pulled the door open. Then he gave a howl of surprise and staggered back, his face dripping.

A tittering mass of schoolgirls swept past him, with Alice at their head levelling a large and efficient water-pistol. She fired accurately at Bob and then turned to me. Before she could fire again I held my hand to my mouth and stuck out my tongue to lick an imaginary ice cream. Alice understood at a glance and lowered her weapon, scowling disappointedly.

'Disarm her, Jamie,' called Bob bravely. But Alice waved the pistol at both of them until, cowed, they sat meekly. Eyeing me cautiously, she handed the pistol over to a hard-faced assistant.

'Cover them for me, Sally, while I negotiate from a position of strength.'

Bob blew a raspberry. Alice ignored the interruption. She turned to me.

'We need fifty pence more for the memory card.'

Bob and I looked at each other and then turned our gaze firmly onto Jamie. He muttered and whinged. Eventually he produced the required change from a well concealed pocket. Alice's sister Rosalind snatched it eagerly, examining the coinage with care. She tossed back one coin scornfully.

'We don't accept toy money.'

Jamie picked the coin up incredulously as Bob and I laughed.

'Just wait till I get back to the Co-op!' he howled. 'I'll demand an apology. I'll have the manager himself out to explain…'

We threw several cushions at him. Relenting, he produced an alternative coin. Rosalind went to the length of biting this one. Then she gave an almost invisible nod of satisfaction.

Alice smiled sweetly as the girls filed out again. 'We'll see you tomorrow morning. We're not coming here again - it's too obvious. When we're at school you can come to the arbour by the playing field. When we're at home, our rendezvous can be the little shed at the bottom of the chapel yard where Wilfred Corn keeps the chapel lawn-mower. The girls all know where it is - it's one of the Cabal's regular meeting places. See you there at ten hundred hours tomorrow.'

The girl Sally with the pistol stared malevolently at Jamie and Bob. As Alice closed the door, Sally fired a couple of final bursts at them.

Shortly I was enraged to discover that the lads had shielded themselves from the water pistol with two of my cushions, which were now sodden. The recriminations were so sharp that both of them stalked off for a walk. This was just as well, since my darling - oh! - gorgeous oodles-of-sympathy sweet Jessica arrived ten minutes later, and stayed for all of a most delightful afternoon.

■ ■ ■ ■

Next morning I concluded that my leg must have died in the night, since it was clearly under the influence of rigor mortis. When the lads appeared they were surprisingly sympathetic. I cheered up when Bob said he had an idea for something to help me and went off to fetch it.

When we arrived at the chapel garden shed for the meeting with the Cabal I was in a much worse mood, having been trundled all the way by Bob in the chapel wheelbarrow. Bob rolled me in next to the lawnmower and dropped the barrow thankfully. When I demanded to be lifted out he declined, citing backache. Since Jamie was too busy going through all his pockets and biting all his small change, I was still in the barrow when our spies arrived.

To my relief, the girls seemed to regard my eccentric seat as quite acceptable. They clearly had higher things on their minds, and there was a hush as Alice and Rosalind stepped to the front.

'Take a look,' said Alice, holding out a small camera with an air of high satisfaction.

We looked. 'It's the case! And it's got EGGS in it!'

The top photo showed a now familiar piece of luggage. The square attaché case was open. It was lined with what looked like black sponge. In the sponge were ten round depressions. Four were empty: the other six contained what appeared to be large, white eggs.

'Was the case unlocked?'

'No. It had a very good lock. Ailsa had to try every one of her Dad's special keys to get it open.'

I was puzzled. 'It must have cost a lot, that case. Not the usual sort of eggers' equipment. Still, it's obvious what they're here for. They want more matching eggs to complete their collection. I hate to think where the others came from.'

'What will you do? Will you arrest them?' Alice's eyes gleamed, and a hiss of excitement came from the rest of the Cabal.

'We have to have proof.'

'We've *got* you proof.' Alice and Rosalind fairly danced with indignation. 'We've got the photos!'

I examined the prints meticulously. 'There are no labels on the eggs.'

'What does that matter?'

'If we don't know where the eggs are from, we can't prove them stolen. They could have come from anywhere.'

Alice was violet with anger - a new colour for her. 'But you're not going to let them steal our eggs?'

I thought hard. 'We have to catch them in the act; catch them as soon as they leave a nest.'

'Which nest? Can we mount a guard on the nest?'

'We don't know where the one they're after is, yet. We're still looking for it ourselves.'

Carmen's voice piped up. 'What thort of birdth are we looking for?'

I scowled. 'Forget the "we". I'm not having you lot plodding all over the Reserve in the middle of the nesting season. I'm keeping the birds to myself.'

The Cabal erupted into wolf whistles. Bob grinned. 'Look out, Jessica! he's got a whole flock of 'em hidden away!'

. . . .

As the clamour faded, Alice and Rosalind started whispering to each other. Then they nodded in satisfaction and Rosalind spoke up.

'What you need is efficient communications!'

'Eh?' I frowned. My temper was deteriorating as the wheelbarrow became more and more uncomfortable. I had already developed a fine set of bruises.

Alice nodded vigorously. 'A way of sending secret messages: you need a chain of observers able to signal the enemy's position.'

Rosalind muttered to Cynthia, then wrinkled her brows. 'We could buy a couple of short-wave radios for, say, twenty each–' She was interrupted by three simultaneous snorts, after which she huffily refused to say anything more.

Alice was a realist. 'No, silly, they're not made of money. And two wouldn't be enough. We need lots of spies.'

'Where would we put them?' asked Bob, curiously.

Alice warmed to her theme. 'Here! - and everywhere! We want an observer stationed at every house that overlooks the Reserve. We'll have one here or at our bungalow, one at Lifandoy House, one at the Home Farm, one at Liffen Farm, one at Ginger Farm...'

The others were getting the idea. 'I'll fix Liffen Farm,' called leggy Patricia, 'That's my Auntie Kathleen's and I'll tell her I'm coming to stay for a few days.'

'I'll arrange Ginger Farm. My cousin Glynys lives there and she'll do anything for spearmint chewing gum.'

'Spottie Mattie will do the House Farm. She owes me two favours and a bag of liquorice.'

'Lavinia Ponsonby's mother is a maid at Lifandoy House.' Hard-face Sally had an anticipatory gleam in her eye. 'Lavinia will do it for us. She'd better - I owe her a broken leg after she clouted me at hockey last week.'

Jamie stretched his large form impatiently. 'Fine. Will do what?'

'Thee where the thpieth go!' said Carmen, endangering her brace.

I scowled, wriggling around desperately in the wheelbarrow to find a less awkward position. 'So what does Rosalind want now? The funds to buy five pairs of binoculars? Lots of other people visit the Reserve, you know. How will you tell the eggers from ordinary bird-watchers at a distance?'

'Tim can't tell twitchers apart even when he's ambushing them,' added Bob helpfully.

I gave Bob a vitriolic look and rolled from side to side. I was sure I was getting bruises on my bruises.

Alice shook her head, impatient to reveal her flash of genius. 'We don't need binoculars to see a black Volkswagen,' she declared. 'All we need to do is to signal its movements and you watch for our signals through *your* binoculars.'

We gazed at her in admiration. 'It might work, you know,' said Bob, 'What will you use for signals?'

'That's easy. If the coast is clear we'll hang a white sheet out of a bedroom window at each place. When the car appears, we'll change it for a red one.'

I squirmed around the wheelbarrow, convinced that I was suffering from something at least as serious as chronic bedsores. 'Right. That's settled. Is there anything more to decide?'

Rosalind advanced grimly. 'Red dye is a pound a packet. Five quid, please.'

The wheelbarrow fell over.

11. - Red Alert

The plot advanced rapidly. The only hiccough was persuading Rosalind that the sentries could each at least find a piece of red cloth for themselves. This done, Rosalind revealed a ruthless drive for efficiency. As Alice's experienced aide-de-camp she provisioned and dispatched the members of the Cabal directly on their various missions of bribery, persuasion and threat.

Bob and Jamie condescended to carry me home between them. As we emerged from the shed, we observed Alice surveying the multi-coloured expanse of the Reserve meadows with interest.

'It's all bumps and hollows and pools,' she said scornfully, as if I was at fault for failing to level the Reserve as flat as a playing field. 'I don't think our bungalow windows *or* the shed will be high enough to signal from. If you were down in the bottom of the valley you wouldn't see the signal beyond the first marsh.'

I nodded 'That crimson fence of yours doesn't help. We'd never notice a red flag over that. What about changing the colour of our signal?'

Alice grinned. 'No, I've a better idea. I'll use the chapel. That big window at the back of the chapel balcony is quite high and faces the right way.'

I scowled. 'You'll get told off if you keep sneaking in and out of the church. Someone will object.'

'No they won't.' Alice purred. 'Mr. Corn has told me I can go into the chapel whenever I like, to practice my solo for the choir concert. You are coming to hear me, *aren't* you?'

∎　∎　∎　∎

The Cabal planted more spies to watch for the eggers' car along the several roads out of Doytown and extracted from us a grudging promise to refund the cost of any phone calls from them. But there was no stir of activity from our quarry for the rest of Saturday; and on Sunday it rained soddenly all day, turning into one of those blank island days when everybody went into hibernation.

When Monday dawned fair, my ankle was almost back to normal. I was feeling more cheerful than for some days when the threshold of Little Cottage was darkened at breakfast time by the austere form of Rosalind.

'We need dosh,' she demanded. 'Carmen just phoned.'

My sunny mood dimmed. Grumbling, I complied. '*More* money? It had better be worth it.'

Rosalind bit the coin carefully, then pocketed it. 'Your Volkswagen drove out of the Doy Hotel car park fifteen minutes ago.'

'What? Where to?'

'You'll have to find that out for yourself. The girls are just off to school. But anyone in the Cabal who sees it before they go will leave out a red signal. We'll have done our side of the job then.'

I dashed back inside and swallowed a scalding cup of coffee. Then, for camouflage, I pulled on an old gardening anorak and an equally old woolly hat, grabbed my binoculars and returned to the gate. Rosalind had gone: I looked hopefully up and down the street for Jamie or Bob, but there was no sign of them.

The only spectator was Uncle Wilfred, standing peacefully at his own gate. I slammed my gate noisily behind me and set off up the street, scarcely noticing Wilfred as I passed him with black thoughts of vengeance in my mind.

'*Good* morning, Timothy. It doesn't surprise me, you know.'

Wilfred's voice in my ear startled me. 'Eh? What doesn't?'

'The fact that your gateposts disintegrate, when you treat your gate as casually as that. I hope it's only your gateposts that get treated in such manner.'

I was in no mood for chit-chat. 'Come to the point. I'm in a hurry.'

'I was referring to your eternal soul, my lad. That's something that is in even more drastic need of regeneration than your woodwork.'

'Hmph! My woodwork simply needs prosperity, even if my soul doesn't.'

'You missed a lovely time with the Lord's people in chapel yesterday. Don't forget, you always have an open invitation to worship with us. The choir is really on form at the moment.'

A vision of Alice floated before my eyes, and I grimaced 'No *thanks*. I had all that years ago. I'm a tone-deaf atheist now, so you're wasting your time.'

'An atheist? You don't believe in God at all any longer?'

'You said it.'

He wrinkled his brow. 'What sort of a God don't you believe in?'

'What a stupid question!'

Wilfred looked hurt. It occurred to me that a couple of minutes religion-bashing would not be wasted if it both got my adrenalin up and allowed time for the lads to appear. I looked Wilfred in the eye. 'All right, I don't believe in a God who created all sorts of uglies to shoot and trap the birds He made, and to steal their eggs.'

My uncle beamed. 'Do you know, I don't believe in that sort of a God, either. So you aren't as far away from my God as you think you are.' As if he had won a major argument, he gave a satisfied smile. He looked at his watch. 'Is that the time? Well, I must get ready to go.' He started back up the path to Big Cottage.

I saw red. 'And nor do I believe,' I grated after him, 'in a God whose followers spray the land with poisons and who crucify the wealth of the natural world He made.'

Wilfred paused, his shoulders slumping slightly. 'That's your decision, Timothy. You have your own set of values. That's your decision.' He continued his retreat at a steady pace. But his neck, and the tips of his large ears, had become bright pink.

Just then my assistants appeared at last, trudging like half-asleep bears up the street. Feeling virtuous and justified, I strode towards them. It wasn't often I could argue Wilfred into blushing like that. I had a feeling this might be the start of a good day's work.

■　■　■　■

Bob and Jamie came instantly to life at the news of the eggers. We held a high-speed conference and the conclusion was unanimous. The doughty pair pointed their noses toward the Reserve - after, that is, that I had recovered the keys of my beloved Ford from Jamie.

'Make sure you *grrrab* them if you find them at a nest,' he growled. 'I'll have a *worrrd* with them when I see them.'

'I've no doubt you will, Jamie. But don't stand there rolling your r's all morning. They've not come into the village, so they must have gone up the valley. Walk fast up the main track and see which signals are red, then start stalking. I'll drive up and park near their car, then follow them from the road end.'

'A pincer movement. I like it,' said Bob.

'Aye. We'll *crrrush* them in the middle.'

'Not yet,' I cautioned. 'We want to see what they've found first.'

Jamie snorted. 'They had better not be after my marsh birds!'

'Or my terns!' added Bob, vehemently.

■　　■　　■　　■

Once out of the village, I turned left across the burn and followed the road up past the side gates of Lifandoy House. The many windows in the main wall of the huge residence were bare. But from a gabled casement at the base of the slated roof a bright scarlet silk scarf dangled feebly.

'Not exactly a sheet,' I complained to the car. 'We'll have a job seeing that from the Reserve. Let's see if the House Farm does better.'

The House Farm was its usual morning bustle of life and work. The farmhouse wall was in shadow from the rising sun. But a red sheet of reasonable proportions was plainly signalling, from one of the bedrooms, that the enemy had passed by. I made a grudging note of thanks to Alice's clever planning and carried on.

The lane was empty of Volkswagens. At Liffen Farm, the sheet hung out was the largest yet, a maroon cloth of huge proportions like a warship's battle ensign. There was no sign of the enemy car; but hereabouts the road was fringed by tall hedges and narrow gateways and tracks that could conceal it and a dozen others. Leaning up against the gate of the farmyard was a familiar shepherd, wearing a battered flat cap. I gave him a dirty look as I passed.

At our last post at Ginger Farm, the blanket draping the wall was white. With an exclamation of annoyance I did a fast three-point turn and reversed my course.

'Rats and mice! I must have missed them in one of these tiny gateways. Or did they turn off at Liffen Farm for Liffen Cross?'

At the latter farm the gate was still being propped up by my least favourite shepherd. I braked and leapt out.

'Have you seen a black car going up this road?' I waved back up towards Ginger Farm.

He rolled something well-chewed around in his mouth and yawned. 'No, boyo. Not since April.'

'Well, have you seen a black car going up to Liffen Cross?'

'No, not a black car on either road, boyo. Not this morning.'

I stared. 'So you haven't seen a black car at all?'

'Not at all. Not except for the one parked behind you.' He resumed chewing.

I swung round as if singed. In the entrance to the narrow lane opposite me was my quarry! The VW was empty. Feeling like an idiot, I muttered a hasty thanks, reversed my vehicle into a different small opening and leapt out again. The shepherd watched me, his face expressionless but his interest indicated by the velocity of his chewing jaw, now slowing dramatically.

He ventured a question. 'Are you the new warden?'

'Yes.' It occurred to me that in the interests of public relations I ought to give him some indication of my sanity. I stuck out a friendly hand. 'Timothy Corn.'

'*Thomas* Pandy.' He relaxed as we shook. Then he looked interested. 'Are you related to that Wilfred Corn?'

I felt it would do no harm to impress him by dropping the name of a senior fellow agriculturalist. 'Yes. He's my uncle.'

The shepherd dropped my hand as though stung. '*Wel*, the nephew of mad Wilfred!' he muttered feelingly. Mumbling worriedly in Welsh, he reached across and clamped his horny hand onto a nearby wooden post. It was not apparent whether this was from superstitious appeal or from a simple need for support.

This was not quite the reaction I had anticipated. Thomas Pandy was now regarding me with an expression that had an air of pleading about it. To reassure him, I gave him a friendly, broad grin.

He changed his look to one of unmitigated horror. With a hiss of indrawn breath he leapt backwards. This was an unwise thing to do, for the farmyard gate behind him was only loosely roped shut. The rope promptly uncoiled: as the gate swung back hard Mr. Pandy went rolling across the filthy yard floor, shouting in horrified Welsh.

As his bewailments reached their peak, two black-and-white Border collies leapt like missiles over a closed half stable door nearby. The dogs looked savage. To my jaundiced eye they had the air of animals trained to dismember anything they encountered other than sheep or shepherds. They barked once in unison and rocketed at me.

I was saved momentarily by the gate. On reaching the limit of its travel it bounced back, blocking the angry sheepdogs' path. They skidded reluctantly to a halt and opened their mouths impatiently to alert everything within earshot to my presence.

The baying awoke a deep-seated phobia in me - doubtless derived from watching too many repeats of *The Hound of the Baskervilles*. As the gate drifted open again, I lost all interest in public relations. Leaving Thomas Pandy to clamber muddily to his feet, I did a desperate about turn, bounded across the road and, calculating that there was insufficient time to reach my Escort, set off down the track past the Volkswagen at the fastest pace I had run in years.

Savouring the chase if not yet my flesh, the hounds followed. In the yard above us, their master was whistling like a demented steam locomotive. But they ignored him and, slavering, began to catch up.

'Get back, you bloodhounds!'

The dogs slowed as a rabbit shot across the track. Before they resumed the chase I managed to gain ten precious seconds. But within half a minute they were nearly at my heels again. Suddenly, I realized the egg-collectors must not be far ahead of me. At my present rate of progress I was more likely to flatten them than to catch them red-handed. At the bottom of a slope the hedges lining the path came to an end. After a short section of fence I could see the stile that marked the boundary of the Reserve. To my great relief, the path up to the stile was empty.

A little way beyond the stile, three dark figures were walking swiftly across the marsh, following the only footpath. If I crossed it into the Reserve I would instantly be in view should they turn their heads.

'Oh, no! I can't go over the stile. I'll have to get off this path some other way!'

The only possible escape not leading to the marsh was over the fence on the left where it approached the stile. I was on a track I had walked but rarely and I could not remember what was beyond the fence. I would just have to trust to a soft landing. With a last burst of speed, I reached the fence just before the snapping hounds, then hurdled it with all the steeple-chasing desperation of an Olympic finalist.

Unfortunately, I had forgotten that steeplechases include a water jump. The water of the West Burn in which I landed was penetrating, cold, and very wet. I sank to my thighs in the dark, peaty water, yelling horribly.

'Aaargh!' Then my cries rose to a higher pitch. 'Leggo! Gerroff me! Geroff!'

It was bad enough to remember too late that the fence was actually the parapet of the burn bridge. But my latter yells were in response to a different sort of agony.

I had landed near the far side of the West Burn, sinking into a gravel slope, which was the edge of a deep, murky pool under the bridge. Landing, I had nearly slid back into the depths. So I had grabbed urgently for a handhold in one of the small willows on the bank. But as I had seized the shrub, something unseen had seized me simultaneously from behind.

The unseen assailant was hooked around my groin. Inexorably, it continued to strangulate a part of my anatomy of which I was particularly fond. The pull of it was sufficient, quite apart from the excruciating pain, to start clawing my feet from their precarious hold. The swirling waters sucked at my legs.

At first I assumed that the dogs had leapt in with me, sinking their teeth into my clothing. But it slowly dawned on me that both dogs were still on the bridge, where they were baying hysterically. Surprised, I twisted round to see behind me.

My new assailant, floating round lazily in the pool, was simply a decaying fallen bush, doubtless a casualty of the recent rain. Coated with all sorts of debris and slime, it had obviously been circulating in the pool for some while. Now wholly waterlogged, it looked more like a disintegrating corpse than vegetation.

The pull of the vile thing revolted me. With a galvanic recoil I kicked away the sunken branch of it that was hooked between my legs and lunged towards the bank. Seeing above my head a stouter bough of willow than the one I was clinging to, I made a grab at it. The tree I was assaulting defended itself, smashing twigs into my face. The main casualty of this was my old woolly hat, which flew off and landed neatly on the 'head' of the thing rotating in the pool.

Not willing to give up my headgear, I reached down for the nearest appendage of the floating bulk and gave a mighty heave. The dead weight of the thing in the burn was more than I expected. It moved slowly over the lip of the pool towards me. But then it began to accelerate as the force of the burn's current caught it. Far from bringing my perched hat towards me, I found myself being dragged out after it. The tree from whose branch I dangled gave an ominous creak and began to tilt over the water.

The choice was the loss of my hat or being crushed into the stream under a tree. Reluctantly I released the drifting wreck. The thing moved away downstream, bearing my hat as a prize, cocked jauntily at an angle upon its amorphous dark form. Freed from part of its burden, the tree above me leaned back again, pulling me with it. Trying to find a way through the net of twigs, I became as completely entangled as if I had been trussed and bound. Encased in willow branches, I lay helpless and gasping.

From where I lay buried in the foliage, I could see the dogs still going spare on the bridge. Once I had been sucked into the bankside greenery I saw them transferred their hatred to the flotsam in the stream. They focused on my receding hat as the object of their ire and began throwing themselves into the air with vexation as they saw it disappearing.

At that moment, Thomas Pandy appeared panting on the bridge. His face was red and both it and the flat cap he was wearing were bespattered with mire; it was quite impossible from his expression to tell which vigorous Welsh emotion was presently exciting him most.

He peered down the burn in astonishment. I was in no mood to attract his attention, even if my ensnared state and the noise of his hounds had not made it nearly impossible. As I watched, he perceived the thing in the water, topped by my hat, as it made one final pirouette in the current before drifting slowly round the first bend downstream.

His faced went milk white. He clutched the fence before him for support and said something half strangled in Cymric. With a stricken expression he snatched the cap from his head. Clasping it with shaking hands to his chest he bowed his head brokenly. Then he stared for one last, horrified moment at the dark water, turned, and with stumbling steps retreated at speed the way he had come, leaving the dogs to follow, squabbling, at his heel.

12. - One Egg

By the time I had extricated myself from my leafy strait-jacket the coast was clear and I was livid.

'Wait until I see that shepherd again! Leave my supposed corpse to float away without a word, would he? I'll do more than make him fall over the next time he crosses my path!'

I indulged in a short, pleasant daydream about the likely effects on Thomas Pandy's nervous system of our next meeting. Then reality woke me to action.

Keeping an eye open for ravening canines, I squelched back to the stile. I peered over it to make sure that my quarry was far enough away for safety, then hopped over and scuttled quickly into cover. From behind a stunted common sallow I could see the path across the wet pasture. The valley here was flatter here than lower down; and the path was obvious as it cut across a broad curve of the West Burn to meet the stream higher up its course on the far bend. After that the path joined the one through the bog which the lads and I had raced up just before we met Sir Charles; Bob and Jamie had since christened this route the Mud Path in my honour.

The sight of three distant figures showed that the eggers had not stopped to inquire into the commotion made by the dogs.

'Hey, how did they get that far away?'

I abandoned some of my caution and started to gallop from bush to bush along the path. Before long, the bushes petered out at the edge of the open marsh. I stopped for breath behind the last one.

Down the valley furtive movements were taking place. I squinted hopefully. Jamie and Bob were bush-hopping as I had been. When they stopped, I waved a white rag to attract their attention. Happily, they had their eyes about them. When I got my binoculars on them I saw Bob waving back while Jamie held his optics on me to see my response.

Bob stretched out one arm, horizontally then vertically. Then he held both hands out, palm uppermost, to indicate a question.

'He wants to know whether they're to follow the marsh path or go up on the ridge,' I told the bush. I nodded and pointed my own arm at the skies. 'You'll never get up the valley unseen. The ridge, Bob, follow the ridge!'

The lads gave me a thumbs up and started scampering up the steep path along which they would overtake their quarry. That left me to sneak across the pasture. The enemy had, by this time, passed the curve of the West Burn and were on the Mud Path, where they were doubtless slithering their way up the valley.

'That's got to be suspicious,' I growled. 'After all that rain, anyone who knew the Reserve would avoid the Mud Path like the plague; and anyone who didn't wouldn't find it anyway.'

I set to catch them up. To start with, I had no cover at all. I would have to trust to my shabby old anorak blending into the vegetation - which, with all the willow twigs garlanding it, would not be difficult.

A swift jog of a few minutes brought me to the loop of the West Burn. The stream was shallower here above the bridge and was divided into a lacework of channels that percolated the bog below the Mud Path. My quarry were now only five minutes slither ahead of me - I liked the hint of snake in their character which this thought gave me - and from here I would have to stalk cleverly.

The three tall figures never looked back. Just in case, however, I served the cause to the uttermost. Dodging from tussock to tussock I was soon as muddy as the path. The fact that I was already saturated to my thighs actually helped, since I did not mind any more what happened from the knees down. I waded through all sorts of filth with equanimity - the need to keep a low silhouette was paramount.

What did worry me, however, was what to do if our foes actually carried out a crime. On my own I was helpless - a mental vision of me rising from the swamp to terrify the eggers into flight was briefly funny but provided no useful ideas.

'I'd better keep as near to them as I can,' I decided. 'I've got a view from the bog and the lads can see from the heather. But what do we do if we catch them in the act? I wish I'd thought to phone Sergeant Farquhar: if we had him waiting at their car it would have been easy.'

The men were now approaching the knoll that overlooked the bowl at the valley head. To one side I glimpsed Jamie and Bob coming down from the ridge. Realizing they were in view of the enemy, they descended the hill hastily to land in the first mound of bracken. From there, a waving of the vegetation betrayed their progress as they wormed through the bracken into the heather where the vegetation became acid on the distant edge of the moor.

I tensed, as no doubt did they, as the eggers approached the knoll. The men stopped directly on top of it, gazing around. Snatches of their conversation, quite unintelligible, drifted to me on the strengthening wind.

'If there's Anyone up there I'd give my eye-teeth to know what they're after!' In agony I offered an unusual bargain to the heavens. There was no response: presumably Wilfred's God either did not approve or else had no use for my teeth; and as a self-confessed atheist I was probably up against it expecting a reply anyway.

'All right, I'll find out for myself.' Giving up on divine intervention I settled for native guile. By now camouflaged like a native, I scuttled to a protruding rock and unearthed - literally - my muddy telescope. I levelled it angrily.

The men were surveying the head of the valley with binoculars. With relief I noticed that Jamie and Bob had crawled to a position where they, too, could overlook the bowl. Glancing across at my assistants, I took my eyes for a few moments off the enemy. When I swung my gaze back, one of them - the biggest of the three - was stooping over a tuft of grass on the knoll.

He had his back to Bob and Jamie so that they could not see what I could. As I observed him, the big man was standing bent over, looking at something in his hand - something which was easily identifiable to my shock as a large, white *egg*.

'YOU...!' Now I was really angry. Bile welled up in my throat. If there had been time it would have emerged as a stream of invective. But all my concentration had to go into keeping the telescope steady. The big man pivoted away from me slightly. Desperate to see what he did next, I found my rock awkwardly placed. I tried to lean the telescope at a different angle. But I lost my balance and nearly dropped it.

The knoll was out of my ken for a few seconds. When it came back into focus again I had a shock. The men were gone! Over the top of the knoll I saw their bobbing heads. They had turned to the left and were walking through the heather towards the Raw Head path. Their course would take them directly under the hidden eyes of Jamie and Bob.

Casting caution to the winds, I stood up and started to semaphore wildly. From the distant movement in the heather I knew the lads could see my waving arms.

'Stop them!' To illustrate my meaning I pretended to grab myself by the wrist and then by the throat. 'They've taken an egg! There's a nest on the knoll!'

But there was no response. I couldn't understand why. The lads were within a stone's throw of the eggers and had their glasses trained full on them.

'Get after them, you pair of hooligans!' I shouted aloud; but the wind carried my voice away. I started to run: but the consistency of the marsh was such that I might as well have tried running through a treacle pudding. It took several minutes to reach the heather. By the time I got to my recalcitrant assistants, I could see that the egg-collectors had long since disappeared towards Raw Head. I came to a halt in the heather, almost unable at first to say a word.

'You - you - *you...*' I gasped.

They looked puzzled. 'Calm down, Tim. We can catch them up in five minutes. You didn't need to panic; we weren't going to leave you behind.'

'You blind idiots,' I raged. 'There's a nest on the knoll. They had a big egg! We've got to get it back from them!'

'A nest?' They were thunderstruck. 'Do you mean a snowy owl nest?'

'It must be. It's a classic site: snowies in the Arctic always nest on hillocks, to have a wide view and to catch the most sunshine. The first egg must just have been laid. The big fellow was holding it in his hand. He walked right past you with it!'

'He couldn't have.' Jamie surprised me. 'Why do you think we were examining them so closely? All three of them are wearing tight jackets - very smart ones, too. Their pockets were empty: in those outfits even a quail's egg would have made a bulge!'

I spat feathers. 'Morons! Don't you know that eggers carry stolen eggs in their binocular cases?'

They frowned. 'None of them had cases! They all had bins hung round their necks - nothing else.'

'What?'

The argument raged for several more seconds. In the end, the lads' flat denials forced me to back down. Jamie was particularly scathing.

'Yon telescope of yours looks like it came from a sunken Spanish galleon. It's probably half full of water. Ye've magnified a blob of mud, that's all!'

Few insults are better guaranteed to enrage a birdwatcher than the maligning of his optical equipment. I was at shouting pitch with Jamie when Bob grabbed us by the throat to bring us to our senses.

'Morons, you say?' he snapped. 'And what kind of morons is it who would shout their heads off at each other a stone's throw from a snowy owl nest?'

We shut like clams and dropped into the heather, red-faced. They both looked at me, expectantly. 'Well? Which way?' asked Bob expectantly.

'The nest or the eggers... Should we jump them and thump them?' It was a hard decision. All of a sudden I wasn't sure I liked being a warden. The other two hung on my words.

'We've got to know about the egg. If there's only one egg, they might have left it so they can come back for the whole clutch.'

Bob nodded. 'If they stole one, the bird could desert and never lay the rest.'

Jamie was sceptical. 'It won't be there. There isn't one.'

'There's only one way to find out. The knoll, and quick!'

Watching every way for white wings, we jogged low and furtively to the knoll. There was a moment's hesitation as we gazed around. Then I gave a bark of warning.

'Mind your feet! There, Jamie - in that hollow ahead of you!'

We dropped down instinctively and scuttled up to it. Unadorned, the hollow was simply that - a shallow depression that happened to contain one large, pristine white egg.

Bob spoke in an awed whisper. 'Look how clean it is!'

I nodded. 'Newly laid,' I stated knowingly. 'Probably fresh this morning. She won't start sitting until they are all laid.'

Jamie's eyes were locked on it. 'So new! Will it be warm?'

I reached out and touched it with a shaking finger. 'Yes! It is!' I trembled with excitement. 'In fact, I could swear it's positively *humming* with life!'

Bob sniffed. 'It's you that's vibrating all over! Come on, turn your energy into speed. Let's get out of here!'

■ ■ ■ ■

Our suppressed excitement converted into an urgent scuttle, then a mad gallop. Full of wrath, we thundered across the moor, scattering meadow pipits and shocked rabbits. The moor gave way to the flowery sandstone grassland of the Raw Head cliff path. The slow ascent forced us into single file. After a week with my feet up I was in poor condition as the other two overtook me, striding on until a junction of paths made them pause.

The path fork overlooked what is possibly Lifandoy's most famous landmark. The much-postcarded Great Stack of Lifandoy is a huge detached block of cliff whose sheer sides are encrusted annually with the nests of thousands of breeding seabirds. In summer it is one of the finest bird spectacles in the country. On hot days it is also one of the smelliest as well: a sea breeze rising up the cliffs brings with it a stench which can be detected half-way across Lifandoy.

Today the breeze was thankfully offshore. The cacophony of myriad kittiwakes and auks arose as we appeared: then the birds returned to their nuptials.

I waved an arm angrily. 'What are you standing here for? Jamie, you go inland over the hill. Bob and I will keep to the cliff and meet you at the lighthouse.'

Jamie bore a pensive expression. 'What do we do if we catch them?'

I had not thought of that. 'I see what you mean. No evidence.'

'Nor even a crime.'

'Unless they take some other eggs.'

'But Raw Head won't produce any rare eggs for them without ropes. I mean, there are falcon nests on both sides of the headland but they are out of reach on the cliffs.'

'No, that's no good. We have to catch them red-handed.'

'Or should we challenge them anyhow?'

'That could work against us. If they know we are spying on them they will work at night. That will make our job a lot harder.'

I made my mind up.

'We must dog their footsteps wherever they go. We'll mount a guard on the nest too whenever we can. But one guard couldn't arrest all of them. Stalking them, with Sergeant Farquhar alerted and ready to intervene, is the best bet. Now - let's go!'

13. - More Visitors

Our quarry escaped mysteriously again. When Bob and I came within first sight of Raw Head, the three in black were on path approaching the lighthouse. The latter was a typical construction of its kind, comprising a squat, white building - the now disused keepers' house - beneath a stumpy tower. The single light overlooked a small yard with outbuildings. The whole was surrounded by a low white wall, pristine except for the eggers' moving shadows.

Before we could get close, Bob and I had to descend a narrow gully, at the base of which the path crossed a tiny but noisy burn. When we emerged cautiously two minutes later beyond the gully we crept along a shallow ditch to a viewpoint. But the view was suddenly un-peopled. There was no-one on the path or in the lighthouse yard; and the vehicle track running from the building was empty for a good five minutes walk.

'They've vanished! Surely they couldn't have got that far down the track - not without running?'

Bob agreed. 'Perhaps they went round behind the lighthouse?'

'They would fall over the cliff if they tried that. The cliff has crumbled away, right to the foot of the wall.'

We watched the lighthouse suspiciously for a few minutes.

'Could they be in the building, Tim?'

'The Lighthouse Commissioners have kept it all locked up since the light went automatic, Bob. Only the Estate Office has a key.'

'They could be in the yard. Perhaps they climbed over the wall.'

'The wall wouldn't hide them unless they were sitting down. The only place they could be standing out of sight is just outside the gates, behind that detached outbuilding.'

'Is that a garage?'

'Yes, locked, of course. There could be a vehicle parked in the gateway behind it, I suppose, which we wouldn't see from here.'

'But we already know where their car is, don't we, Tim?'

'Yes, of course. Silly me.'

'Could they be sitting down with some sandwiches somewhere?'

'If they weren't carrying an egg, how could they be carrying butties?'

Our fruitless tactical discussion was interrupted by a surprise development.

'Hey! There's someone walking up the track. It's... oh, it's just Jamie!'

Jamie was shambling along the track toward us, as languidly as if he had all the time in Lifandoy. We signalled to him with urgent arms.

'Here! Keep down! We're over here!'

The object of our gesticulations strolled up nonchalantly and gazed down into our ditch with disdain.

'So, you've joined in the mud-larking too, Bob? Well, you're both wasting your time. Yon eggers are long gone. Did you not hear the Land Rover?'

'*What?* Not again?' I could not believe it.

'I saw it from behind just as I topped the hill. It must have left the lighthouse just before you got there. I just got my bins on it before it went out of sight.'

We clambered wearily out of the ditch and walked across to the lighthouse. 'Did you see the driver or the licence plate?'

'I told you, Tim. I had about two seconds to see inside the back. They were there, all three.'

Bob was outraged. 'That means someone on the island must be helping them! Who is the Judas?'

'Not necessarily, Bob. They could just have been lucky,' I pointed out. 'Most people on Lifandoy would give strangers a lift if they asked. And there are plenty of Land Rovers on the island. But who would drive one up here?'

Jamie's eyes glinted. 'There's one Land Rover we know has been up here twice recently. Did you ever find out why Wilfred was up here that day he rescued you?'

I searched my mind. 'He said he was looking for something.'

'So he came back for another search.' Bob nodded. 'Would he pick up three strangers?'

Behind the garage, we gazed sourly at a set of fresh vehicle tracks in a muddy puddle.

'Wilfred?' I groaned. 'If he thought he was being helpful Wilfred would give a lift to a whole busload of tourists. That's it, of course. He must have been parked behind the garage, having a kip or something. He's whipped them from under our noses.'

■ ■ ■ ■

We returned in foul tempers across the Reserve. We watched for a short time for the snowy owl without result, so to the egg on its knoll we gave a wide berth. Bob went off to the beach to count his terns. Jamie, happy to potter among his marsh birds in the valley bog, agreed to take first turn at keeping a distant eye on the knoll.

I decided to walk back to West Doy for a change of clothing, leaving my car for collection at the end of the day. With the countryside positively throbbing with wildlife it was a delightful walk; by the time I reached Little Cottage my good humour was restored and I was ready to wish well to the world. Until, that was, the world arrived.

Standing outside my home was a small group of unkempt-looking men in an assortment of worn green overwear. They were all bore expressions of apparent unhappiness, although from somewhere they had all acquired cups of steaming beverage also.

For a moment, I wondered if they were a gang of international coffee thieves who had invaded my meagre stocks. Then to my relief I recognized the china as belonging to Big Cottage, not Little. Martha had taken pity upon the hapless travellers, who from their array of expensive bins and 'scopes were clearly not the criminals I had at first supposed, but a party of amateur naturalists.

Monday seemed a strange day of the week to receive an influx of tourists to the Reserve. However, I put on my most welcoming smile and approached the group with the air of helpfulness that Keith Potts usually affected on such occasions. Beaming, I even chose to overlook the fact that one of the newcomers was leaning rather heavily against the weaker of my two gateposts.

'Welcome to the Lifandoy Reserve! I am the acting warden, Timothy Corn. Have you just arrived on the island?'

The group snapped to attention. At the same moment Martha appeared at my side with an enormous plate of biscuits. I was not clear as to whether it was myself or the biscuits that were of interest.

One of the group spoke up informatively. 'Yeah.'

Martha held the biscuits under my nose. There was a brief scramble as the best biscuits were expertly selected, with muttered thanks, by many hands. Mine was not last among them.

'Thanks, Martha. You're a life-saver.'

'Not me, young Timothy.' There was a twinkle in her eye. 'Saving is done by the good Lord, as I trust you will one day discover.'

I mumbled something into my biscuit. The visitors waited patiently. The party eyed my filthy clothing without dismay; probably they thought it was my normal uniform. When I finished my biscuit I heard the leader speak again.

'Sparrow around today?'

It was an odd question. It was delivered with an air of laconic intensity, the reason for which escaped me. As I took in the visitors more carefully, they went down in my estimation, from naturalists to mere tourists. Behind them a dusty female house sparrow was pecking at something on the lawn of Little Cottage. I indicated it disdainfully.

'That's a house sparrow. *Passer domesticus.*' I added the Latin name to awe them with my warden's knowledge. 'Although you won't find many of these up on the Reserve. They are rare away from human habitation. On one of the headlands we have a couple of pairs of a little brown finch called the twite, which looks very similar. But we have more attractive birds around there...'

I paused. The leader seemed impatient. I fixed him again with my helpful look. 'Have you visited the Reserve before?'

'Nope. Didn't expect to, either. We were over on the Isle of Man, so we didn't have far to come.'

'Ah, you came on the Saturday ferry?' Saturday was the only day when there was a ferry service running directly between the two islands of Man and Lifandoy.

He looked puzzled. 'No, we didn't hear until Saturday night. Couldn't get a boat until we found a lobster boat coming over this morning.'

A trip on a rolling lobster boat explained something of their appearance. It also seemed unusual dedication, and I said so. The leader, whom the others addressed as Mike, waved my plaudit away airily.

'Nothing to speak of. Right - where is it, then?'

His question seemed to produce a charged atmosphere in the group. Everyone hurriedly started passing their cups back to Martha and gathering expectantly. My gatepost gave an ominous creak as the weight of its occupier lifted rapidly from it.

'Where's what?'

He laughed. 'The biggie. The lifer. The megatick!'

Martha cleared her throat. 'The what?' she inquired gently.

'We were on the Isle of Man cleaning up on the red-rumped gulp and the Steller's,' explained Mike mystifyingly. 'Picked up a Bonaparte's too, as an extra goodie. But this is bigger than any of those. New for the Western Pally, isn't it?'

Martha looked at me curiously. 'Are they speaking English, Timothy?'

I was slowly making connections. 'It?'

Mike sighed. 'The lesser crested yew sparrow, of course!'

I gulped. 'Ah - er - of course...'

'Came over on National Birdpage as a red hot report.' Incongruously, he held up an expensive-looking electronic paging device. 'Place called the Doy Hotel. We've already been there - they said you would be the chap who knew. We ran all the way up the hill - would have died without that coffee!'

Light had dawned on me at last. 'You're twitchers!'

There was a general snarl. 'Thought *you* would have known better. *Birders,* please - twitchers is an insult. You'll be accusing us of using Twitcherspeak next. Well? When was it last seen? Today?'

Mike was a big fellow, and he was towering over me in a menacing way. I realized that I was rather warm under the collar.

'Er - well - no. Tell me, are there any more of you coming?'

He looked disappointed. 'Hundreds, I expect. What about yesterday?'

'N-no. That is–'

'Saturday?'

I said nothing. The group adopted a pose of collective severe dejection. Complaints began to issue forth.

'Looks like a dip-out to me.'

'Knew we should have gone to Fair Isle instead!'

'Second busted clean-up on a biggie this year.'

'This is really gripping me off...'

But their leader held up his hand benevolently.

'Wait a bit. Have you actually looked for it over the weekend, Tim?'

'No, Mike. Look, I...' Miserably, I opened my mouth to start an explanation. But I was given no chance.

'Say no more!' Mike interrupted, speaking like a machine-gun. 'Lads, remember who Timothy is. We see before us an underpaid, overworked servant of Joe Public. Dedicated to the cause of environmental protection, striving every hour against the evils of eggers, gamekeepers, wildfowlers and prairie farmers, he needs our help, not our whingeing. Overworked wardens have no time to sit watching even super-rarities for us. If the biggie is still here we'll find it ourselves. We're the experts, remember. Now, which way was the wind blowing on Friday?'

'It was a south-easterly,' said Martha helpfully. 'Dried my washing a treat.'

'South-east?' Mike glanced at the clouds. 'It still is. That means that if the bird started from the hotel it would have come straight up the valley - this way! There won't be much cover further north, so it could still be in any of these bushes in the village right now.'

Cries of excitement arose. 'With all that rain it can't have gone far. What's that, over there?' 'Or that?' 'I don't recognize that jizz?' 'Lesser or greater crested, could be either! Where's it gone?'

Mike held up a magisterial hand. 'Order, please. Tim, where is the thickest shrubbery in the village?'

I gaped. Martha replied for me. 'Oh, I should think Mrs. Bull's garden next to the chapel must have the most bushes. She's even managed to grow a few ornamental yews.'

The crowd erupted and began to jog away, giving whoops and shouts.

'Let's stake out Mrs. Bull's garden!' yelled Mike. 'Quietly, now, we don't want to alarm anyone. *Let's go.*'

Martha smiled as they thundered off. 'I really must get back to my sewing. But it's so nice to see such enthusiasm in the young,' she said.

'Huh!' Feeling as though I had just taken a right to the chin, I sagged wearily onto my gatepost. It gave another threatening creak.

'Except...' Martha frowned '...just one thing, Timothy. What on earth is a red-rumped gulp?'

With a savage crack, the gatepost disintegrated under me.

■ ■ ■ ■

As usual, Martha was immediately sensitive to the agony of a soul in distress. Before I could think clearly I found myself dressed in clean clothes and placed in my best armchair holding the largest cup of coffee I could imagine. Martha sat by me, patting my head while I expounded to her in sobbing tones about the rarest birds of the Western Palearctic region and on how to tell a red-rumped swallow from a Bonaparte's gull.

Martha rarely fails to cheer me. I do not know what it is about her, but she has a brightness about her that is as encouraging as a sunny morning on the *machair*. My psyche was approaching a healed state again when my landline telephone rang. She picked it up and passed it to me. The voice which inquired hurriedly after me at the other end was that of Keith Potts.

'Tim? Is that you?'

'Keith! I thought you were still in hospital!'

'I am. I can't talk long. I've tried to reach you four times. Where have you been?'

'Well, I... Never mind. I haven't got time for excuses.'

'Excuses? We've got things well in hand here.'

'What do you mean, in hand?' Keith was obviously at odds with the world. 'I know you, Tim Corn, and I don't like the sound of that. Talk business! Have you found the you-know-whats yet?'

'That sounds cryptic.'

'This isn't a private call. Sixteen other patients are sitting in other beds around here and listening to me. Have you found the nest?'

'Yes. We found the first egg this morning. It took a lot of finding.' I thought it unwise to explain exactly who the finders had been.

'Brilliant! But speaking of eggs, have you heard–'

'We know about the eggers, too. We're watching every step they take.' My tone was warmly reassuring, my best bedside manner.

'You are?' He sounded surprised. 'Well done! But...'

Keith's voice began to crackle as his battery started to fade. He spoke louder. 'Are you listening, Tim? I don't - I mean - I didn't think you would have seen them yet. When I last heard they were still on the Isle of Man...'

There was a loud click, then silence. I put the receiver down, frowning.

Martha looked concerned. 'Bad news, nephew?'

I grinned. 'No. Keith's mobile phone just ran out of battery, that's all. That was Keith Potts, from hospital.'

'How is he? Will he be back on the island soon?'

I grinned again. 'I've still got the Reserve to myself.'

Martha gave me a stern glance, with just a hint of a smile in it. 'In that case, you had better not sit for very long. I've no time for malingerers! Anything could happen while you're relaxing. Couldn't it?'

14. - Constable Williams

After saying my thanks to Martha and swallowing a brief meal in my kitchen, I headed back out of the cottage. On reaching the street, I had a wonderful surprise. Standing on the pavement was sweet Jessica. There was a look of puzzlement on her face.

'You *are* here,' she exclaimed. 'I saw the door was open, but there was no car. I was expecting one of the lads to emerge.'

'Jessica, darling.' After a glance up and down the road for small girls, I held out my arms to enfold her in a romantic embrace.

'So, you want to call me darling, do you?' Jessica avoided my passionate lunge with a neat side-step. She gave me a piercing look. 'In that case, tell me why I shouldn't think up an apt name for *you,* Timothy Corn!'

I stopped, startled. 'Eh? What name?'

'Hah!' She walked round me, eyeing me as though I were on public trial. 'A scurvy knave is the first that springs to mind. Or better, how about Peeping Tom?'

'Peeping? Who's been peeping?'

'Not you. I mean your customers - the gang of mainlanders you've sent to peer through every window of our house.'

'Eh? Oh - the twitchers.'

'In one.' Jessica had a stern expression. 'Mummy was so upset that she retired to bed with one of her migraines. Then she found them pointing telescopes right at her bedroom window.'

I winced. This was a disaster of large potential. If there was one person in the whole of West Doy whom I dared not offend it was Mrs. Bull. I tried to repair the situation.

'They aren't staring at your windows - just the bushes around them. And in any case, I didn't direct them to your bungalow.'

'Some of them said you did.'

'It wasn't me. I didn't tell them. Martha did.'

'What? Dear old Martha? She wouldn't do a thing like that! What does she know about rare birds?'

'That's not the point. I didn't–'

'Forget it.' Jessica thawed suddenly. 'I'm not angry at you - yet. And yes, I *would* like a kiss, best beloved. You look like you need some comfort.'

'I do!' As we cuddled, I played for all the sympathy I could get. 'I've been working hard.'

'It will sort itself out, sweetheart,' she cooed. 'If the bird they want is in our garden I expect one of the children will have seen it. When Alice and Rosalind get home from school they will tell your twitcher friends all about it. And if the twitchers have any more questions, I'm sure they will all come looking for you straight away.'

A chill ran all the way from the back of my neck to my heels. That probability had just occurred to me also.

Jessica inquired where I was going. When I said that my first call would be on Sergeant Farquhar at the Doytown police station she was taken aback.

'Have you been doing something nefarious?'

I laughed. 'No. I'm strictly on the side of the good boys. In fact, I'm about to give our dear sergeant some business.' I explained about the eggers. When I told Jessica about the egg on the knoll she was excited.

'Is that what they're after? How evil! And what villains they are. Dear Timothy, you are brave to take them on! You will be careful, won't you?'

Being cast as a hero by an oodles-of-gushing-admiration Jessica was quite enough to turn my head. By the time we had walked down the hill to Doytown I was living in visions of grandeur. Jessica and I had already made a plan for the seizure of the gang. We were moving on enthusiastically to holding them for ransom, enticing more eggers into the same trap and perhaps even penetrating an entire international eggers' syndicate.

Then, as we rounded the last corner talking excitedly, we came face to face on the street with a familiar figure.

'Ulp - er - Sir Charles, how *pleasant* to meet you.' I came back to reality with an abrupt sinking feeling. 'Have you finished your report yet? May I offer you our further assistance with your survey?'

Sir Charles Hamilstone-ffrench was just passing the diminutive station of the Lifandoy constabulary. He took in my appearance blankly. Then recognition dawned and he gave a regal nod, followed by a sudden smile. The latter was regrettably directed not at me but at Jessica.

'You say, *our* assistance, Mr. Corn? I hardly feel that such a mundane subject as land use ought to occupy the time of such a charming lady. Surely this is not one of your assistants from the Reserve?'

'Er - no.' Anything that raise my standing in Sir Charles's eyes was worth a try. 'This is my girlfriend, Jessica. She comes from an old Lifandoy family - and she feels the same about the Reserve as I do.'

'And with reason, I am sure.' The old buffer took Jessica's hand eagerly: he was clearly a lady's man. 'Delighted to make your acquaintance, my dear.'

Jessica surprised us both. 'You have already made it, Sir Charles. I work at the Estate Office.'

'Of course you do. I see Mr. Corn has a friend in an influential establishment.' Said another way it could have sounded sinister, but Sir Charles sounded affable enough.

Jessica smiled. 'I thought you had returned to London, Sir Charles?'

'One cannot ignore the demands of the world, my dear. When business calls I must respond. But I am back for the moment. I hope to finish my report for the Earl by the end of this week. Good day to you both.'

The land agent ambled away. I gazed at Jessica speculatively. 'Well! Why didn't you tell me...?'

'Oh, Mr. Corn...' Sir Charles spun on his heel. 'Tell me - have you seen the lesser crested yew sparrow again?'

I drew a long breath. 'No, Sir Charles.'

'Please let me know if you do. It will be in your interest to do so.'

I looked a question.

'When I was in London, I mentioned your sighting to a friend from the Ornithological Society. He was *most* interested. He said he would pass it on to the Society immediately. He was also most expressive on the wildlife value of small islands in general. He went a long way towards convincing me that somewhere like the Reserve was a key sanctuary on a heavily populated island for such a rare bird.'

I gaped.

'I have therefore decided to make the case of the - er - yew sparrow a central example in my report. Any news of its protection and survival here will greatly enhance your case for the Reserve. In fact, I shall make a *point* of following up for myself any information I hear concerning the bird. Good day again, Mr. Corn.'

At my side, Jessica gave a sigh of admiration as he strolled away. 'Oh, how nice of Sir Charles to help you like that. Isn't he thoughtful?'

I gave a strange grating noise through my teeth. There are occasionally times when even Jessica's sweet nature can be hard to live with.

■ ■ ■ ■

Sergeant Farquhar listened to my tale with growing, if dour, indignation.

'I've heard about these egg-collectors. There have been none on Lifandoy in my time, and I don't want any now. Who did you say gave you the car number?'

'It was Angus Donald from the *Bagpipe,* Sergeant. You know Angus, don't you?'

'I ken the man. A good man, Angus the *Bagpipe.* Just let me think...' he tapped his pen for a few seconds, frowning at some scribble on a pad by the telephone. 'The thing is, I haven't time to deal with this myself. I've just had a report of a missing person that I must investigate straight away. An incident that's in progress takes precedence over one that hasn't happened yet. You need someone... aye...'

The burly sergeant turned his head and bellowed at a doorway behind him. 'Williams? Are you still there?'

Immediately, a fresh-faced young constable with a mop of carrot hair bounded into the room. 'Here, sergeant. Have you a job for me?'

Farquhar nodded. 'I want you to follow up a black Volkswagen car. Mr. Corn, here, has the number.'

'Yessir! Stolen, is it?'

'No, Williams. Calm down, laddie. It's the three men in it who deserve your attention.'

'They're egg collectors,' I offered. 'We would like to catch them red-handed.'

The constable scowled. 'It beats me, sir, the sort of scum who would do things like that.'

Sergeant Farquhar eyed his deputy warmly. 'I'm giving you this case all to yourself, Williams. You will need to keep in constant contact with Mr. Corn on the Reserve. But don't be afraid to call for help if you need it. These egg-collectors have a rough reputation. I don't want you outnumbered if you manage to make an arrest.'

Williams grew visibly as we watched him. 'I'll not let you down, sir!'

I produced a folder. 'I've brought a few maps of the Reserve. If Constable Williams has the time now, we can sit down and show him the lie of the valley and the places where we've seen the eggers so far.'

Farquhar reached for his cap. 'While you're doing that, I have to see someone urgently up at Liffen. Williams, you can hold the fort here for an hour until I get back.'

'Aye, Sarge.' Williams bade the closing door farewell. 'Mr. Corn, would you and the young lady like a coffee?'

'Certainly would. Call me Tim. And this is Jessica.'

'William.' The constable grimaced. 'William Williams, if you can believe it.'

'If you're treating us to coffee you can call yourself what you like! Now, here's the first map...'

■　■　■　■

Before long, we were in vigorous discussion over a table covered with sketch maps and cups. Ideas flew back and forth. I was more than a little chagrined to discover that of the three of us it was Jessica whose grasp of the situation shone forth. It soon became evident that she had a fine tactical brain and my original crude plans were greatly refined by her contributions. I began to feel that the prospect of reporting a major success to Keith Potts on his return was a real one.

After some time there was a heavy tread at the door. Sergeant Farquhar marched in, bearing a worried expression.

When he saw me, his face brightened sharply. He peered at me.

'Now, Mr. Corn, were you at Liffen Farm this morning? And is that your Ford parked in the lane there?'

I sat back stiffly. 'Yes and yes. Don't tell me I parked illegally?'

He gave a long sigh of relief. 'No, you're safely parked. But you've left a very worried shepherd behind you.'

I had a sudden fit of the giggles. 'Not Thomas Pandy?'

He nodded. 'The poor man has been dragging the West Burn looking for a body. When I told him I'd just left you in Doy he burst into tears.'

Under Farquhar's stern gaze I submerged my mirth. 'Er - did you see any other cars there?'

'No. Only yours.'

'In that case it's time we were going. Can we take your constable with us?'

'As long as you don't lose him. What are your plans, Williams?'

The young officer looked at the clock. 'First stop the Doy Hotel, Sarge, to take a look at the hotel register. Then I thought I'd take Mr. Timothy and Miss Jessica down to the harbour to meet the *Bagpipe*. She'll be in the harbour before five tonight with the wind the way it is. I'd like to have a word with Angus Donald, the helmsman, to see if he knows anything more about the eggers and their car.'

'Give Angus the *Bagpipe* my best wishes, laddie, and tell him I'll see him soon. For the Doy Hotel, it might be better if you weren't seen there yourself. We wouldn't want the mice running from the trap. Perhaps Mr. Corn or his friend could look at the register for you?'

'Good idea, Sarge.'

'Right. What are you waiting for? Get off with you, then.'

∎ ∎ ∎ ∎

From a distance we could see that there was a black Volkswagen in the hotel car park. Williams brought his tiny patrol car to a halt at the roadside short of the building, just past the entrance of the island school. 'One of us had better walk from here. My car would stand out like a sore thumb.'

I opened the car door and stepped out. Jessica looked out at me. 'Is this something you would like me to do?'

'It's an idea. Do you mind?' I took her hand to help her out. 'It might help if both William and I keep out of their sight for the moment.'

The constable looked doubtful. 'You'll need to look in the hotel register without anyone noticing. Perhaps I should speak to the manager. And we could really do with the full addresses, to run a check at the station. It won't be easy if our suspects are nearby.'

'That's what you think! *Nothing* to it, that's what we say!' An indignant voice broke into our conversation without warning. The three of us looked up in astonishment.

From behind a bush by the school gate there emerged the grinning figure of Alice, with her usual entourage in tow. The Cabal broke into cheerful whistles.

'Oooh, look at them! Hand in hand, and with a copper watching them too!'

'Give 'er a kiss! Go on, don't be shy!'

'I like the copper myself. He's young and handsome.'

'That's more than can be said for Timothy.'

'Shush! He's going to buy us all a cornet at the Summer Fair, remember!'

Constable Williams jumped at the appearance of the mob. He made a cautious enquiry. 'Are these children friends of yours?'

'Children!' The Cabal erupted with cries of derision. 'You've only just started shaving yourself, Mister Plod!'

I sighed. 'Yes, I'm afraid so. They have been useful to us for running errands. With careful instruction they can perform simple tasks.'

Alice was caustic. 'Yes - not complicated ones like climbing a tree to look through someone's–'

'Ahem!' I cut her off sharply. 'Alice, was there something you wanted to tell us?'

She sniffed. 'You were going to sneak in and get the eggers' addresses out of the hotel register, weren't you?'

Williams looked stunned. 'What? What do you mean?'

Alice held out to him a grubby scrap of paper. 'We've saved you the trouble. Carmen wrote them down this morning. We thought of it ages ago!'

Williams took the paper as if it was coated with gold. He peered at it in amazement. 'Er - I'll keep this, if you don't mind.'

'That's what it's for.' Alice gave a pleased wave. 'Meet us at the shed after tea. We'll have a report for you by then. Oh, and Mister Plod can come too, if he likes. We won't bite him if he's good.'

15. - The Unexpected

I squinted, gazing out to sea. 'The *Bagpipe* is still nearly half an hour out, William. You were right about the wind, so I expect the tide must be against her.'

The constable got out of the car and tipped his cap down over his eyes against the bright afternoon sunshine. 'We shall have to possess our souls in patience, Mr. Timothy. I'm sorry if I've brought you and Miss Jessica here to waste your time.'

I grinned. 'There's always someone to talk to in Port Doy. It's surprising what I can learn just by meeting people.'

'Is that so? Do you mean about the wildlife?'

'Yes. The lobster fishermen often see interesting things around the coast - seals, otters, porpoises, sometimes a dolphin or a basking shark. It all helps to put together a jigsaw of the wildlife around the Reserve. It all goes in my boss's big black diary.'

Jessica looked interested. 'Do they know the birds?'

'They know some of them. They tell us when the first puffins and guillemots are back off Raw Head in spring, for example. And they know the storm petrels, although they're not happy to see one. It means bad weather when the stormies fly inshore.'

William gazed across the haven. 'Do you ever go in the boats yourself?'

'Occasionally. I help with the lobster-pots in return for a free landing on one or other of the offshore islets. One of them has a few pairs of rare roseate terns, which we keep an eye on. And one of the fishermen sails the tourists up to the Great Stack and Raw Head when the sea is calm in mid-summer. I cadge a free lift with him so that I can do a rough count of the nests on the cliff while I give the tourists a running commentary.'

'I wish I had a job like that. Police work on Lifandoy doesn't often get beyond the mundane.'

I laughed. 'Wait until our eggers need arresting. That could be exciting enough!'

Constable Williams looked thoughtful. 'I've not come across egg-collectors myself. Are they - I mean, it doesn't sound like the sort of thing someone clumsy or rough would do?'

I grimaced. 'Yes and no. They aren't serious naturalists, or they wouldn't do what they did. They care about the eggs, not the birds. In fact, most eggers - they don't deserve their proper title of oologists - know almost nothing about birds. They couldn't tell the call of a tern from that of a crow, I shouldn't think: and still less care. They just frighten every bird in the colony and take what they want, or go up a crag and abseil straight down to the nest. They can climb well, by the way. I've seen one climb fifty feet up a pine just to see into one nest.'

'Are they often caught?'

'There are anonymous tip-offs, but not often. Mostly wardens rely on the good offices of farmers who keep an eye out for strangers on their land. Building up a dedicated network of local observers ready to phone the police is our best policy.

'But eggers aren't fools: they're out-and-out criminals. When they go for a nest they treat it like a military operation. Sometimes they send in someone without previous convictions to look over the site. If he's caught he just pleads ignorance. Then the real team goes in in the dead of night.

'They have all sorts of other tricks, too. They put fake eggs in place of real ones so that a warden won't see the nest empty if he looks. And catching eggers can be a real pain. They have even been known to use decoy cars, for example.'

William scowled. 'Don't they realize they could wipe out a rare bird?'

'No. They all say it won't make any difference - the birds can always lay again. But the rare ones often don't. Those species are sensitive to disturbance to start with - that's why they're rare.'

Jessica looked dismayed. 'Do they just take one egg, or all of them?'

'Oh no, they collect the whole clutch. And not just one, either - the bigger collectors collect lots of clutches from the same species, to compare all the variations in the markings. That's why ospreys are so vulnerable - their eggs are particularly varied. Our visitors seem quite content with plain white eggs, though.'

'And they have a whole case full.' William was horrified.

'You saw the photographs. There were two spaces left in the case.'

. . . .

The three of us strolled along the quay, chatting. Then someone shouted a cheery greeting.

'Well now, Timothy! You're not leaving the island, are you?'

It was Uncle Wilfred. I snapped back a reply. 'Of course not! You can, though, if you like!'

Wilfred's smile faded only slightly. 'I'm here for life, m'boy. Or for as long as the good Lord wills it, at any rate.'

'Hmmm. No, I'm just looking for Angus the *Bagpipe,* that's all. And you're a long way from the House Farm.'

'There's a new plough coming for the farm. It might be on this ferry or the next. And I thought I'd drop in to console Jack Dooley while I'm here. He still hasn't found Cocky, you know.'

My ankle throbbed at old memories of cocker spaniel bites. 'Er - that's a shame,' I said, unconvincingly.

Wilfred glanced at me. 'That's a valuable pet he's lost, you know.'

William nodded. 'That's right. I thought Mr. Dooley's name rang a bell. We've been keeping a look out on our patrols.'

I frowned. 'Do you know what to look for? One looks very like another to me.'

Wilfred looked puzzled. 'There can't be another like Cocky on the island. I could tell him from a long way away.'

I was not aware that Wilfred had unusually good eyesight, and it seemed unlikely to me that he could tell one spaniel from another at a great distance. But the point was not followed up, for at that moment the approaching *Bagpipe* sounded its deafening siren at a meandering lobster boat. We all turned automatically to watch as the fine new ferry creamed majestically into port.

As the ship came up to its pier, I grimaced. 'We could be out of luck, ladies and gentlemen. That doesn't look like Angus at the helm to me.'

Jessica agreed. 'No, it isn't. That's the relief helmsman. Angus must have the day off.'

William looked sad. 'Let's walk down the pier and ask,' he said. 'I must talk to him as soon as I can, in any case.'

At the gangplank, a bearded seaman shook his head. 'Angus would have been on today but he swapped with his relief. He'll be back on Wednesday, that will be his last trip for a week. And no I'm sorry, Mr. Corn, your plough will be on the Wednesday sailing as well.'

Wilfred was phlegmatic. 'Never mind. I'll go and see Jack. He's just bought a load of interesting scrap iron I'd like to look through.' He ambled off pleasantly.

I turned to William. 'What next? Do you want to meet Alice and her friends again?'

'No, thanks. I shall head back to the station and check on these addresses. At least I have something to work on.'

An unusually large number of foot passengers began trotting eagerly down the gangplank.

'Is the fine weather bringing an early wave of tourists onto the island?' enquired Jessica.

'Er - no.' I had noticed that many of them were carrying binoculars and telescopes in cases. With a sinking feeling, I realized that our lesser crested yew sparrow was gaining a wide reputation. I turned my head away from the band of twitchers in case any old acquaintance among them should recognize me.

A stream of cars started pouring off the ferry. Most drove around the harbour and off up towards Doytown, but a few dropped into parking places on the quay or sidled up one of the narrow streets of Port Doy itself. We walked back towards the patrol car, ignoring the traffic.

'Do you want a lift up to West Doy?' asked William. 'I don't mind going that far.'

'Thanks.' I accepted gratefully. 'That will save me at least part of the walk back for my car. I can easily - oh!'

We all came to a sudden halt. Parked on the quay a few spaces short of William's police car was a black Volkswagen, with three men in it. They were talking animatedly and staring out across the water.

'Don't stop!' hissed Williams. 'We'll check the registration number and walk on before they see us.'

The rear registration plate faced onto the road. It had changed since our previous views in that it was slightly damaged: the eggers had evidently backed into a wall or something.

'That's them all right.' William hissed again as he groped for a piece of paper covered in numbers. 'The last letter on the rear plate has the corner broken off - it's not obvious that it's a G, not a C. But it's obviously them.'

We got into the police car, not daring to look back. 'Is it worth watching to see what they're doing?' I wondered.

'I doubt it,' said William, glancing back. 'They've just got out of the car. It looks like they are going for a drink in the Harbour Inn. I could do them for the number plate but we're after a bigger prize than that. And I can't stay here until they've finished boozing. Do you want to stay and watch them?'

'No. I must be getting Jessica back home; and I did say I would meet Alice and her band. Let's go!'

■ ■ ■ ■

Back at Little Cottage we found Jamie sitting peacefully in one of my kitchen chairs outside my porch. As Constable Williams drove away I led Jessica through the gate - now swinging loosely with no post to hold it - and up the path.

Beside Jamie on the grass was a mangled pile of wooden shards that looked rather as if they might once have belonged to a deckchair. Jamie gave an apologetic wave.

'Is all the wood you possess rotten?'

'No,' I snarled. 'What have you done to my only deckchair, you hulking great oaf? It wasn't built for the likes of you!'

'It was rotten,' he protested, giving the remains a kick. 'And I needed a rest after an afternoon's hard work.'

'I doubt that, you scurvy knave!'

Jessica interposed sweetly. 'Scurvy knave? That's my insult, Timothy. I didn't give you copyright to use it. What's mine is mine until we're married.'

I choked on what I was about to say. 'I didn't - yeeagh! Until we're *what?*'

'You heard me,' said Jessica.

'But - but when did...?' I glanced at Jamie for moral support. But the chair was empty and Jamie had silently vanished.

Jessica leant forward and planted a firm kiss on my lips, silencing me. 'I'm sorry, that wasn't the way I meant to say it,' she said softly. 'You're right to be angry.'

I would have been a statue had I not melted at such an apology. 'That's - that's alright.'

'But it is something we will have to talk about when we're alone, isn't it?' She gave me no chance to reply. 'Goodbye, darling. Unless I'm here this evening I'll see you tomorrow night if you're out and about. I have a feeling Mummy needs me at the moment.'

Smiling at her as she went down the path, I changed my expression to one of thunder as I went into the cottage.

Jamie had no sympathy for me. 'None of my business.'

'You traitor to our sex! What are friends for? What happened to moral support? Why did you creep off like that?'

He snorted. 'It's not for me to lecture you! Why should I suppose that a nature reserve warden would need telling about the birds and the bees?'

'But - but I've never said anything to her about getting married!'

'She obviously has other ideas. I can see there are going to be changes at Little Cottage.'

'What? I can't have a woman living here! Jessica in Little Cottage? She'd wreck the place!'

'Well you shouldn't be leading her up the garden path, then.'

'Me?' I fumed.

Jamie shrugged. 'There are a lot of young men on Lifandoy who would like to be in your place. Jessica Bull is no ordinary girl. She may look soft, but there's steel in her somewhere.'

'That's what I'm afraid of!'

'Ach, if you're a weakling yourself–'

'Listen, you Scottish ray of sunshine, I've got a mind of my own. No girl of any sort is going to bounce me into making a decision in a hurry. When I get married it will be because I choose it.'

'*When,* eh? Plenty of people don't bother nowadays.'

I paused. 'Jessica wouldn't stand for that.'

'She's not religious, is she?'

'No, certainly not. She used to go to chapel but - well - something happened and she hardly sets foot in the place now. She says she's an atheist, like me. She wasn't always, but she certainly doesn't believe in a loving God and all that now.'

'But she won't be moving in with you, though? Have you talked about–'

'Sleeping together? I have dropped the odd hint. But Jessica isn't that sort.'

He laughed. 'You're telling me she resists your charms?'

I spoke softly. 'She always has done so far, anyway. You're right, she is a special girl. She says that if she couldn't trust me with her now she'd never be able to trust me with other girls later.'

'What about you? Do you care?'

'I never did until I met her. Now I might, for the present at least. I can see there are advantages in knowing that if she stuck to her guns with *you* she would do it with all the other chaps too.'

'I know what you mean.'

'If you're prepared to wait, if you really believe this is the person for you, that you could spend your whole life with them - well - as Wilfred sometimes says, when God made time He made plenty of it–'

'Eh? I thought you were an atheist? But you would have no principles yourself against sleeping with her?'

'None. Wilfred and Martha would say living in sin was plain wrong, but I have no scruples. But Jess has convinced me to take a longer term view than some people. It's simply a matter of what works - and what doesn't.'

'I've known a lot of marriages that didn't work.'

'So have I. But the ones that do can be rather special. I suppose I have to admit that for all I say about Wilfred, if I had a marriage like his and Martha's I wouldn't care how many failures filled the Sunday papers...'

Jamie looked surprised. 'I'm getting worried about you, Tim lad. I see the rot has set in deeper than I had realized.'

I laughed hollowly. 'It comes to us all in time, dear boy. One day you too will face the prospect of that awesome walk.'

'Hah! My marsh birds are the only ones I intend to fall in love with for the moment. Speaking of which, I've something exceedingly odd to tell you...'

16. - Searchers in the Valley

Jamie had decided to have a rest after our long walk up to Raw Head and back. His researches had made him familiar with all of the mosaic of wetland and water along the West Burn; once in the valley he had headed for a favourite quiet vantage point. One of the few dry spots in the fen, this was a reed-surrounded outcrop of rock which rose to a very small elevation. Although invisible itself once the vegetation had grown, it commanded a view of the valley as far up as the important knoll as well as overlooking the homes of many of Jamie's precious marsh birds.

He had settled down to a peaceful afternoon of counting, with binoculars, the flights of trilling waders over the bog, when he had been surprisingly disturbed. Over a rapidly cooked meal, he described to me what had happened.

'I'd finished plotting the snipe territories, Tim, and I was half way through my dunlin count when they appeared.'

'The three eggers?'

'Only two of them - the big man and one of the others. I wasn't expecting it, actually. They came over the stile from Liffen Farm as before. But they turned straight down the valley, away from the knoll.'

'Towards you?'

'Yes.'

'Did they see you, Jamie?'

'No. But they came close. They walked down through the main nest area, disturbing every bird that could fly.' He was furious. 'My waders were up as thick as a cloud of midges! It was all ah could dae not to stand up and let them know what ah thought of them...'

'I'm not surprised. How did they miss you?'

'Ach, they didn't know the fen. It's a treacherous place, as you well know - one of them fell into ditches a couple of times. And my little pile of boulders might as well not be there once the reeds start up around it. They wouldn't have found it if they'd been looking twice as hard.'

'*Looking?* That sounds ominous.'

Jamie nodded. 'They were quartering the marsh, obviously on the lookout for something. But they weren't after ordinary nests. I know the positions of some of those wader nests down to the last tussock and I'm quite certain they stepped right over a couple. There are so many in the marsh they could hardly avoid the odd one. At least one sitting snipe flew up from right under their feet.'

'They didn't pick up any eggs?'

'That was something that puzzled me. When I first spotted them I could swear the big chap was carrying something. But by the time they passed me his pockets were empty. The bulge had gone.'

'He probably just ate an apple he was carrying.' I dismissed the observation as irrelevant.

'Perhaps. But that wasn't the only odd thing. When they were well past I followed them. I wanted to see whether they would walk down to the village and off the Reserve this way.'

'And did they? There's only this path or the Liffen Farm one unless they cross over the ridge to the *machair.*'

'That's what I thought, Tim. But you're wrong. There is another path.'

'Eh?' I racked my brains. 'Oh - well, there once was a bit of a path down from the House Farm. It crossed the West Burn by some stepping-stones nearly at the bottom of the valley, just above the last pool, the one by Mrs. Bull's little marsh. But you can't mean that path. No-one would find it now anyway. Wilfred's boss had it ploughed up last summer. Keith told me that Graham Fytts claimed that it wasn't a legal right of way and last autumn he planted wheat all over it.'

'Did he? Well, someone at the House Farm has cut a path through the crop again. Only a very narrow path - if I hadn't been watching the eggers I wouldn't have noticed it. They went straight across the stepping stones and up through the wheat to the road.'

'*What?* But the wheat is half grown! I must ask Wilfred what he's up to. And I can't have people wandering onto the Reserve from all directions without me knowing about it!'

'How did the eggers know the path was there?'

'Perhaps they spotted it from the road end. Anyway, never mind. You say they searched the whole valley?'

'Except for Mrs. Bull's marsh, if that's what you call it.'

'But they didn't find anything, Jamie?'

'They were a pair of elephants. I thought even eggers would have done better than that. I was sure they would spot my teal, but they didn't.'

I chewed over Jamie's news. 'That's good news, I suppose. Mind you, it's the snowy owl nest that matters. Everything else is small fry - to them at least. And speaking of small fry, where's Bob? Has he taken a turn now?'

'Small fry? He'd roll you into the Burn if he heard you saying that. Yes, he came back just after they disappeared, so I told him to sit up on the ridge opposite Liffen Farm until you relieved him.'

'I'd better get going, then. I've arranged to see Alice and her mobsters in their shed shortly. Do you fancy giving me some moral support?'

Jamie laughed hollowly. 'Lead on! Or do you want me to fetch the wheelbarrow?'

■　■　■　■

When we reached the shed - after a detour to keep out of view of the twitchers - I found that the Cabal were even more full of themselves than usual. I was chagrined to discover that little of what Jamie and I had to tell them was news. Alice dismissed our revelations with an airy hand.

'Patricia told us all about it. She wangled a visit to her Auntie Kathleen's at Liffen Farm and then pretended to sprain her ankle. I'd lent her my old toy telescope: she sat all day in the bedroom watching you...'

'Ahem.' I dreaded the next bit. 'When you say, all day...'

'When when you jumped into the West Burn. That was a bit of quick thinking!'

I relaxed. 'Do you think so? I couldn't let them see me.'

'Of course not. They must suspect nothing.'

'Did you see who it was brought them back to their car?'

'Yes. Nice old Mr. Corn gave them a lift.'

I clutched the air. 'When I see Wilfred I shall kick him all the way up his garden path.'

Alice shook her head. 'Don't do that. Pump him for information. He might have heard something useful.'

Jamie was impressed. 'Good idea. We could do with more hard information. For instance, it would be useful to know how long they're on the island for.'

The Cabal looked at Carmen, who nodded. 'I thall find out how long their room ith booked for.'

Alice nodded happily. Then her sister Rosalind nudged her. 'What about their car? One of Daddy's old friends in the harbourmaster's office could look at the arrivals and departures list for us, to see if they have a return ferry booking.'

Her younger sister gave a whoop. 'Nice one, Rosalind. I hadn't thought of that. Will you get onto it for us, please?'

There was a moment's silence. As the sisters exchanged looks they appeared to remember something else. Frowns appeared on their faces. 'Speaking of arrivals…'

I had a nasty feeling about what was coming. I leapt up. 'Right! Jamie, I must be off. Bob will be wanting his tea.'

I bounded to the door and out of the Cabal's shed with as much nonchalance as I could muster. Behind me, Alice's voice followed angrily. 'Hey, wait! Rosalind and I want to know why our house is surrounded by lunatics looking for a non-existent bird…?'

■　■　■　■

On the ridge, Bob had found a place where he could simultaneously watch both the valley and the beach. When I reached him, he had his back placed firmly towards the valley as he trained his telescope on the *machair* beach with his precious terns.

'Hey, you! A fine guard you are!'

'Sorry, Tim.' He apologized and reversed his gaze smartly by one hundred and eighty degrees. 'Can't afford to waste time - I thought a bit of sea-watching wouldn't hurt. All the girls' signals are white and the marsh has been deserted all the time I've been here.'

I sniffed. 'Well, it isn't any more. Someone is coming down from the House Farm.'

'What?' Bob was mortified. 'Where - oh, I see. Sorry again, Tim. He's not actually on the marsh yet, is he?'

I sat down beside Bob and we both scrutinized through binoculars the faraway figure, which was descending the new path through the wheat. Slowly he came into recognizable view.

'That's no egger,' I said. 'It's... *Wilfred?*'

'You could well be right.'

'I know I'm right. I know my lunatic uncle when I see him. You know, I'm coming to the conclusion that my most inexplicable relative really *is* going - oh, what did you say?'

'I said, what's that thing he's carrying?'

'What thing? Oh, I see - it looks like a long pole. What is my mad uncle up to this time?' I got up hurriedly.

'Where are you going? Aren't you staying on watch?'

I made a face. 'I've known Wilfred too long not to know when he's up to something. I don't think the eggers will come back tonight - they would have taken the one egg this morning if they were going to.'

'I'll come and watch the fun.'

When Wilfred reached the West Burn we descended the ridge and slunk across the marsh, taking an inconspicuous path. Although the traverse took us quite some time, Wilfred did not appear: whatever he was doing he was doing it either in the Burn or close to it. Eventually we spotted him, standing in shallow water close to the stepping-stones.

'There he is - at the top of the pool above the little marsh.'

'I see him. He's poking in the pool with his long pole. What's he after?'

We crept closer. Wilfred was wading down the pool, systematically probing the depths. We waited until he was completely engrossed. Then we walked to the edge together.

'Wilfred! How nice to meet you. But I'm afraid spear-fishing is illegal on the Reserve.' I applied maximum sarcasm.

He gave a satisfyingly large start. '*Ow!* Er - ah, Timothy. There you are!'

I gave a pitying smile. 'What are you doing, uncle?'

Give Wilfred his due, he can think fast when he has to. He withdrew his long pole, looking at it reflectively. Then he grinned.

'It's for you, Timothy.'

I took a step backward in alarm. 'Eh? What do I want with a beanpole?'

'It's not a beanpole. It's from Ferry Garage. Jack has a very interesting load of scrap iron in at the moment. Came from an oil rig supply vessel, so he says.'

'But why are you poking it in the pool? You've not been talking to Thomas Pandy, have you?'

He laughed. 'Oh, the body in the burn! Yes, I've heard the tale. Sergeant Farquhar has spread it all around Doytown. Poor Thomas was sounding the depths of every black hole in the stream. He was finding all sorts of rubbish, too. In fact, that's what gave me the idea–'

'The idea for what?'

'I - er...' Seemingly I had caught him on the hop. But not for long. 'I thought of bringing this for you, nephew.'

'I've told you. I don't grow beans.'

'Ah - it's not for your vegetables. It might do for your gate.'

I looked at it curiously. 'Oh. It's a bit thin for a gatepost, isn't it?'

For some reason Wilfred looked enormously relieved. 'I suppose it is. Never mind - it was just an idea. I'll find a use for it on the farm. We'll find another for Little Cottage.'

'You do that. I wouldn't mind a thicker one, though, if you came across one.'

Losing interest, I gazed across the little marsh towards the distant splash of colour of Mrs. Bull's vivid fence and West Doy beyond. Still trying to penetrate Wilfred's strange behaviour, I was only half aware of a flicker of wings as some small wading bird fluttered away from the other end of the adjacent pool. Something about the bird was unusual. It awoke some long-buried memory in my brain. I was half-consciously trying to trace the connection when I realized Bob was saying something.

'I agree. He was up to something. But *what?*'

I awoke from my reverie. 'Oh! He's gone. That was a fast exit.'

Bob concurred. 'He didn't want any more questions from us.'

'I'm not surprised,' I snarled. 'He probably answers all his questions to himself. I really think my Uncle Wilfred has become two cents short of a dollar in his dotage, you know. Can you believe he actually told me he has no ambition ever to be rich?'

'What? Well, that's different. Perhaps he's just too old to want his world to change. Not that I meant–'

'No offence taken,' I reassured Bob. 'But I agree he is far too old mentally to change. He thinks he's ultra-modern and ultra-efficient with all his intensive agribusiness, but in fact he's a dinosaur. He clings both to an ancient religion and to a modern one. I could almost put up with the ancient one, if only he would recant over his intensive farming, with all those chemicals he uses–'

'Or at least, modify it to avoid serious damage to the environment?'

I threw Bob a horrified stare. 'Oh, no, Bob. Organic farming is the only way. It should be enforced by law.'

My assistant frowned. 'No. Not for everyone? Surely even you, Tim, know that organic farming can't feed the world, or even a large portion of it, at the moment? In fact, almost no-one seriously believes it could. Your law would have to choose who lived and who starved. And I thought it was extremism that you were *opposing?*'

'Huh. Perhaps some people should starve. My extremism is perfectly sane. Uncle Wilfred's is bonkers; it's utterly unjustifiable. And, more to the point, utterly unchangeable. He will never see even a glimmer of green common sense. You mark my words.'

'Mark them? I'm not your teacher, Tim. You're a big boy - life is your teacher, now. And that's full of surprises.' Bob paused and gazed after Wilfred. 'Anyway, I could see your uncle didn't want any more questions. But nor do I. I'm starving. If you have no objection I think I shall–'

'Sure, Bob. Go and get some dinner. I'll see you tomorrow. And thanks!'

Left alone, I stood for a while beside the calm burn, gazing around the marsh. The little vanished bird had irritated me with its suggestion of strangeness. Slowly I walked down the pool, watching for another flutter of wings. I was nearly at the end, where the West Burn narrowed into its final stream course, when it came.

Something stirred, but not where I expected it. I caught it only in the comer of my eye, a movement so fleeting that it was gone before I could focus on it. I turned my head in vain.

But when my gaze fell upon something lying right at my feet, I forgot completely my original quarry.

'Ah-hah! My other gatepost!'

At my feet, half embedded as by a substantial impact among the rushes was another familiar, bright orange tube. I bent and extracted it with difficulty, whistling cheerfully.

'Come to daddy! You're the first thing that's gone right today. I can't imagine why anyone should be laying cable to a new telecommunications mast in West Doy marsh, but so what? A bit of black paint and a hammer, and my gate will be better than Wilfred's! Who could object to that?'

17. - Freedom to Change

I had just finished disturbing the tranquil village evening with my hammering and painting when the sound of many feet reawakened the echoes.

'Hey, Mr. Warden! Nice gateposts you've got there!'

Mike and twenty more like him were grinning from above their binoculars and telescopes. I gave a guilty start. 'Ooops! Er - any luck, lads?'

The chief of the twitchers nodded pleasantly. 'Not bad. Good, in fact.'

'*What?*' I was startled.

Mike grinned. 'We haven't found your biggie yet. But that Mrs. Bull's garden is a hot patch, a real migrant trap. See if these grip you off: two barred warblers, a white-spotted bluethroat and a wryneck, all in the same bushes. One of the most interesting days I've had all month!'

'You're joking!' I started to laugh hysterically. 'I must see this for myself. Er - by the way,' I swallowed nervously, 'have you met the two young girls who live there?'

'You mean besides that gorgeous blonde? Yes, they were very friendly. They said they would tell us about anything they saw. They know you, don't they? The smaller one said she was sure you would go out of your way to be helpful.'

A plaudit from Alice sounded distinctly sinister, particularly as I had been expecting her to drop me in it. I smiled weakly.

'Are you leaving the island soon?'

Mike shook his head. 'The softies are. But us real birders are going to hang around. We've been talking it over and we think your little island may hold some surprises. It's relatively unknown. A few days working over the likely spots could be a real clean-up, even if we don't get the old yew sparrow. That's assuming you don't mind?'

'No, certainly not.' Wheels were turning in my mind. 'In fact, I might be glad to have you around.'

'Really? Why's that?'

I lowered my voice. 'Bad news. I have reason to suspect we have *egg collectors* on the island.'

There was a collective hiss of indrawn breath, followed by a furious muttering. It was evident that I could not have more rapidly gained my audience's sympathy. Mike spoke for them all.

'The swines! Put them in front of us and we'll tear them limb from limb! What do we look for?'

'Three big chaps in a black Volkswagen. An hour ago they were boozing in the Harbour Inn.'

Mike clasped my hand feelingly. 'The Harbour Inn? *In* the *harbour* would be more like it if we caught them in the act!'

I decided not to overdo things. 'Don't do anything silly, lads. The law is already keeping an eye on them. Just let us know of anything you see, that's all. If we want you, we'll shout loud enough.'

They bristled en masse. 'We'll come at the run!'

■   ■   ■   ■

West Doy was becoming an eerie place. No sooner had the sound of the twitchers' feet died away, than more approaching boots took up the rhythm.

It was Uncle Wilfred. Avoiding a glance at Little Cottage, he was about to pass by. But when the new gatepost caught his eye, he changed his mind.

'I say, Timothy, I am impressed! That was quick work. Have you got a secret scrap source that Jack Dooley doesn't know about? Your gate looks fairly acceptable now.'

I had no objection to my work being praised. 'Yes. Much better.'

Wilfred continued his critical examination. 'Mind you, it's not quite straight. It leans this way a little.'

'I know. I think there's a rock down there. I can't knock it any further over.'

Wilfred flexed his muscles. 'Just a minute. I'll get my big sledgehammer to move it.'

He was back in moments, with a tool as high as my midriff. I looked at it uneasily but Wilfred responded by giving me a broad grin, which made me feel distinctly anxious for my post. He lifted the sledge experimentally, swinging it back and forth a couple of times. Then he hit my post, with a shuddering impact.

'Hey! You'll put a dent in it, not to mention that I've just painted it.'

Wilfred grinned again. 'A post like this won't take a dent very easily.' He swung again, twice more. 'There! That looks a bit straighter.'

I scowled. 'You *have* dented it. I said you would.'

Wilfred bent and fingered the damage with impatience. 'It must be poor quality metal. They don't make steel like they used to. It's cheap and too soft.'

He looked closer at the dent. 'I see it was orange before you blackened it. I can't understand this modern preoccupation with dull hues. If bright colours were good enough for the Almighty's rainbow, they're good enough for me.'

'Rainbow?' I sniffed. 'I shan't be encouraging it to rain. The weather is lovely at the moment.'

'Yes - just what's needed for the Summer Fair on Thursday. You will be going, won't you?'

'Of course. Are there any special attractions this year?'

Wilfred beamed. 'Certainly. Our chapel choir has been asked to perform an opening rendition. We intend to repeat two of the best items from the programme for the choir concert on Wednesday evening. I don't know which two they will be; we must see which pieces go best on Wednesday.'

'Really.'

'You would be very welcome at the concert as well, if you're interested! I have given you an invitation, haven't I? It starts at seven-thirty in the chapel.'

I opened my mouth in haste to decline. But I was overtaken. From behind us as we contemplated the gate came a sweet and familiar tone.

'That sounds delightful, Wilfred,' said Jessica. 'May I come with Timothy?'

Wilfred's cup was clearly full to overflowing. 'Wonderful! Magnificent! Martha will save you two tickets. I shall see you there!' Leaving me with mouth agape, he grabbed his sledgehammer and retreated rapidly before I could raise any objection.

I turned to Jessica wide-eyed. 'Darling, what did you say that for?'

She took my hands in hers and returned my gaze meltingly, in a way she knew I could not resist. 'Oh dear, I am sorry. Have I put my foot in it? I just thought it would be nice for us to go to the chapel together on Wednesday...?'

We exchanged stares carefully. 'What if I were to say,' I said quietly, 'that I don't think I have any interest in doing that?'

Her expression was no longer melting. Jessica had a full-blooded look in her eyes, a firmness about her that I could not recall ever having seen so clearly before. For the first time ever in our relationship, something like a chill entered the atmosphere between us.

'If you mean that you shan't set foot in the chapel for any religious reason, then I agree, Tim - nor shall I. But for a reason of my own I wish to go on Wednesday to the concert, and I should like you with me. And I must ask, are you or are you not in love with me?'

A man can reply to a question like that in one of only two ways. Either I could fling my arms around her and assure her of my lifelong adoration, whatever whims she inflicted on me, or I could reply brusquely, with consequences that I did not dare imagine. I pondered the alternatives until I was certain what to do. Then I spoke.

'Coffee?' I inquired, lamely.

■   ■   ■   ■

Jessica rested warmly on the sofa beside me. We gazed across the small sitting room of Little Cottage, unwilling to inspect each other's faces. Eventually she voiced the thoughts of both of us.

'Where do we go from here?'

'Should we go anywhere? Why can't we stay as we are?'

'Because neither of us is content to live in suspended animation.'

'All right, let me rephrase my answer. Should we go anywhere fast? What's the sudden hurry in life?'

Jess smiled sweetly. 'I'm not in a hurry. I have a great time with you, Tim. But I think it's time we knew that we agreed on the direction we're taking.'

'By which you mean the altar? No chance!'

To my surprise, she laughed merrily. 'Did you think that I was proposing to you? Dear Timothy, you are *so* funny.'

I was rattled. 'I'm surprised you consider it a joke,' I snapped.

She ceased in mid-chuckle. 'I *don't* Of everything in the world, that commitment is the least frivolous of all...' her eyes had a faraway look '...*whatever* the world may think.'

Somewhere remote inside me a warning bell sounded. 'Just a minute, Jess! What's happened to you? You've been doing some deep thinking, or I'm a stuffed whale.'

She nodded. 'You see? We understand each other well. Too well! None of my previous boyfriends would have perceived the things you see in me. You're a special person for me, Tim.'

I ignored the compliment, waiting sullenly for her to tell me.

'Yes, I've been doing some deep thinking. Not that I've produced any deep conclusions. But I just feel uneasy.'

'Uneasy?'

'Something is going to happen soon. Something - no, I don't want to talk about it just now - is weighing very heavily on me. And it will on you, too. We are going to change - or split.'

I was angry now. 'Someone *has* been talking to you, Jess. Was it your mother?'

'No. Not a word.'

'Who, then?'

She hesitated. 'It wasn't someone else talking to me that upset me. I was unhappy before I went to her.'

'Her?'

'I'm sorry. I should have told you. I've had a couple of long talks to Martha.'

'To *Martha?*' I was relieved. Martha was one of only two or three of people I might have thought of for myself. 'What did she say?'

'Not a lot. I told you, Tim, I did most of the talking myself. But there's something about Martha that makes you think even when she just listens to you.'

I chuckled. 'I know what you mean. All right, no, I don't mind. If it had been anyone but Martha...'

She relaxed suddenly and put her arm around me. Slowly, intensely, we kissed.

At last I leaned back. 'So, what did she say to you?'

She smiled. 'Nothing in particular. Nothing religious, if that's what you're worried about. But there was just one question that she asked that stuck in my mind. She asked me, 'Do you give yourself enough freedom to be able to change when you need to?'

'What an odd thing to ask someone! To change in what way?'

'I suppose we all change as we grow, don't we? Especially when we grow serious.'

'I should think we already *are* fairly serious.'

Jessica sat back. 'I'm getting serious about a lot of things nowadays, not just you. Life in general! I'm full of questions about my life. I'm sorry, I'm not explaining this at all well. But I have this odd sense that something is happening to me which might change me a lot. And if it changes me then it must affect you as well: which gives you the right of reply.'

I looked worried. 'That sounds like a bad thing for you.'

She frowned. 'A bad thing for me? Why?'

I grinned, pouncing on her. 'Because you affect me quite a lot already. So much, in fact, that I'm going to have to tickle you unmercifully to get my own back...'

■   ■   ■   ■

'The thing that puzzles me,' said Bob slowly, 'is that we haven't seen the female snowy owl on the nest yet. I'm not surprised about the male: he's probably keeping out of sight somewhere on Ginger Hill where you saw him before - which is all to the good from our point of view. But the hen must be around. The egg was warm, so we know the bird wasn't far away. And we can't see the actual nest from here. I know that even very obvious birds can keep themselves incredibly well hidden near their nests - that kingfisher on the West Burn fooled me completely last month. But a big white bird flying to that nest should be visible from a mile away...' he raised his bins briefly to his eyes then lowered them again '...which it hasn't been.'

I listened thoughtfully. It was Tuesday noon and I was seated in the grass on the ridge that divided the valley of the West Burn from the coastal *machair*. The crest of the West Ridge, as it was sometimes called, was a pleasant place with the midday sunshine being nicely balanced by a light easterly breeze. And although Bob had arrived to leave me from an eventless morning's sentry duty I was happy to chat before Reserve duties intervened.

'Some birds don't start sitting on the eggs until the whole clutch has been laid,' I pointed out. 'According to the books, that doesn't include snowy owls. But Lifandoy is so far south of normal snowy owl range that anything could happen here. For instance, perhaps they only visit the nest at night to begin with?'

Bob shifted to a more comfortable position in the grass. 'It would be nice to at least see the number of eggs growing.'

We gazed out across the valley. Far below we could see the figure of Jamie patiently wending his way around the fen on one of his regular surveys. I frowned.

'I'm pondering a different enigma. I've been re-reading Keith's letter.'

'What about it?'

'I still don't understand what he meant about seeing the birds in a place that was very *yellow.*'

'I'd forgotten that. Can't you phone him and ask?'

'From the way he talked when he rang it sounds like a whole crowd is listening in on every call. In any case, I'd feel a bit of a fool. I've already told him everything is in hand.'

Bob gazed around the valley. 'There are various yellow flowers in bloom. But most of them are in the marsh. The knoll we're watching is all green and brown.'

'I know. The best splash of colour is at the other end of the valley - Mrs. Bull's red fence.'

'It's been red for a whole two weeks now, hasn't it!' Bob laughed. 'It must be due for repainting in another colour soon.'

I stood up. 'Right. If all is quiet perhaps I can get back to some genuine Reserve work for once. It's nice lounging on the grass up here on the West Ridge, but - *oh!*'

Bob looked up. 'Something the matter?'

'Not yet. But there's a tractor coming down from the House Farm towards the burn. See it? It's in that field of young whatevers-they-are.'

'It looks like it's going to do some spraying.'

'It does. And it's going to do it horribly close to the West Burn. I've warned Wilfred again and again about watching the wind direction. With this easterly, the spray will drift right across the marsh!'

I looked closer, then leapt up and started to trot down the hill. 'Wilfred, you never change, do you? You're asking to be buried in the marsh. If your pesticides murder my orchids I'll take you to court, I swear I will.'

18. - Voices in the Lane

I kept up an urgent pace, angling down the West Ridge towards the lower valley. It would take me at least ten minutes to get to a place where I could attract the tractor driver's attention. I was so angry that I jogged all the way to the main Reserve path below the ridge. By this time, the tractor was operating its spray. It was progressing steadily alongside the West Burn, followed by a small cloud of droplets being dispersed by the wind.

I stopped for breath, thinking aloud. 'I'll murder that driver! I'd better run along the path for a little way. I can save myself some distance before I cross the fen to catch him. No, wait, though - he's stopped.'

The distant tractor had come to a halt. The driver climbed out and bent to pick something white from the ground. I yelled loudly and waved: but there was no response. The driver remounted and continued his way. I kept going.

The path I was on ceased heading towards the Burn and angled away down the valley. I was just about to take a deep breath and plunge into the marsh when my plan was interrupted.

'Excuse *me*. Are you the Reserve warden?'

'Yes, I am. Er - can I talk to you later, please?'

The speaker was an elderly lady equipped with binoculars and a similar companion. She advanced with determined tread.

'No, young man, you may *not* talk to us later,' she stated. She was tall, with steel-grey hair, steel-rimmed spectacles and a manner to match. 'We have been waiting a whole hour at your cottage for someone to appear. My sister Violet and I have both been faithful supporters of the Nature Reserves Society for forty-three years, and we expect better than this. We have visited every other Society reserve and this is our first visit to Lifandoy. *Never* has a reserve warden failed to greet us kindly and to give us, however busy he was, a short introduction to his or her reserve. *Never* have we been let down before.'

That did it. There was no way that a mere cloud of spray could force the name of the Lifandoy Reserve to be placed at the bottom of the list. I sighed, gazed in anguish at the receding tractor, and turned my attention briefly to my visitors.

The first lady's name was Edith. Edith and her sister Violet looked stern but in fact they turned out to be a delightful pair, full of excitement and interest as I pointed out some of the treasures of the valley around them. They were thrilled by the display of orchids and exclaimed at the snipe displaying over the fen and the redshank flickering over the wet marsh.

While they were engrossed, I cast a few quick glances towards the tractor. I could see that the driver was dressed in House Farm overalls but otherwise he was unrecognisable to me. To my surprise, he did not spray the field thoroughly. In fact, apart from stopping once more to pick another white object up from the soil, he spent only a little more time in the field. Shortly the sprayer had been turned off and the tractor was creeping back up the hill to the road.

'Odd, that! I wonder why he was doing that. Oh - yes, Edith, that *is* a dunlin flying over there. Well spotted! Now, would you like me to take you up on the ridge to overlook the *machair?* Then I can make sure you won't get lost on your way to the Great Stack and Raw Head.'

The top of the West Ridge was another place for the ladies to do some exclaiming, at the gleaming white of the beaches beyond. It was also a good place to exchange notes with Bob.

'You never reached the tractor, then, Tim?'

'No. He stopped before I reached him. And I'm being a good warden. This is Edith, and Violet. Ladies, this is Bob, our seabird man. Anything doing, Bob?'

'Not on the bird front at the moment, no.' He lowered his voice. 'But look at Liffen Farm, Tim.'

I lifted my binoculars and scanned across the valley. 'I see what you mean. Alice's signal there is red. That has to be my next destination. The day is getting busy!'

I returned to the ladies. 'The path to Raw Head is that one over there. If you keep along the cliff path, you can't miss the Great Stack. That is the best seabird nesting site, especially for photography. But you could find nests anywhere, even beside the path, at this season. Make sure you don't tread on any eggs! Now, have you any other questions?'

'You have been too kind already,' Edith smiled. 'Perhaps we'll see you later.'

As they left me, I examined Liffen Farm closely with my bins.

'I haven't seen the car,' said Bob, 'but it would be easy to miss behind those tall hedges.'

'OK, Bob, I'll take a closer look. Don't forget the kite, will you?'

He laughed as I set off back down the hill. 'Anything for Jessica!' he cried.

■ ■ ■ ■

The kite was Jessica's idea. At the police station, Constable Williams and I had argued about how a sentinel on the West Ridge could signal the whereabouts of a prowling egger. Walkie-talkies were out, as they might easily be picked up by our all-too-sophisticated quarry. None of us had mobile phones that were much good anywhere on the island and certainly not on the Reserve. I had suggested signalling by mirror, but that depended on sunshine. William had thought of a flag, but the eggers could see that as well as ourselves.

'What about one of those childrens' kites with a bird motif?' Jessica had asked. 'You could fly that over the West Ridge and it would look just like a hovering hawk. The eggers know nothing about birds so it would mean nothing to them. If you devise a simple code you could use its movements to signal how many eggers there were and which way they were going.'

'Will the wind blow enough?'

'On the West Ridge it hardly ever stops. The wind will blow.'

■ ■ ■ ■

She had certainly been right on the last point. Now the regular island breeze was ready to lift the kite the moment Bob spotted intruders near the knoll. Leaving him, I made a circumspect and rapid approach to the stile below Liffen Farm, hoping that Patricia's red signal did not mean that the car had merely gone past on its way elsewhere.

I sidled over the stile and up the track. I had still to round the last corner to the farm when there came the roar of an engine. A car accelerated away rapidly down the road from the farm. Whether it had started from there or had come down the road from Liffen Cross I could not tell. I raced back to the last field gate I had passed, in time to glimpse a black VW with three occupants driving very fast down the valley road towards Doy. The rear registration plate was still broken.

'I wonder what alerted them? Anyway, they haven't come onto the Reserve, which is what matters.'

Shrugging my shoulders, I retraced my steps toward the stile and the Reserve. I was ambling down the track listening to linnets in the hedgerow when I heard voices behind me. One of them was unmistakably Wilfred's.

It came to me that it was about time I discovered what Uncle Wilfred was up to. I did not particularly want to be observed on the track myself - certainly not if Thomas Pandy's dogs were about - and a convenient hiding place was to hand.

I slipped over the bridge to stand in cool greenness beside the West Burn. Right under the bridge itself was a dry alcove, just large enough to sit in. The voices drew closer. As they approached the bridge Wilfred asked a question.

'How did you get on in the field?'

I squeezed further into the dry niche. Above me, to my alarm, the footsteps halted on the bridge. A voice unknown to me answered Wilfred's question: to my astonishment it had an American accent.

'No problem, Mr. Corn. Thanks for your help. A blind man could have done it. And that tractor is a useful machine, too.'

'Will we see the results by the weekend?'

'The weekend? You can see for yourself tomorrow.'

'And what about the marsh on the other side of the stream?'

'Except for where the village overlooks it we'll have finished there by Thursday if not before.'

Under the bridge my jaw dropped. Was Wilfred preparing to spray the Reserve marsh? Were the House Farm men planning to take their tractors over the West Burn? It was unthinkable.

Wilfred continued. 'Can't you finish the job now?'

'What do you think? That's what we walked down here to see. When I was on the tractor I could see one of the wardens poking around in the marsh - a big fellow.'

'That sounds like Jamie MacLeod. Let's see. Yes, I can see him down there still.'

'We mustn't be seen on the Reserve by the wardens. I think we've done it all for now.'

The footsteps restarted. This time they went back up the track toward the road. I sat still for a few minutes, stunned by what I had heard.

'Wilfred is planning to have our orchids sprayed!' I couldn't believe it. 'He wants to present Sir Charles with a *fait accompli*. The House Farm is going to kill off the marsh...'

For once, I was really shocked at Wilfred. Somewhere, I had always felt that deep down inside my uncle there was a soft spot, a faint sympathy toward the natural world. He believed in a Creator God - which should, at least, put him one step behind his money-grabbing boss Graham Fytts in a scale of their relative rapaciousness. But even Fytts had never gone this far. I felt almost physically sick. White with wrath, I emerged from hiding place and stood, appearing from below the bridge careless of whoever might now be present.

As I rose, the face which stared down at my pale visage was not that of Wilfred or his mystery helper. It was that of Thomas Pandy, who was passing over the bridge with his dogs.

There was a momentary hiatus. It was broken when a stone I was balanced on tilted, throwing me bodily into the stream. After that, things got confused. There was a banshee screech from the shepherd and an instant declaration of war by his dogs. As they leapt in upon me, I expelled a mouthful of brown water with a bellow. Thomas Pandy fell to his knees, gibbering. He was oblivious to the fact that his beasts in the burn were trying to make me as deceased as their master feared I already was.

'Get your bloodhounds off me! I'm not a ghost, as you very well know!'

Thomas gaped at me, his face pasty. He pursed his lips for a whistle, but only a feeble hiss emerged. Livid, I went onto the offensive. I grabbed one of the snapping animals by its ears and ducked it hard. When the other got the same treatment it, too, spluttered away. I seized the opportunity of a rapid exit from the stream. Thomas Pandy, on his knees before me, stared as if he thought Glyn Dŵr himself had come back to life.

'*Wel,*' he wheezed. 'And I thought you were dead, man.' From shock, his accent was as inspissated as though he were speaking through a mouthful of clotted cream. 'We found that hat of yours at the top of the green sink, the one that swallowed two of my sheep last year when the bottom fence broke. We were dragging it for a corpse.'

I gave him a sour look. 'So Sergeant Farquhar told me.'

He looked crushed. 'Man, you must come back to the house right away. I don't want you dying of cold now you're alive again. Here, take my jacket...'

The man was so mortified that I accepted his offer. Calling his sobered hounds to heel, Thomas led the way up past the farmhouse to his miniature cottage with his equally miniature, shyly smiling, Welsh wife.

■ ■ ■ ■

The hospitality of the Pandys was enormous. My empty stomach was in the first stages of rebellion when, after a warm shower and clad in Thomas's old clothes, I found a spread laid to feed a stream full of Reserve wardens. 'Help yourself to everything, Mr. Corn. Will you take a bowlful of Blessed Bran?'

Not doubting that the reputation of my office was at stake, I set to readily. A line of very small Pandy children sat on the floor to watch me eat. In the background their parents hovered silently. That they were dying of curiosity was obvious; that they would not consider conversation until every possible crumb was gone was equally so.

When the polite moment came, Thomas cleared his throat and a hush fell.

'It wass a fine morning, wass it not, Mr. Corn?'

I agreed. At that moment, I was feeling agreeable to almost any sentiment that anyone might express.

'And tell me, what wass it that you were doing in the burn. Wass it fishing that you were after?'

'That was a magnificent spread, Mrs. Pandy. No, Thomas, I wasn't fishing.'

'It's a strange place to watch birds, but I suppose…'

I hesitated. I was thinking rapidly. 'Thomas, did you see anyone else on the track before you saw me?'

He blinked at the change of subject. 'No. I heard voices. But whoever it wass, they were going up the hill. I came into the lane from the field gate, you see.'

'Oh, pity. You don't know who was on the bridge before you came there, then?'

'No. Does it matter?'

Thomas's answer decided me to settle for a small lie. 'I was under the bridge because I was spying on some egg-collectors.'

'Egg collectors? *Wel,* that's bad. Is that who was in the lane? Do you know what they look like?'

'Three men in a black Volkswagen. One of them is very big.'

Suddenly, Thomas was all ears. 'Three, you say? Mainlanders?'

'Yes.'

'I don't suppose they could have been in the bar of the Harbour Inn last night?'

I sat up straight. 'Did you see them there?'

'Heard them, rather. They were in the next corner, see. They were talking about the Reserve. And I heard them mention the name Ginger.'

'Ginger? Ginger Farm or Ginger Hill?'

'I don't know. But they followed it with something about taking turns picking up the *eggs.*'

'Thomas, where's your telephone? I want Constable Williams to hear what you've just told me, right away!'

19. - Memories

William arrived at speed at the Pandy cottage and was delighted with the shepherd's report. 'That's hard evidence, that is,' he declared. 'Sarge will be chuffed to hear all this. It gives me what I need to spend more time on the case. Do you know where the suspects are at the moment?'

I glanced out of the window towards the distant ridge. 'They're not in Bob's view,' I reassured him. 'The kite isn't up yet.'

'Where was the car going?'

'Down the valley road to Doy, very fast.'

He nodded thoughtfully. 'I think they were frightened off. Perhaps they saw Wilfred or Thomas and that made them change their plans. I'll go back to Doytown and see if I can spot them.'

I stood up. 'And the ghost had also better get back to work. I know two ladies who will be looking for me for a start.'

William scowled. 'Some fellows have all the luck.'

. . . .

Back on the Reserve, I gave both Jamie and Bob a distant wave and betook myself off down the valley. A small trickle of tourists were plodding up the Reserve track and it took an hour to carry out my public relations duties with them all. Then I had some work to carry out in the form of repairing one of the Reserve notice boards which had suffered in the winter storms. I was just banging in the last nail when there came a piercing greeting.

'Dear Mr. Warden. Oh, Violet, doesn't he work hard!'

I turned. 'Hello, Edith; Violet. Have you had a good walk to Raw Head?'

Apart from getting lost briefly on the return, they had had a wonderful walk. The ladies were full of their memories of the seabird cliffs, of the soldierly packed ranks of the guillemots, the onomatopoeic crying of the kittiwakes, the curiosity of the fussy puffins.

'Oh Mr. Warden, we even saw a seal! It was enormous, quite the biggest we have seen.'

'That would be a grey seal, then. The Atlantic grey seal is much larger than the common seal.'

'And the cliff flowers! We have never in all our lives seen such an array of colour. What species are the tiny bluebells that carpet the cliff tops?'

'That's the spring squill. It's only found on western cliffs like these.'

'And the nests! There were nests and eggs everywhere, just as you said. We found them in the most remarkable places. Violet even found one large egg wedged in the branches of a thick bush.'

'That would be - eh? What did you say?'

Violet was as definite as her sister. 'A large white egg was wedged into the base of a bush. It was well hidden: I only spotted it because I dropped my spectacles under the bush. It wasn't on a nest - it looked as though it had fallen there. But there was no nest in the bush.'

I was intrigued. 'Really? Did you leave it there?'

They both looked worried. 'No,' said Edith. 'When we lifted the egg out it was still warm. I do hope we did the right thing: Violet wrapped it in her spare headscarf and we looked for a nest with eggs like it.'

'But how did it get there?'

'We saw a raven stealing a smaller egg. We wondered if one could have picked this egg up and dropped it into the bush?'

'That's possible. Did you find somewhere to put it?'

'We found a nest some way away. But there was a nest in the grass that was a perfect home for it.'

I laughed. 'Oh, well. There'll be a surprised mother bird somewhere, then.' The ladies departed. I had barely collected up my tools when Bob appeared. 'Hi, Bob. Have you handed over to Jamie already?'

'Yes, Tim. I called him up to me because I had some news to pass on.'

'Action from the eggers?'

'Not on foot. But there's been a black VW going up or down the valley road three times so far. They're clearly spying out the land. In fact, I was watching the road so intently that I nearly missed the real action.'

'What? Someone at the knoll?'

'Actually, there could have been. When I remembered to look at the knoll there were a couple of your tourists wandering across the moor not far away.'

'That settles it. I shall have to do something to keep them straying from the Raw Head path.'

'I didn't mean them, though. I was just watching them when I spotted it.'

'It? A snowy owl from the nest?'

'I think so. It was right up the valley by the time I got a scope on it - just a white speck. But it was so brilliant white that I can't think what else it could have been. Anyway, when I saw it I decided to take the risk.'

I got his meaning. *'You've been to the nest!'*

He nodded. 'I reckon those tourists put the bird off the nest. You can't see the nest from the ridge, of course. But when I knew the bird had flown I thought I could chance a quick look before it came back. And there are *two* warm eggs now.'

This was big news. 'Magnificent. But I shall have to make sure no-one else disturbs it. A roll of sheep fencing along the path should be enough.'

'I'll help you lay it out. Do you want to do it now?'

■   ■   ■   ■

Back in West Doy, Bob and I sneaked up the street. To my relief we were unseen either by twitchers or members of the Cabal. It was definitely my day, for the one person we did bump into was Jessica.

'Hello, sweetheart,' I said. 'Do you fancy a ride with Bob and me down to the harbour? Come on, let's go before anyone else appears.'

The early evening sky had clouded over and as we drove down through Doy the fickle island weather turned to rain. The street emptied and only an odd car heading for the ferry indicated the presence of humanity. As we passed the Doy Hotel we all looked across at the car park, but it was empty. At the port there was no sign of the ferry and the rain was like stair-rods. I pulled up outside Ferry Garage and gestured.

'Let's try Jack. He's almost certain to have a roll of old wire netting amongst his scrap.'

We dashed through the puddles into the dark garage. 'Why doesn't Jack have some decent lighting put in? He never spends money on anything around the garage.'

No-one was around to tell us whether the garage was officially open: but on Lifandoy it did not occur to us that our business might be unwelcome at any hour. So we poked around the labyrinthine scrapyard in the rain, marvelling at the variety of Jack's collected junk while shutting our ears and noses to the evidences of his bleating and squawking menagerie.

'Look here! Here's a blacksmith's anvil,' I said. 'And here's the barrel of an old naval gun. What a mixture.'

Bob agreed. 'This heap looks like a whole deep-sea diving outfit! Who on earth does Jack expect to sell this to? Does he think one of the lobster fishermen is going to start chasing his prey on foot?'

We laughed. 'Ah, this is more like it.' I hauled a rusty cylindrical mass from the chaos. As I lifted it, a siren sounded loudly from the harbour. 'I'll pay Jack when I see him. Let's get to the ferry before Angus can disappear.'

The *Bagpipe's* gangplank had barely thudded down onto the puddled quay when Angus came bounding down it, kitbag over his shoulder. 'Hello, Jessica. Hello, Bob. Tim, have you caught the crooks red-handed yet?'

I leapt back to avoid being knocked down. 'No. Are you planning to do the job for me?'

'If you like! I'm off duty for a week now, so I thought I'd come and sponge off your hospitality for a few days - if you'll let me work my passage, that is.'

I grinned. Angus was large and strong enough to make any egg collector pause. 'Excellent. I have exactly the job for you. How about a night shift watching a snowy owl nest from the West Ridge?'

'Night shift? Sitting there watching the dawn wake up the terns on the *machair* and the redshanks in the marsh? Lead me to it, boy. I've spent long enough breathing the paint fumes on our fine new ferry. Some brisk island air will blow them away well.'

We jogged back through the rain to my car outside Ferry Garage. 'Anyone home yet?'

Jack Dooley's moon face emerged from the gloom. 'Oh, it's you, Mr. Timothy.' The three with me disappeared into a café next door to the garage while I explained about the roll of wire. Jack invented a price and I paid him with small change. I was just counting out the last coppers when another customer, heavily proofed against the rain, slipped rapidly past us out of the building.

The other customer was carrying a curious parcel, a spherical mass wrapped in an old tarpaulin. The shape of the object caught my eye but it was not until its purchaser was rounding the corner that I realized he was a heavily disguised Uncle Wilfred.

'Hey! You come back! I want to talk with you - oh, sorry, Jack. I'll pick it up - come back here, you ruffian, oh, where's he gone to?'

I was in a foul mood when I joined the others in the café.

'What's up, darling?'

'*Wilfred.*' At my snapped retort the other three raised eyebrows at each other and left me to simmer alone. Over a huge mug, Angus was regaling Jessica and Bob with tales about Jack Dooley's past.

'He's owned almost every sort of livestock that he could squeeze into that yard,' he was saying. 'Do you remember when he bought that pig, Sally? The lazy one that never stirred more than a yard if she could help it? To get her moving he introduced her to a boar. He thought that if she had a litter, she had to get doing. She started swelling and Jack became quite the expectant father. All of Port Doy was waiting for the happy event. But she was pulling his leg - all she did was get fatter and fatter on all the choice morsels he fed her, and lazier with it.'

'I remember her,' Jessica grinned, 'but I don't remember the end of the story.'

Angus shook his head. 'That was Jack's dark secret,' he said. 'But one day he lost all of his Irish temper. Then for weeks after that there was a strong smell of bacon whenever anyone walked past the garage.'

The thought of a bacon aroma irritated me. It mixed with the smell of rain-wet clothing and the café odours in my brain. I sneezed violently. '*AA-TCHOO!*'

Jessica turned to me. 'Did Jack say whether he's found Cocky yet?'

I shook my head. 'If he has he didn't say so.'

There was a pause. Angus looked out of the café window across the harbour. In the distance we could see the long breakwater which sheltered the outer harbour, with its terminal light warning of the dangerous reefs beyond. 'The rain will clear up in a minute,' he said, peering out past the breakwater. 'You can see the South Rock again now, that's always a good sign.'

Abruptly his face fell. He looked up at a colourful calendar on the café wall, then glanced at Jessica. I followed his gaze; hesitated.

'Ready to go, sweetheart?'

She gave me a strange look. 'Yes. Let's go right away.' She rose and walked with me out of the café, her eyes down. 'I think I might go home now, if you don't mind, Tim. I feel a bit weary all of a sudden.'

We all got into my car. In the back, Bob appeared puzzled and opened his mouth to speak forwards to Jessica. 'Are you...?' But Angus, sitting beside him, placed a large hand gently over his mouth and nodded to me.

'Step on it, Tim.'

Back in West Doy, Jessica got out of the car by the chapel. She stopped only to give me a peck on the cheek and a wan smile, then walked slowly along the lane. I reversed smartly around and drove the minuscule distance back to Little Cottage, then switched off the ignition. There was silence in the car. Bob was worried.

'Did I say something wrong?'

'No.' Angus spoke heavily. '*I* did. Sorry, Tim. I should have remembered. It will be just five years this week.'

Bob wrinkled his brows further. I gave him a thoughtful look.

'Angus mentioned the South Rock,' I explained. 'That's what upset Jess. It reminded her of her father.'

'Her father? I thought he was dead?'

Angus grimaced. 'It's just five years since he died. People who know Jessica try never to mention the South Rock in her presence. I'm not on the island often enough and I forgot. Me - of *all* people.'

■　■　■　■

It was a sombre little group that debated tactics in the sitting room of Little Cottage. I pointed a thumb for Angus's benefit. 'You're welcome to sleep in the spare bedroom,' I said. 'Do you want a nap now?'

'That would suit me fine. I was up at five. If I could get a couple of hours in I could be up on the West Ridge to relieve Jamie before sunset.'

'You won't see much from up there in the dark.'

'I'd see any torches. And in any case, I can get the lie of the land in my mind. Then a quiet spot in the heather down below the hill will give me the best chance of hearing or seeing intruders. Now, if you'll excuse me...?'

'Sure.' I glanced across the room. 'Bob? Have you a quarter of an hour to spare, now? I could do with some moral support next door.'

Bob winced. 'You're going to have it out with Wilfred about the spraying?'

'I am.'

20. - Temper and Nightmare

Bob paused at the bottom of Wilfred's garden path, looking at me.

'Let me do the talking,' I said. 'I've got plenty to do.' I padded quietly up the path, feeling like a carnivore ready to pounce. The front door was closed so I led Bob around to the open kitchen door. There we both came to a halt.

Wilfred and Martha were in the kitchen. Peering in, we saw them both. They were one on each side of the kitchen table. They did not see us, for they were kneeling one on each side of the oak table, their elbows resting on it. Between them lay a closed book: each of them had one hand laid upon it. Beside the book lay a framed painting, lying face upward in the centre of the table.

Even from the door I recognized the painting. It was an original in oils, an amateurish but rather attractive picture of a calm Port Doy roads busy with fishing boats and sailing craft. The centrepiece of the picture was a vessel familiar to every islander - the Lifandoy lifeboat, resplendent with brightly coloured superstructure and life-jacketed crew. Normally the painting hung over one wall of the kitchen, over the polished sideboard. I paused to wonder why it had been lifted down.

The book, a well-worn tome, also seemed familiar. It was clearly a Bible. I was often in Wilfred's house and had had Bibles held under my nose on various occasions. His and Martha's well-worn volumes rested in their usual places on the sideboard - this was neither's.

At my side, Bob held back. He was uneasily starting to withdraw. It occurred to me to follow suit. But something else occurred to me at the same moment, with greater force. I was about to sneeze again.

The Big Cottage garden was overflowing with flowers. The heavy evening scents after the rain were enough to produce in me a convulsion of the grand sort.

'*A-A-TCHOO!*'

Startled, Wilfred and Martha turned their heads and, seeing us, rose unhurriedly. Martha smiled.

'Timothy, Bob, come in. Will you have a cup of tea?'

Feeling as though I had just exploded, I was in no condition to refuse. I nodded weakly and stepped into the room, mopping my nose furiously.

Bob followed. He looked curiously at the painting on the table. 'Have you been to a sale?'

Martha chuckled. 'No. That belongs in its usual place. I just lifted it down because it reminds us of someone.'

I watched as she replaced it on the wall. 'Who's that?'

She turned to face me. 'The painter.'

Something in the way she said it struck me as odd. As I tried to identify her hidden meaning, she picked up the Bible from the table.

'No, thanks,' I said. 'I don't need one of those.'

Martha looked at me sweetly. 'I wouldn't give you this one if you begged for it. It belongs to someone else.' Without ado she turned, placing the book in a niche at the top of the sideboard, beneath the picture. As she did that I knew that that was where I had seen the book formerly. I could not ever remember having seen it lifted down from there before.

Wilfred gestured to two chairs. 'Sit down, Timothy, sit down, Bob. Martha, Timothy and Jessica have said they will come to the choir concert tomorrow!'

Martha looked doubtful. 'Will the choir be in tune?'

I snorted. 'They'll be more in tune than the choirmaster by the time I've finished with him.'

Wilfred was surprised. 'What does that mean?'

I glanced at Martha. 'This may be a bit strong for your tender ears later.'

She settled herself comfortably into an armchair. 'My ears have heard stronger things than you know, nephew.'

I sighed. 'All right. Wilfred? I said, earlier, that you were stark, staring mad.'

'You did. As I recall, you thought it strange that I should not worship money.'

Bob raised an eyebrow. 'Well, isn't it? Doesn't everyone put their faith in it to some extent? Everyone wants prosperity. Or are we talking about the choice between God or Mammon? Jesus's eye of a needle and all that?'

'We are. One can only worship a single God.' Wilfred paused and glanced up at the book on the sideboard for a moment. 'Real faith in Jesus Christ follows the road He took, which was certainly not one of prosperity, Bob. In fact, it leads to a share in His death.'

I spluttered. 'Great! Are you trying to convert us? Great selling point, I don't think. Wouldn't you be better advertising the so-called Resurrection? It has a much better public relations image than the Cross!'

'No.' My uncle was firm. 'That's the point. The Cross is at the heart of what Jesus did. The Resurrection followed because it had to - it was the inevitable consequence of crucifying God; for the Christian the Resurrection is a whole new shore and existence but not the lifeboat that carries one there. And it represents a strictly non-financial bonus.'

'Non-financial? Personally for you, maybe, but have you no corporate conscience?'

'Corporate? Do you mean regarding the farm?'

'I do.' I was going red in the face and did not care. 'Wilfred? Give, over with your religious claptrap. You really are mad, aren't you? Damn you for a *viper!* Why the hell did you spray the bottom field with your poisons when the wind was onto the Reserve? You know how close many of the orchids grow to the stream. Are you a lunatic or have you the ethics of a drug pusher?'

Bob cringed. Martha glanced sharply at her husband. 'What's this?'

Wilfred was clearly searching his mental diary in the hope of a forgotten appointment. He met my gaze reluctantly. 'You're right, of course. The wind was easterly, I admit it.'

I waited for further explanation, but there was none. 'Is that all? What spray is on the menu for tomorrow? Hydrochloric acid?'

'Oh, now, that's ridiculous!'

'Is it? Do you have any understanding what you're doing to your God's creation? Whether you're doing it for money or not, or what order of values you're applying, makes no difference. It's no use telling me I'm going to hell when Jesus comes if you turn His world into hell ready for Him! He'll *have* to make a new earth for you; you will have killed the first one off by then!'

Wilfred's face was white, but he made no reply. I went on. 'I may be a sinner with a God-shaped hole inside me, but you're a viper, Wilfred, with a poison sac that you're using to kill all his orchids. After all, even He considered the lilies of the field!'

Uncle Wilfred set his jaw and faced me reluctantly. 'The spray shouldn't have been used with the wind like that and I'm honestly sorry. All I can plead is pressure of circumstances. But *that* spray wouldn't have killed any orchids.'

'What? Chemicals kill orchids. You're not going to deny it?'

Wilfred frowned. 'I don't expect a diehard green activist to believe me, but yes, I do in this case. I have been researching all our sprays carefully. As it happens, we have just cancelled all spraying of broad-spectrum weed killers around our field boundaries, and in the bottom fields along the West Burn.'

'In all your fields alongside the Lifandoy Reserve? Fat chance! You don't mean that the House Farm has stopped their use there?'

'A permanent ban would be for Graham Fytts to decide. What I mean is that for the moment - and only for the moment, until how we have worked out how to use them where they are unavoidable - for now, *I* have decided to have them all banned.'

'Really? You? Don't make me laugh. You're as likely a convert to environmental sanity as I am to Bible-bashing.'

Wilfred's retort was sharp. 'The fact that you *don't* think doesn't mean that I *can't*.'

I scowled and raised my voice a notch. 'Then I suppose you'll also deny that you're already making plans to spray our side of the West Burn ready for ploughing?'

Wilfred stared. 'What are you talking about? Has Sir Charles told you something he hasn't told us?'

'No. Probably the reverse. But answer the question. Do you deny it?'

'Of course I deny it.'

I seethed. 'You're lying through your teeth, then.'

Bob nudged me. 'Don't go overboard, Tim.'

Wilfred looked me in the eyes. 'In all your life have you ever known me to tell a deliberate lie?'

'No! But everyone has to start somewhere!'

. . . .

When we returned to Little Cottage I was in a terrible temper. Bob and I engaged in an acrimonious discussion that only ceased when we became too tired to continue. Shortly Angus roused, so we rehearsed our debate with Wilfred again for his benefit. Angus had more respect for Wilfred than I had; he declined to take part in further blackening of my uncle's character. The conversation migrated to another subject.

'What was that painting on Wilfred's table?' Bob wanted to know. Angus enquired what he was talking about. I explained.

'The picture on Wilfred's kitchen wall had been lifted down. It's a painting of the Lifandoy lifeboat in the harbour–'

'In oils? I know it well. Or rather, I have another copy myself.'

'Eh?'

Angus gave me a strange stare. 'You'll know who painted them, of course.'

'Should I?'

He lowered his gaze. 'Have you forgotten that Jessica's father was an artist - as well as being coxswain of the lifeboat?'

Not getting an audible answer, he went on. 'We were all given a copy - the crew of the old lifeboat, that is. But Wilfred isn't a sailor. How he and Martha came by a copy, I don't know, though I think I could guess. I think Jessica gave it to them. It may well be the original.'

I replied slowly. 'You're right. I remember now. Yes, she gave away everything that came to her from her father. She told me her mother gave her a lot of his small belongings but she didn't keep a single one.'

'Why not?' asked Bob.

'She took her father's death very badly. She said that if she couldn't have him she didn't want anything to remind her that she'd lost him.'

'But why give them to Wilfred?'

I looked at Angus. He nodded. 'Wilfred was Ian Bull's closest friend,' he said. 'They were inseparable.'

Bob raised his eyebrows. 'Does that include in religion?'

'Especially in religion. In those days they ran the West Doy chapel together. Ian was as keen as Wilfred.'

'But I thought Jessica never goes to chapel?'

'Only once in a blue moon,' I answered. 'Her mother still goes, though I think mainly from habit. But Jess doesn't. She doesn't believe any more than I do; less if that were possible. She gave up on any notion of a loving God when she lost her father. On the surface she's the sweetest, fluffiest girl you could imagine: but inside she has a core of ice, particularly where God is concerned.'

That night I slept badly. Still seething about Wilfred, I had resorted to downing spirits, an unusual thing for me both from habit and from expense. I scarcely noticed when Bob and Angus separately bade me farewell and after finishing what there was in the bottle I dropped off to sleep on my living room sofa in the small hours, only to toss restlessly.

I woke late after an outrageous nightmare. I had been dreaming of the Reserve being ploughed up by Wilfred's ploughs. My uncle was riding on the foremost machine, holding a hymnbook and singing loudly. Beside him, also singing, was Alice. But instead of a hymnbook she held her appalling picture of Simon Splutter in one hand and an ice cream in the other. Suddenly, the other members of the Cabal jumped into view, steering the other machines.

Jessica and I ran to escape being crushed. We tripped over something white among the orchids, which appeared to be an egg. But when I tried to pick it up it turned out to be the bald head of Jack Dooley, emerging from the slough with a squirming creature in his grasp.

'I've found Cocky,' he yelled. But when he threw the creature at us it turned into an orange tube, which grew into a Volkswagen driven by murderously grinning eggers. The eggers tried to run us down and we avoided them only by squelching at high speed across the marsh. We were about to wade into the burn to escape. But as we reached the water's edge something horrible rose out of the stream, barking like a dog and wearing my old woolly hat pulled down over its face. As we recoiled, the thing removed its hat to reveal the angry face of Sir Charles Hamilstone-ffrench. He shouted at me, levelling his finger accusingly.

'You haven't found the yew sparrow. Find the yew sparrow. Find the sparrow, you!' He waved at me threateningly and water splashed my face. His voice grew oddly squeaky. 'Back to the sparrow, you! Get back to the sparrow, you! Get back in your barrow, you!'

Another splash of water hit my face. I screwed my eyes up, then opened them slightly. The source of the squeaky voice tittered in a most un-aristocratic manner. I opened my eyes wide.

It was Alice. I was still lying on the sofa in my front room. The door was slightly open and she was aiming a water pistol through the gap. Her next assault caught me right on the mouth.

'Hey! What do you - *groogh!*' Spitting water, I sat up. 'I'll ram that - ouch, my head - ram that pistol down your throat-'

'Tsk, tsk.' Alice opened the door wider. 'It smells like a shebeen in here.'

'Oooh! Do me a favour, put the kettle on for some coffee.'

She snorted. 'You've no time for coffee. I'm here on business. Do you know that there's a black Volkswagen parked at your gate?'

I leapt to the door. The effect on me was devastating: reaching the doorpost I embraced it and peered out through a seasick haze.

Alice was right. I tottered down the garden path, feeling like death out for an early morning walk. The VW was badly parked but otherwise innocent in appearance; its owners were not to be seen.

I shambled down the path and stepped to the rear of the car. When the number plate came into focus it read as I expected. Alice eyed it suspiciously and took out a notebook.

'The corner is broken off. The last letter could be a C or a G.'

'I know. The police have already noticed that.'

She started to prowl round the car. 'Never leave anything to chance - that's the master spy's motto. I'll check the front plate - oh!'

She stopped half way and peered in excitement through a side window. 'There's a broken eggshell on the floor!'

I agreed. 'Well spotted. It could be a hard-boiled egg, though. We need more than that.' I pushed my nose hard against the glass.

Behind me, a deep male voice spoke loudly. 'More than what?'

21. - A Warning

'Eek! Er...' I turned, in shock. I was feeling sufficiently fragile for the strange voice to put my recovery from hangover back to square one. But it was not the eggers. Mike and his fellow twitchers stood there, grinning. 'This is the eggers' car, isn't it? Have you caught them?'

'Not yet, Mike.'

'We're keeping them under observation for you. They were in the bar again last night. We couldn't overhear anything useful, though.'

Alice sniffed. 'Not very good, are you? I reckon all you lot could do with a bit less to drink.'

The band of twitchers muttered and recoiled in surprise. As they did so, Alice yanked my arm down and hissed in my ear. 'They're in a nice bad mood now. Give me my picture of Simon Splutter, quick, or I'll tell them you invented the yew sparrow.'

I hissed back desperately. 'Can't. It's in my other trousers!'

She glared. 'I'll settle for *two* ice creams at the Summer Fair instead.'

'Done. But if you tell them, you forfeit the lot, picture too.'

'Crease that picture and I'll have you arrested, Mister Burglar.'

The twitcher Mike towered over Alice. 'Is this a private conversation with a lady or can I join in?'

Alice simpered. 'Charmed, I'm sure. I'm off to school. Timothy, don't forget it's the choir concert tonight. Jessica says you're coming.'

I threw a look after her that should have lightly fried her all over. I had just turned back to Mike when there was another interruption.

'Good morning, Timothy.' Wilfred, on his way to work, was his usual breezy self with no ill-will after my insults of the previous evening. He, too, stopped to look at the car.

'Friends of yours visiting?'

'Certainly not!' chorused the twitchers and I together, jumping back as though the car were red hot.

Wilfred nodded. 'In that case I won't offend you by pointing out that it's very badly parked.' He turned to Mike. 'Welcome to the village. Have you come to visit the Reserve?'

'Just a minute!' I scowled. 'I'm the warden, not you.'

Mike laughed. 'We're just having a walk up to Raw Head. We've had a good look around here.'

I caught his meaning. 'You're going soon, then?'

He nodded. 'On tomorrow's ferry, I think. The griff is that a couple of blockers are over from America - a belted kingfisher in County Tipperary and a yellow-bellied sapsucker in the Shetlands. We could tick them both off with forty-eight hours' hard travelling.'

I frowned. 'Are they birds you haven't seen before?'

The other twitchers mostly nodded, but Mike shook his head. 'I've seen both in the last five years. It would be nice to see them again, of course, to recall the finer details of the plumage and so forth.'

'And they're only rumours? Not even definite reports?'

'Actually, I doubt either is genuine,' he admitted. 'Wrong time of year for birds getting blown across the Atlantic. But we have to check them out, don't we?'

Uncle Wilfred eyed the twitchers in wonder. 'Is that the sort of life you live all year?'

'More or less - money permitting.'

'Do any of you have jobs?'

'Not many. Really dedicated birders are virtually unemployable.'

He was dismayed. 'Are any of you married?'

Mike gave a sad smile. 'Some of us were. But commitment to the cause is everything.'

Wilfred grimaced. '"The pearl of greatest price"? Listen, are you sure there's no more worthwhile cause you could follow?'

Mike looked down at him. 'I do wonder, sometimes… Tell you what, I'll give it some thought. Really.' He went on chatting to Wilfred for a couple of minutes while I completed my examination of the interior of the car.

When I returned my attention to the bystanders Mike was just turning to his followers. 'Right, lads. I hear there are a few bushes in the Raw Head lighthouse yard. If there's not at least one barred warbler on the headland in this weather I'll be very surprised. Let's go!'

I watched them go. When I turned back, Wilfred was inspecting the car critically again. 'This car's been badly driven,' he observed. 'That rear wing is dented.'

I snorted. 'Huh. Why don't you have a go at it with your sledgehammer, then?'

Wilfred was, as ever, amiable toward my sarcasm. 'Did you sleep badly, Timothy? You sound as though you got out of bed on the wrong side. Your face has a green tinge to it.'

His healthy manner infuriated me. 'Green is most certainly not the wrong side, you murderer of orchids.'

'We've already discussed that thoroughly.'

'Oh, I'm sure I can list more crimes. What about all the field hedges you uprooted? What about the nitrate fertilizer that runs into the West Burn? What about the silage you cut so early that all the corncrakes on the farm have gone? What about the autumn stubble that you plough up and reseed immediately after harvest so that it can't feed the small birds all winter? What about the marsh you tried to drain on your side of the Burn, where the water table is so high that your wheat there spends the summer swimming backstroke in a chemical lake?'

Wilfred said nothing, but his smile vanished.

'And don't come back at me with another religious reply, either. *Nuts* to your creator God giving you dominion over the earth! I tell you - if you won't go green, I certainly won't be thinking about coming to Jesus!'

'That subject often comes to your lips, doesn't it, Timothy? Do you sense an inner prompting?'

'I might as well expect the dead to rise as to get sense out of you. If you've nothing more to say, go to work. You make me sick.'

To my annoyance, Wilfred stayed where he was. 'Your arguments would be more convincing, Timothy, without your resorting to the bottle that *did* make you sick.'

My reply to that was terse. Wilfred's eyebrows shot up in dismay and, to be honest, I was a little sorry. There was still liquor in my veins: I decided to let it talk no more.

'All right, I didn't mean that. Now go, unless you've anything else to say.'

Abruptly, Wilfred grinned. His face lit up in such an alarming manner that I grabbed my garden gate for support. 'A parting gift, Timothy: your mail.' He held out a letter. 'It's got Keith Potts' name on the back. I brought it round because I knew you would want it straight away.'

He left it in my hand and walked off down the street, whistling. He was clearly delighted that he had been able to love his enemy.

■ ■ ■ ■

I was already feeling queasy and Uncle Wilfred's famous grin was the pits. I staggered back into Little Cottage and was as ill as a seasick mainlander. Eventually, things began to brighten until after a couple of coffees I felt well enough to take an interest in my letter.

This time Keith had written in his own spidery hand. The letter was short and pointed.

> *'Dear Tim,*
>
> *'My mobile charger must have been nicked by another patient on the ward. I have had to write to give you an urgent warning. Head Office has now confirmed the eggers' car did not return to Man or Heysham and must be on Lifandoy. I'm glad you had news from Angus in good time - though I still don't understand how you could have seen the eggers so soon. But here's some news you haven't had. We now know who the eggers are. And the big man of the three is a known ruffian with a violent record as long as my arm. On no account tangle with him! It is even possible he may be armed with a small handgun. Don't try to be clever - let the police do the heavy handling. Do your best for the birds, but not at the expense of your own skin.*
>
> *'Be careful to look after those "Fetlar" birds (you know which ones I mean) - and look out for Wilfred!*
>
> *Yours,*
> *Keith Potts.'*

I sat up straight. Keith's news bad sobered me more than coffee. I reached for the phone and tapped out a number.

'William? I've just had a letter from Keith Potts. He says - oh, you've had the same information. Listen, their car is parked outside my gate! No, I'm not joking. They must have arrived when it was still dark, or they'd have seen my warden's signboard.

'Could you drive up the valley road and watch for our signals with the kite? Good. Remember - if the kite dips five times they've taken an egg and you can arrest them in possession. Any other signal and you won't catch them red-handed. OK?'

Slamming the phone down, I grabbed my bins and made for the slightly open front door. 'Speaking of kites, that reminds me of Angus. He's been up there twelve hours. Where are - what? - hey - *ouch!'* Reaching the door I was knocked flat as it opened. Bob and Jamie bounded in.

'Tim, do you know what's parked at your gate? And what are you doing lying behind the door? Are you drunk?'

'A plague on both your houses!' I staggered up. 'No, I'm not drunk. Yes, I've seen the car. I've also had this letter from Keith.'

I thrust the epistle into their hands. They read it with horror. Jamie scowled. 'Where are they now?'

'I've no idea. I was going to start at the chapel balcony window. We should be able to see the kite from there, if Angus is still flying it.'

There followed a mad gallop through the village. We thundered up the lane and into the chapel yard. Then we stopped in embarrassment. The chapel yard was not empty. Martha stood in the corner, where she was cleaning the glass on the chapel notice board. She saw us and smiled.

'Good morning, boys. The old poster had been up so long, I really felt we ought to have a change. But Wilfred has been so busy recently, I didn't like to ask him. And all the younger church folk are so willing, but they have their families to look after...'

We gazed at the colourful new poster. It read:

'JESUS CAME TO FIND YOU.
ARE YOU COMING TO FIND HIM?'

We glanced at our feet. When I looked up, Martha had a twinkle in her eye. 'Now, you've not come to admire the poster. And you've certainly not come to the choir concert twelve hours early. What are you after? Is some rare bird sitting on the chapel roof?'

'Ah - not that we know of.'

'I did see one unusual little bird behind the chapel, actually.' Martha had plenty of time to chat. 'I've never seen one quite like it before. A pretty thing - it was spinning round and round on a pool in the marsh below Mrs Bull's fence—'

'*Martha.*' I broke in, not listening. 'Would you have any objection if we went up to have a quick peep from the chapel balcony window?'

'Not in the slightest, Timothy, although I could show you the way to the Promised Land without your having to climb all that way up to look—'

'You're a dear.' I grinned and blew her a kiss as we raced for the door and the steps.

The balcony window commanded a wonderful view of the valley. At any other time we would have revelled in it. But not today. 'The kite is flying!'

'I see it. I can't tell where it's pointing to, though.'

'It's certainly not pointing to the valley,' I said. 'It's turned toward the sea, if anything. It's definitely flying on that side of the hill. Do we agree on that?'

'So what are they after?' asked Jamie.

Bob was already jumping up and down. 'My terns! The roseate terns! They're after the tern eggs!'

I nodded. 'You're right, of course. We should have foreseen that they would be the easy target. The eggers can't reach most of them without a boat, mind you, but there are a couple of pairs of roseates among the other terns in the main colony. The eggers will create havoc among all the terns if they start hunting for them there.'

I looked hopefully at the other two. 'Lads, I know you were thinking I could give you some time off…?'

Jamie shook his head. 'No need. It will do when the emergency is over. I'd better relieve Angus. I can do some map work from the top of the West Ridge anyway. And if I see that you need me I'll come straight away.'

Bob needed even less persuasion. 'I'd coming with you, Tim. Try and stop me! If the eggers frighten off all my terns I won't have any project left to work on!'

. . . .

The normal way to the tern colonies was up the main track and through the gap in the West Ridge to the south of our lookout hill. This was probably the way the eggers bad gone. But Bob and I knew we could get to the shore much faster by scrambling straight over the West Ridge above the village. We set off at our maximum pace.

Twenty minutes later we paused for a desperately needed rest. The whole of the west coast lay before us, the emerald *machair* separated by a sandwich filling of milk-white sand from the turquoise sea.

'Can you see the eggers?' I gasped. We collapsed onto the grass and balanced our binoculars for extra steadiness on convenient tussocks.

'I can see two of them,' wheezed Bob. 'They're a good half an hour ahead of us - on the path above the beach. I see them. They must be only a couple of minutes from the first terns.'

There was despair in Bob's voice. 'We're too late. When they reach the end of the beach, about four hundred arctic and sandwich terns - to say nothing of the roseates - will leave their eggs and chicks and fly up in panic. If the eggers stay there until we reach them the whole colony could desert for the year. Do you know, if I had a rifle in my hand I would be tempted to use it.'

I sympathized. 'They're blackguards. I just hope the arctics have a good try at lacerating their scalps, that's all.'

We watched in agony as a cloud of screaming terns drifted up before the intruders. The men waved sticks at them as the birds dived slashing with their razor-sharp bills. Then the men paused.

'Who's that? There's someone in front of them. He just stood up. See him? He was sitting by those rocks above the beach. He's dressed in grey–'

'And he's not the third egger.' Bob was equally puzzled. 'He's only a small man. Is he an accomplice?'

'No. *Look.* He's waving them back! They're arguing with him. He's shaking his fist at them.'

I peered more intently. 'It can't be. But I know that outfit. It's Sir Charles. Sir Charles is ordering them back. He's stopping them from going into the colony!'

Suddenly we both had the same thought. I got up and, tired legs notwithstanding, began to run. Bob followed. 'Come on! He's on his own. If the eggers turn nasty he could be in real trouble.'

The hillside melted away before our urgent strides. Leaping bushes, boulders and rivulets we risked broken limbs and necks in our kangaroo descent.

The distant argument visibly continued. Bob shouted in surprise. 'They've turned back! He's won. They're going back along the shore!'

Amazingly, we reached the shore in fifteen minutes. We burst dramatically through the final barrier of bracken and bramble. Sir Charles was still there, standing by the rocks watching the eggers go. He turned as we staggered up, his face stern.

'I have to say, Mr. Corn, that my opinion of your management of the Reserve declines hourly.'

My lungs were on fire. '*Aaah!* Sir Charles - you're all right? They left you alone! You stopped them - but - what did you say?'

He stabbed his finger up the path. 'If those two are examples of the visitors you set such store by, I am appalled. Your whole Reserve is evidently full of people who vary from the irresponsible to the mentally deranged.'

'Eh?'

'Yesterday I met two ladies who proudly informed me that they were carrying an egg in a headscarf. Today, on ascending the ridge to see the sunrise I came across a grown man flying a child's toy kite. Now I have been roundly abused by two scoundrels who were ignoring all your signs and entering a restricted area–'

'And you stopped them! Sir Charles, how did you do it?'

'I did it without the help of yourself and your companion, Mr. Corn. As usual, you wardens were engaged in your favourite game of racing down hillsides and leaping from bushes - from healthy shrubbery which you have done your best to demolish.'

We gaped. Sir Charles went on. 'Your clients, Mr. Corn, include egg-thieves, kite-flyers and trespassers. For all I know you might have armed intruders wandering the island to boot.'

'How did you know?' said Bob. 'Did someone - yeeow! - Tim, what was that - oh, I see.'

Sir Charles fixed me with gimlet eyes. 'My report will be nearly ready for the Earl by tomorrow. Mr. Corn, I regret that you now have little chance of convincing me of the value of your case. As a last opportunity for you, have you found the yew sparrow yet?'

'No, I'm sorry, you see—'

'Enough. My report will reflect my dismay. Unless the House Farm manager fails to tender one I shall strongly advise the Earl to accept his new Reserve management plan - including the modern farming methods it must employ.'

'But - but - but ...' The only sound I could emit might have come from a farmyard.

'Mr. Corn, I see little point in continuing this conversation. The only advice I can leave you with is to place a proper guard on these beautiful seabirds, and to control your visitors forthwith.'

22. - Mysteries

Sir Charles began to walk away. Then he turned his head. 'Oh, Mr. Corn: have you any giant parrots on the Reserve?'

I gazed at him. 'No, Sir Charles.'

'That's what I thought. In that case, I think that the two ladies I met may need attention to their eyesight, as well as to their kleptomania. Good day Mr. Corn and, quite possibly, goodbye.'

As he departed along the shore Bob and I collapsed onto the turf, broken physically and mentally. We lay on our backs, too numbed to move. As he stared upwards, Bob inquired dully. 'What's this about a giant parrot? Have Edith and Violet reported something odd?'

'I've no idea. That's the least of my cares. Bob, I've blown it! I've let Keith down completely.'

'Why don't you tell Sir Charles about the eggers?'

'And let him find out that one of our visitors could have taken a pot-shot at him? What good would that do? Besides, he'd be bound to tell Wilfred; and that could make things worse, if worse is possible. There are still the snowy owls, remember.'

I left Bob to watch over his terns in case the eggers came back, and made my sad and weary way up and along the West Ridge to the kite hill. When I reached the top Jamie was there; to my surprise so was Angus. The look on his face told me that the limit of my woes might not yet have been told.

'What's happened, Angus?'

He bit his lip. 'I'm sorry, Tim. I didn't think fast enough. Lack sleep, I suppose.' He answered the enquiry on my face. 'The eggers have realized that there's something important on the knoll.'

'*What?* How did that happen?'

'It was the two who were after the ternery. I don't know where the third is - I've not seen him. But the other two came along the *machair* after they left the terns. They were going to walk through the gap in the ridge but something they saw alarmed them.'

Jamie nodded. 'I think they saw me on the way up to relieve Angus.'

'Anyway,' said Angus, 'after that they kept on up the shore. Either they were too lazy to climb the ridge, or else they didn't know where they were going. They came right up to the start of the Raw Head path, then cut inland across country.

'I could see they were going to walk right past the knoll. I had to do something. I'd no idea whether there was a bird on the nest - there hadn't been one visiting at all in daylight - and I couldn't risk them flushing the hen right off her eggs in full view.

'So I went down and got in their way. They didn't like that - they were in a foul temper already. But they did as they were told and headed back for the village down the path Jamie says you call the Mud Path.'

We looked at Angus. With his massive form and short, powerful limbs it was unsurprising the eggers had behaved meekly.

Jamie scowled. 'But they will have the scent.'

I nodded slowly. 'You're right. They already think they were ordered away from the ternery because of the roseates - Sir Charles could easily be mistaken for a warden - so they will assume that they were also warned away from the knoll for a reason. That means that we're in trouble on all three fronts.'

The other two frowned. 'Three?' said Jamie. 'The ternery, the knoll - that's two. Isn't that enough for this time in the morning?'

Gloomily I explained about Sir Charles. The expressions of the other two darkened further. Jamie was particularly depressed. 'I've a good mind to give up natural history. It's all being destroyed before our eyes. Even otherwise nice people like Wilfred are agin' us. How can we fight in every corner at once?'

Deep down inside me, something started to smoulder. 'We must because we have to, Jamie,' I said slowly. 'There are plenty of people for whom there are still hope. The decent people will help us in the end.'

'Are there any decent people?'

Angus smiled grimly. 'Are we decent people?'

I paused at the thought, then sighed. 'You're right. We're all implicated in some degree. None of us is blameless. There are plenty of Third World habitats that have been ruined by coffee plantations! Wilfred talks loads of rot, but at least what he says about us all being sinners has more to it than this atheist likes to admit. We all help to spoil the world. We're all at sea in some way. So unless we're going to pray for a miracle, or start walking on water, we must keep up with the enemy vessels and sail them out of our ocean.'

Jamie startled us with a roar of approval. 'RIGHT! And I say we must go down fighting. The captain must go down with his ship!'

'Er...' I hesitated, uncertain whether I wanted to hit this level of support.

Angus yawned. 'But first I must go down for a bit of shuteye. I'll be back this afternoon to see what's what.'

■　■　■　■

Jamie was happy to watch out the morning, so I walked back with Angus. At the village we found the street empty of Volkswagens of all shades, so he went into Little Cottage while I watched the usual trickle of visitors gathering. Among them were Violet and Edith. I approached them curiously.

'Good morning, ladies. Have you seen anything else unusual on your travels?'

Edith was excited. 'Young man, are you aware that you have a huge parrot flying around your Reserve?'

'Have I? When and where was this?'

'Yesterday evening. We went for a walk to see the sunset from the big hill at the top of the valley. There was no path but we walked up from the valley road through a little wood of stunted trees–'

'On the side of Ginger Hill? That is what we call a relict ashwood. The trees are very old and some rare flowers grow around the wood. If you go there again please ask me to take you. There are a few dangerous clefts in the limestone rock: we *do* like our visitors to come back–'

'And we were walking very slowly when the parrot flew past us. It was very large and white.'

'*White?* Did you say white?'

Edith was very sure. 'It was pure white, except that we thought it had a yellow patch on its head.' She opened a glossy book with a title something like *Birds of the World.* 'We found a picture of it in this book.'

She pointed. The picture she indicated was indeed one of a large, white bird. I read the text under it with amusement.

'A sulphur-crested cockatoo? From Australia? That certainly is a large white parrot.'

Edith scowled. I know when I am being humoured, young man. We are experienced birdwatchers and we are not used to having wardens humour us.'

'Ah - of course not, Edith. I'm sure you checked the bird's identity thoroughly. We wardens would be very happy if everyone was as eager. Goodbye, now, and have a nice day on the Reserve.'

It was with glee that I watched the ladies go. Sulphur-crested cockatoo, my foot! The ladies had seen one of the snowy owls, doubtless the smaller male. They had even noted - wrongly - the yellow of its eyes. The place they had described was a little visited spot, close to where I had been attacked by the bird myself. As Bob had pointed out, the absence of the male bird from the nest area must mean it was frequenting a quiet part of the Reserve. Now we knew for certain which part.

■　■　■　■

Having given all my introductory talks I excused myself and headed into Little Cottage for a coffee. My kitchen, however, held a shock. Beside the sink stood several unwashed mugs - and an empty jar of coffee.

I glared at the closed bedroom door. 'Angus, I'll string you from your yardarm, if you still have such a thing. You've used a day's supply of coffee in a single mug. Doytown Co-op, here I come.'

A few minutes later I was gazing in guilty admiration at the massed jars of instant coffee on the Co-op shelves when a fellow shopper offered a greeting. It was Jack Dooley. The scrap merchant was in a warm mood for once, his moon face wreathed with a smile. I enquired the reason.

'Someone has seen Cocky, Mr. Timothy,' he said. 'I've had a definite report of him.'

'Good,' I said unconvincingly. 'We'll all be glad to see him home again, won't we?'

Jack shook his head. 'Most people will,' he muttered, 'but not everyone.' I could name a few who've spoken badly to me because he's flown at them. He's a beautiful creature and he's got a right royal temper at times. They don't understand that he's a pedigree, you see.'

I decided not to mention my ankle. 'Who reported him, then?'

'I don't rightly know. It was Sergeant Farquhar who told me. He said some walkers had seen him - visitors, not island people.'

I thought for a moment. 'Most of the visitors come to the Reserve at some point.'

Jack brightened further. 'If you hear anything...'

I smiled half-heartedly. 'If anyone tells me they've seen him run past I'll let you know,' I promised as I moved away.

As I walked off with my coffee, Jack's expression was one of gratefulness mixed with surprise. He was still staring oddly after me through the shop window as I drove away.

After an early lunch I set out back up the valley to relieve Jamie. I was nearly at the foot of the kite hill when I saw the kite suddenly soar into the sky above me.

'Trouble on this side of the hill,' I muttered to myself. 'But that's odd: I've passed no-one in the valley. Surely Jamie can't have mistaken me for an egger?'

I jogged up the hill. My sentry was sitting quite still at the crest, peering intently down at the marsh behind me. 'You walked right past them, Tim.'

'What? Are they in the lower fen?'

'Yes. They're wearing camouflage jackets, all three of them. Very clever - they've always been in black before. They're obviously up to something - they must have hidden when they saw you coming. I spotted them when they stood up again as you passed.'

We watched for a while. 'They're not going anywhere fast, are they? They're just walking slowly through the marsh.'

'They're doing more than that, Jamie. They're *quartering* the marsh. And what are those things they're carrying? They look for all the world like metal detectors.'

'Whoever heard of metal eggs?' Jamie snorted. 'Are you going to tackle them?'

I thought hard. 'Not yet. Let's watch them for a while. They aren't crashing through the vegetation at the moment - they seem to be keeping to the paths where there are any. If we disturb them, they might move to somewhere we want them less.'

'OK. In that case,' said Jamie, 'I'll go further up the marsh and get on with some work. They won't go up towards the knoll when they see me in the way.'

'Right. You contain them. Perhaps they *are* doing metal-detecting: they shouldn't be doing that on the Reserve either, but it's better than egging. If they're stopping in the lower valley I'll settle for watching them for now.'

In fact, that was all I did. I spent a very peaceful afternoon on the ridge top, watching the three mysterious searchers in the valley and chatting to visitors passing to and from Raw Head along the path. Various enquiries were made about the kite: I met these with a prepared explanation about studying the wind direction, which was nonsense but indisputable.

As the sun began to drop faster Bob strolled up from the beach to relieve me. 'Anything doing?'

I pointed out the marsh probers and explained our plans. 'Jamie will stay in the upper valley until dusk. Angus will relieve you here then and he'll move nearer, as last night, to watch the knoll closely. He's keen to see if the owls will hunt at twilight.'

'OK. You'd better get off, now.' Bob grinned. 'I wouldn't want you to miss the choir concert. Are you really going to go?'

I groaned. 'It's a lesser punishment than the one I would get if I stood Jessica up.'

He chortled. 'Have a tuneful evening, then.' He dodged as I threw a clod at him.

■　■　■　■

The only good thing about going to the choir concert at the chapel was that it enabled Jessica and me to meet with the Cabal in the chapel shed before the concert. When they arrived, Alice was unusually silent. She remained so when I enquired sarcastically whether she already knew all that had happened. It was Rosalind who answered me.

'We don't know,' she said. 'Patricia had to come back to school. Her Auntie Kathleen at Liffen Farm called out the doctor and he said Patricia's ankle was fine. He gave her a lift straight back to school.'

'I was hoping you could tell me who was on the burn bridge yesterday morning?'

'Nope.'

'That's a pity. Why not?'

'The doctor came only twenty minutes after Patricia put up the red signal. What happened on the bridge?'

Judiciously omitting certain embarrassing points, I narrated the events since our last meeting. As I did so, Alice's expression darkened. When I finished, the Cabal turned to her expectantly, waiting for her to break her silence. Finally, she did.

'Something smells.'

'What?'

'Something is wrong. I don't know what, but you're missing a key fact. The case smells as fishy as Port Doy quay.'

'Why?'

'I told you. I don't know. But one or two things don't add up.'

'Like what?'

Alice picked some wax thoughtfully out of an ear, then ceased when Jessica frowned at her. 'When Patricia put up the red signal yesterday there was a black Volkswagen at the road fork at Liffen Farm. When the doctor's car pulled up behind it, it drove off fast up the Ginger Farm road.'

'I know. I saw it go.'

'But when the doctor drove Patricia the other way down the road half an hour later there was a black VW at the roadside below the House Farm. And she's almost certain it didn't pass Liffen Farm in between.'

Jessica raised her eyebrows. 'They must have driven terribly fast if they went round by Doytown.'

'I think they could have done it,' I said. 'Nothing would surprise me about these characters.'

'And then again,' Alice said. 'We both saw the car at your gate. But Carmen says that the one at the hotel was–'

'Hold on,' I broke in. 'Don't get too hung up about the car. I tell you, these eggers are devious characters. It's a known trick of theirs to employ decoy cars, for example.'

Alice frowned. 'I suppose. I don't know what sort of people eggers are–'

'Then let me tell you that they are scum!' I warned her. 'And to add to that, here's a special warning. We've heard from good sources that it's possible at least one of them may be armed.'

There was a shocked hiss. Alice turned to Rosalind. 'Where do we stand, quartermaster?'

Rosalind shook her head. 'We don't.'

'You're damn right you don't,' I said. 'Nor do I, nor does Bob, nor Jamie. The boys in blue are in sole charge there.'

Alice curled her lip. 'Mr. Plod to the rescue? We'll see. But we reserve the right to be prepared.'

Jessica stood up. 'But you won't be prepared for your concert if you stay in this shed much longer. I think it's time to go.'

The Cabal roused itself obediently and began to move. Alice yawned. 'See you tomorrow. We'll be waiting for our ice creams at the Summer Fair. You'd better be there!'

23. - The South Rock

Even from the last row of seats in the crowded chapel, the choir sounded off key. I squeezed Jessica's hand. 'Is there something wrong with my hearing?'

'I don't know,' she replied. 'Why? Does the choir seem distant?'

'No, it's too close.'

She gave me a kiss on the cheek. 'It won't be long, now. We've just Alice's solo and the last two hymns to go. What do you think of the music?'

'I suppose the songs aren't bad. Some of them were a bit heavy on the preaching side. But they were mostly quite lively and one or two were thought-provoking. But part of the choir sings them as if it were being tortured by the Spanish Inquisition.'

She chuckled. 'I know what you mean. Hush now, here's Alice.'

The chief plotter of the Cabal stood up. Her hair was amazingly tidy now, and her face gleamed as though it had been plunged into a bowl of olive oil. I reflected that that was a task I would have been happy to perform. She opened her mouth and the congregation tensed expectantly.

The sound that came forth was extraordinary, even by present standards. My first reaction was to think that the heat of Wilfred's frenetic conducting had finally set off the smoke detectors. When it dawned on me that the high-pitched bleeping was actually Alice's voice, I sat back in awe, too stunned to complain. What she was singing, I had no idea. Her diction was non-existent and her solo would have sounded little different had she performed it on the oboe - or even the smoke detector. I realized that her voice had been audible throughout the concert, rising above the other parts. But until now I had dismissed it as the product of some unfortunate feedback over the public address system. I nudged Jessica in wonder.

'Is that her, or the microphone?'

'I think it's Alice.'

'Why can't we recognize any words?'

'You never normally want to hear what Alice has to say.'

'Touché... Well, what's the song?'

'It's supposed to be *Morning has Broken.*'

'I'm not surprised it's broken with a noise like that–'

There was an irritated 'Hush!' from the seats in front. I subsided. When Alice at last shut up, the choir stood for a rousing chorus. To rouse it further, Wilfred added his own powerful baritone voice, with the result that Alice's shrilling was for once nearly drowned. The congregation stood up en masse and joined in. To my alarm, a couple of women started to clap in time and a man near the choir raised his arms high. Most plainly regarded the singing as a demonstration of enthusiasm in itself. When the organ stopped, the audience carried on with an impromptu celebration, with the eager, semi-orderly manner of a football crowd.

I stared around. 'This isn't the chapel I used to know! I mean, people always sang lustily, but they usually stopped when the music did.'

'It seems everyone has their own peculiar form of worship now,' agreed Jess. 'Look! Half of them don't know what the other half is doing, because they have their eyes shut.'

The members of the choir were also having a good time, some belting out the chorus again while others sang softly with closed eyes and looks of rapture. I felt thoroughly disconcerted; although I noticed a fellow sufferer in Alice herself, standing quietly amid the choir with a puzzled look on her face.

■   ■   ■   ■

Eventually, the ballyhoo subsided. As everyone sat down, I nudged Jess hopefully. 'Can we go now?'

'Not yet. Wilfred is going to say something. I'd like to hear what he has to say.'

'Can't you ask him later? The night's still young.'

Jessica turned to me and there was the same odd expression in her eyes as there had been when Angus mentioned the South Rock in the café. 'I'd like to listen now, Tim. In fact, this was the thing I really wanted to come for.' She looked frightened, almost old.

I slouched down, puzzled and annoyed. Shortly Wilfred stood up and cleared his throat. I steeled myself for a horrible little speech of self-congratulation.

'As you all know,' said Wilfred as the mutter subsided, 'each year I normally give a short word of thanks. Tonight the thanks will be even briefer than usual. Thank you, choir, for *all* your hard work. Thank you, audience, for coming. Also a special thank *you,* for coming, to those visitors who are not often among us. That is all the thanks I shall offer.

'But one other thing can be mentioned tonight. In fact, I *must* mention it.' A deeper hush fell, and more than a hush: as Wilfred's words fell I sensed an emotional sea-change among the people near me. The air of expectancy was painful. I sat up.

'Tonight,' he said, 'is the night of our annual concert. This year, as many will know, it also happens to be an anniversary.' Wilfred gave a long pause. 'It is an anniversary none of us is glad to reach. Five years ago tonight, in one of the most dreadful storms to fall upon this island, the Lifandoy lifeboat was wrecked on the South Rock, with the loss of three of its crew - of Luke, Rakesh and Ian - three utterly irreplaceable lives.'

At my side I felt Jessica stiffen. She grasped my hand; I squeezed it in reply. Now I knew why I was here.

'In that storm nearly all of us lost precious friends,' said Wilfred, 'and a few lost far, far more. The loss of the coxswain, Ian Bull, was one of the greatest burdens any family at this chapel has had to bear. Martha and I, like many of you, continue to uphold the Bull family with our prayers to this day.

'This is not the place, nevertheless, to re-awaken an old tragedy or to disturb the dust of the past. But before we go I do want to share, as a special word from the Lord, two short readings from this Bible.' He reached behind the lectern and lifted into view a familiar, worn brown volume. Beside me, Jessica gave a little gasp. Inquiringly I turned: but she had eyes only for Wilfred. I am not a sensitive person, but the profile of her face against the low chapel lighting was a sight I think I shall never forget.

At the front, Wilfred began to leaf through the book as he continued. 'Nearly five years ago, this Bible was lent to me. Every evening since then, Martha and I have prayed for the healing of the grief it represents. Every night it has rested unopened in its place, awaiting a reader. Every night we have prayed that one day its rightful owner will some day come back for it.

'Yesterday, for the first time since it was lent to us, Martha and I chose to open it. Many of the verses in it are underlined or annotated - this was not a Bible that went unused. But a couple of readings went to our hearts. Both of them were underlined in red. Both had dates written by them which I happen to know were key ones in the life of the book's owner. Those of you who knew him well may be able to guess what those dates were. The first thing we read was from chapter five of the Letter to the Romans.

'Since this is a concert and not a service I will not start actually reading passages from the Bible, but you will recall that is where the apostle Paul says it is rare for anyone to give their life for a good person, but through God's amazing love Jesus died for us even when we still sinners.

Wilfred paused. 'In a minute we shall be singing our final hymn, number ninety-seven: *"Eternal Father, strong to save."* But first, let me just say this. The Bible says that Jesus died for us while were yet in a state of being - or destined to be - God's *enemies*. That act was unique. As *he* would be the first to point out to you were he here, not even Ian Bull's unforgettable self-sacrifice compares with that.

'And what would Ian say to you if he were here now? Perhaps you are still an enemy of Jesus Christ? Many, of course, are God's enemies. Some may have become more embittered against Him by events such as the one we are remembering tonight. Of course, their anger against Him is ultimately unfair, unlike His reasonable anger at the disobedience of us all, which is the real problem.

'But it was not God's anger that caused the old Lifandoy lifeboat to founder. Nor do I offer any other explanation. It is not for me to try to tell you why such a grievous thing happened. Our Almighty God who made both men and storms has not explained it to me any more than to any of you. What we do know, however, is that He has sympathy for men and women: real sympathy, of the sort which led Him to come and live among us, and sail through our storms with us.

'The Son of God did many things as a man. To me, one of the most amazingly human things that He did was the making of personal friends. Much of the time, He was very busy; He had a world to offer healing and redemption to. Yet He still had time for such a preciously unimportant thing such as friendship! And He was loyal to His friends in every way that He could be - it was a rare occasion when He was missing in their time of need.

'But one story, about one of His friends, is different. There was one friend whom He was not around to help. The one Bible verse I *will* read to you tells of His reaction when one of His close friends, Lazarus, died.

'Can we ever believe in God's love again? Does He - did He know what real grief is like? Could He? This reading is a short one; in fact, it's the shortest verse in the whole Bible. To those of you who cannot forget or forgive, this is the only message I can offer. From this Bible, on this of all nights, I can read nothing else to you than the thirty-fifth verse of the eleventh chapter of the gospel of John...'

Wilfred put his finger to the page and looked straight down the chapel at Jessica and me.

'"Jesus wept"'.

And he shut the book and walked away with it, as I tried to guess what in the world the woman holding my hand would do next.

■　■　■　■

As we walked hurriedly out of the chapel, Jessica's face was white. I kept my mouth shut, feeling her tension through her grip but not knowing how to respond. I let her lead me as we walked through the sweetness of a calm May evening. Where she was going I had no idea, but I was determined she should not go there alone.

We walked for a long, long time. To my surprise, she first led me down onto the Reserve below the chapel, then onto the steep slope by which Bob and I had ascended the West Ridge that morning. At the top of the ridge we turned left, following the ridgeback south. To our right, the setting sun was over the sea; it was a clear evening and, in the far distance, the backlit shadows above the horizon were the Mountains of Mourne in Ulster.

To our left, most of populated Lifandoy unrolled like a map as we walked. The ridge path snaked for most of a mile until it reached the cairn that marked its southern extremity. Beyond the cairn, only the crumbling granite parapets of old Doy Fort concealed the crowded anchorage, sheltered by its long breakwater, which lay outside Port Doy harbour proper.

Jessica led the way down onto the small lane that leads out to Lifandoy's southern headland. When she declined to take the steep road down to the harbour and turned up onto the track leading to Doy Fort, there was no longer any doubt where we were going. I decided it was time to speak.

'Jess?' She halted and turned, her face glowing in the light of the setting sun. 'Jess, do you need to do this?'

'I do.' Her voice was low and unsteady.

'Why?'

'We all have to face our memories eventually. Wilfred and Martha are right: the book must be reopened one day.'

I hesitated. 'Would you prefer to be alone?'

She held out both hands. 'Dear Tim - do you think I would have had the courage to come this far without you?'

We clenched hands, then relaxed and walked on slowly, hand in hand, to the partly ruined fort on its little hill. High on the green slope, on a little platform below the fort walls which overlooked the anchorage, there was an old wooden seat. During the day it would have been laden with camera-bearing tourists, but to our relief it was empty. Jess stopped dead as the seat came into view.

'This was Daddy's favourite place,' she whispered. 'He used to let me sit here with him. They were our closest times together. I've never... Put your arm around me, please, Tim.'

Holding her like a fragile crystal, I led her to the seat and we sat there, huddled against a chill sharper than the cool onshore breeze. Below us to the left, the corner of the broad anchorage was shielded by the long breakwater stretching from the cliff foot below. Nearby, the corrugated red bulk of the lifeboat station hunched broodily at the head of its long ramp. Offshore from a tiny beach lay constellations of sailing boats, moored fore-and-aft or swinging, rocking in the slight swell. In the distance the elegant masts of a tall ship - a schooner on a training cruise - rose above the stubby hulls of moored lobster boats. Everything inside the breakwater was a picture of calm and safety.

But outside, it was madness. To our right, the cliff fell below us to no beach or mooring. The safe haven was replaced by a very different scenery. A harsh mosaic of reefs stretched out to sea, disappearing slowly and weedily beneath the incoming tide. The sea, calm as it was, roared through gaps in the reef to pound the face of the breakwater. It tugged impatiently at every jagged outcrop, foaming white and then sucking noisily back again.

Yet nowhere did it tug more or foam whiter, or suck back more greedily into its depths, than on the reef's outermost set of fangs, the set which terminated in the misshapen, high mass of the blackened and hated South Rock of Lifandoy.

■　■　■　■

By the time dusk had come and we had walked down onto Port Doy quay my shirt was wet with many salt tears - not all strange to me - and my arms ached from holding a warm, shivering body more tightly than they had ever done for pleasure. I was tired. The long walk back to West Doy stretched before us as a weariness.

So we responded eagerly when the window of a small car on the quay wound down and a familiar voice called in the twilight.

'Would you like a lift?'

'*Martha?*' we exclaimed together, 'what are you doing here?'

The rear door opened invitingly. From the driver's seat came a half-querulous reply. 'That's what I'm wondering myself.'

I stared into the gloom. 'You're alone!'

She nodded. 'Wilfred thought you would turn up here. But he expected he might not be too welcome. We decided I should come.'

I knew the car for Wilfred and Martha's own little vehicle, a rarely used and venerable Mini. I was bewildered.

'But Martha, I haven't seen you in... I mean, you've hardly driven in years!'

She laughed merrily; the lights of the Harbour Inn seemed in response to glow brighter across the water. 'I still have a licence, although I would never drive when it was busy. And I don't want to drive in the pitch dark, so are you coming or not?'

Without ado we piled in, suddenly giggling. As the door shut, Martha started the engine and reversed gingerly. She eased off along the quay at the pace of a pony and trap. Outside the Harbour Inn were a line of cars, illuminated by its bright frontage. Among them was a black Volkswagen with a broken rear number plate. I scowled at it as we passed. 'At least the lads should be having a peaceful evening.'

When we passed the Doy Hotel the car park was empty. I nodded. 'So much for Alice's suspicions. Our eggers are boozing in the Inn, there's no doubt of that.'

Martha crawled up the hill to West Doy. When she rolled to a halt outside Big Cottage we got out and both gave her a hug. 'You're welcome to supper,' she offered. 'Just follow me in if you're hungry; but do as you please.'

When we were alone on the pavement Jess hugged me. 'Thank you, darling. It was a very special thing to have you with me this evening. I needed you very much.' She grinned. 'I'm ready for my goodnight kiss if you're not too tired to give me one.'

When Jessica Bull is in the mood, her kisses turn me to jelly. Our open mouths met with mobile readiness and our bodies pressed against each other for a long time. Several times we broke for breath then started again. When our facial muscles could take no more we simply clung together, content for time to pass or stand still as it chose.

At last she relaxed. 'I must go. Martha will be wondering what has happened.'

I hesitated. 'I don't want to see Wilfred now.'

'You don't need to. You get your beauty sleep. I have something to do alone.' She levelled our eyes. 'I think you know what.'

The night air was suddenly oppressive despite its cold. 'You're going to ask them to return–'

'My father's Bible? Yes, Tim, I am.'

'Because it's his or because it's a Bible?'

She put her hands to her slim waist and stood akimbo. 'Yes and yes. The two are inseparable: you will remember him well enough to know that.'

I glared. 'Are you about to start going to church too? Is religion going to come between us after all this time?'

She was angry now. 'Are you suggesting that emotion will change me as a person? If so you're dead wrong.' She took a deep breath. 'I hoped that you of all people might understand me. For the record, no, I am not about to turn into pew fodder. Nor am I going to claim to be a Christian or, worse, pretend to be one when I'm not. Nor will I start praying or preaching. I'm an atheist! But yes, I am going to change in one way. I am going to ask for the return of Daddy's Bible - and start reading it.'

'Why?'

'Why read it? To find out what it was that made him what he was. Five years ago I got rid of everything that was his. I knew none of it could ever bring him back - none of his possessions held anything of him locked secretly inside them. None of them held any part of him living - only dead and crumbling. But there is one through which I might still feel his love: the one that spoke to him and shaped all his life.'

'Does it have to be that Bible?'

'Possibly not. There's nothing emotional about all this. Perhaps any Bible would do; but this was the one he read.'

'Jess? For my sake, don't do this.'

'I'm sorry, Tim. Martha was right; I must give myself the freedom to change if I need to. You and Wilfred may not believe in change - that's your prerogatives. But I have to read the book that changed Daddy's life. And if it shaped him it may shape me too - or more likely, break me, for I'm sure I'm not willing to be shaped as any God up there would want me to be. It may shape me harshly, but I am prepared to take that risk.'

'Even the risk of - of finding your father's Jesus?'

'I won't find Jesus unnecessarily. I'm grown up, now! But I will take any risk I have to. And worst of all, even the risk of losing you.'

I should have been angry at that. I should have been livid. But there was no fire left in me. I was weary. 'What makes you think they will give you the Bible ?'

Jess smiled. 'You do ask such odd little questions sometimes, darling. Either of them would chop off their hands rather than keep it from me. Goodnight, Timothy. I'll see you in the morning.' She started up Big Cottage path, a slight figure in the gloaming.

'Eh? Aren't you working tomorrow?'

'No, silly! It's Summer Fair day. The office is closed. I can come and help you on the Reserve until the Fair starts.'

． ． ． ．

I walked up my own path and opened the door. To my surprise, the room was inhabited. Gazing at my little TV were both Bob and Jamie. On the table by them was a note which from its creases had been pushed through the letter trap.

I picked it up. It was signed Mike, and it read:

'Sorry, Mr. Warden - we're scrounging a sail out to see your tern islands early tomorrow, so we won't see you in the morning. Raw Head was useful; there were two poms flying past the headland and an icky and an LBJ in the lighthouse yard. Tell the old fellow next door I'll keep thinking about what he said. May you always have the right jizz!

'Cheers from Mike's Mob.'

Bemused by the note, I eyed the lads. 'What are you two doing here? I thought you'd be away writing up your work?'

They gave weary yawns. 'We've been waiting to tell you that tonight may be the night. Angus and William are both guarding the nest. The eggers are prowling in the marsh. They've made one abortive assault on the knoll already!'

24. - Night Raiders

Summer nights on Lifandoy are not pitch dark for long. Nevertheless, I was glad that the Reserve track was illuminated by a nearly full moon as I made my way up the valley.

The vantage point on the West Ridge was well moonlit and would not have been difficult to find, even without the rustling of the kite tethered to its appropriate rock. Although I had a head torch, I had no wish to advertise my presence at a distance. I called softly. As I expected, there was no reply. I supplied the answer myself.

'Angus will be down near the nest. At least, he'd better be.'

Resting from my exertions, I stared out across the inkiness of the valley, which was still in moon shadow. After half a minute, there appeared from nowhere a pinprick of light, which flickered on and off three times. From a little way to the right came a second flash, then further back, a third.

'The blackguards! They're all there. Have they left their car at Port Doy and walked up here to try and fool us? I'd better get down to Angus and William right away!'

I guessed that the likely place to find our sentinels would be on the heathery slope near the knoll, where Bob and Jamie had first found cover. I descended the hill rapidly. When I got near the spot, I cupped my hand over my mouth and emitted a modest imitation of the call of a tawny owl.

'HOOO. HU-HU-HU-HOOO. We don't get tawny owls in the valley without any trees, but the eggers won't know that, though Angus should. Hallo, there's a reply. He's awake and alert.'

Angus and William were so well hidden in the heather that even in the moonlight I managed to fall over William before I saw him.

'Oops! Sorry, constable - didn't see you in that camouflage jacket.'

'Think nothing of it, Tim. A policeman's lot is to be dropped upon.'

'Where's Angus? I hear you've been seeing some action?'

'Aye, Tim. They came up the marsh at dusk, as soon as Jamie left the valley and came up the ridge to Bob and me. They were heading straight for the knoll. I managed to get in their way just in time. I was hooded up, so they didn't see who I was. They headed back as soon as they glimpsed me. Meanwhile Jamie and Bob signalled to William with the kite and he came right away.'

William took up the tale. 'You had warned me that dusk and dawn were critical times, so I was already watching from Liffen Farm. When I saw where they were, I came across the valley towards the ridge and got in their way too. When they saw me they dropped right back down the marsh: they certainly aren't keen on company.'

I stared into the night. 'They're on their way up here again. I saw their torches on the Mud Path.'

'What now?' Angus was worried. 'Do we let them take the eggs, then collar them?'

'It would be tempting to use the eggs as bait.' I hesitated. 'But the clutch may be incomplete - and a laying bird is too easily disturbed. No, catching the eggers isn't worth losing our nesting snowies. We must keep them away from the nest altogether.'

'Difficult,' commented Angus. 'There are clouds rolling in and that moonlight will soon be gone. It *will* be dark then; one of them could easily reach the knoll unknown to us–'

'Or to them, for that matter.' I was thinking. 'Without flashing their torches around they will have little idea of the ground they're on.'

William agreed. 'A sense of direction won't count for much soon. And they could lose that path they're on at any time.'

I grinned in the dim light. 'Just what I was thinking. Now listen - here's what we will do.'

■　■　■　■

Angus was watching carefully. '*There* - I see a light. It's about half way up the Mud Path.'

'That's just where we want them. The path is at its worst there. Right, lads - torches on.'

The three of us lit up. Our torches were pointed at the ground between us. We waved them around enthusiastically for a few seconds.

'Now - *off*'

Overhead, the moon vanished behind the advancing cloud. All the silhouettes of the surrounding land disappeared, leaving the night featureless. William chuckled. 'The moon must have been listening. It was right on cue.'

'Excellent. Now - quietly. Angus, lead the way, please.'

Angus swung his large frame invisibly up and through the heather.

'Right - follow his rustles, William, and I'll follow.'

Angus chuckled. 'They'll be splashes if I take the wrong path.'

But Angus did not lose his way. Earlier he had been studying the lie of the land around the knoll carefully for just such an eventuality. As well as if he had been practicing blindfold, he led us almost silently across the valley.

The plan was simple. At intervals we would stop and show our torches briefly in the same positions as before. The last of the lights at the distant farmhouses had blinked off for the night. With the valley under black cloud even I could have lost my sense of direction in the marsh - especially on the Mud Path. If we could convince the intruders that *we* had not moved then they might mistakenly move down the fen to their right. The only result of that from their point of view would be disaster.

We paused and showed our torches directly in front of the knoll. Then we showed them below it on the slope below.

The faintest glow of a torch showed in the valley. 'They've taken the bait!'

Angus hissed back. 'There's only quagmire between them and the burn. If they hit a bad patch, it will take an Air-Sea Rescue chopper to rescue them.'

I agreed. 'They're in the swamp. But they're still heading to the east of us. There are two torches on now. No, it's all three. Time for us to move again.'

We showed our own lights at the bottom of the slope, just above the stream.

'They're still going. They must be nearly in the burn–'

'If not in it.' Angus laughed. 'Oops, there goes a torch. One is in; and there goes another…'

We watched happily to the sound of distant splashes as the torches lit their owners' struggles in the water. Remembering my own argument with the West Burn's willows, I watched with glee as our enemy floundered.

'They must have good waterproof torches! Not one has gone out.'

After a long interval, the three torches wavered up on the invisible far bank of the burn. They moved uncertainly around like patrolling insects. Then they began to rise swiftly as their owners made a firm retreat from the field of defeat.

'They've crossed the burn,' I said. 'They're walking up through the Ginger Farm fields.'

Angus and William gave a cheer. 'They've given up. We fooled them!'

I watched the bobbing lights fade into the night. 'I doubt they'll come back tonight. Can we go home to bed, do you think?'

'I'll stay here if you want me to,' said Angus.

William had a better idea. 'Let's head back to my patrol car. If they make another approach we should meet them on the path before we get to Liffen Farm. If they head for home we'll see them as we drive down the valley road.'

William's second guess was correct. A mile down the lane from Liffen Farm we passed three bedraggled, trudging figures. Soaked even without the rain which had begun to fall, they had not even the spirit to raise their heads as our headlights caught them.

'They've shot their bolt for the night,' said William. 'With luck they'll be on the ferry tomorrow.'

'We can't bank on that,' I answered. 'I suggest we all go home and get a good night's sleep. One of the lads can go up on the ridge in the morning.'

William grinned. 'Let's hope your kite is there waiting for him. I've enough to do without it breaking loose and drifting across to stampede Thomas Pandy's sheep.'

'Owls are enough for tonight.' I grimaced. 'I'll leave kites for tomorrow.'

∎ ∎ ∎ ∎

Relaxing in my own bed in Little Cottage, I was just dropping off to sleep when I became aware of a weird, rhythmic sucking sound. It did not take long to track it down to Angus in the spare bedroom.

'Oh, *no*. Here, Angus, shut your mouth.' I levered the massive jaw shut and silence fell. But the snoring racket soon recommenced. After five more trips to the spare room I gave up and settled for two tightly shut doors and a sheet over my head. But even then the regular gurgling penetrated my consciousness. When I finally slept, my dreaming was a replay of the previous night's nightmare, but with the additional horror of some lurking monster in the marsh which threatened Jessica and me with snore-like snarls and shone its torch-like eyes at us as it drew ever nearer.

■ ■ ■ ■

In the morning I emerged red-eyed, to find a fresh and eager-looking Angus chatting to Bob over two immense mugs of coffee.

'Do you have any idea how much coffee costs?'

'Payment for services rendered, O Master Acting Warden...' Angus leapt off his chair and grovelled at my feet. '...O Thou from whom we ask little in order to be the servants of Thine inestimable Self.'

'Yes, but why does that little have to come from my inestimably valuable coffee? Thieves and robbers - Woe! - I am beset by bands of thieves and robbers. Speaking of which, where's Jamie?'

'On duty hours ago,' exclaimed Bob. 'Don't you know what time it is?'

I glanced hurriedly at the clock. 'Minutes ago, more like! It's only five past eight, you scoundrel. I'd better go and get tidied up, though. Jessica is off work for Summer Fair day: she should be along soon. Unless she's still reading her Bible, that is.'

Bob double-took. 'Jessica reading *what?* What happened to our favourite female atheist?'

Angus was interested. 'What's wrong with reading the Bible?'

'What?' I glared. 'Don't tell me you belong to the God-squad too?'

He smiled oddly. He seemed about to say something when there came an imperious knock at the door.

I sniffed. 'That will be Alice, I suppose. Just wait while I shift her off the doorstep.' I threw the door open. 'All right, what is it this time - *oops* - er, *Sir Charles*. I wasn't actually expecting you–'

'Good grief, man, you like you've been awake all night!' The land agent shook his head. 'No, I shall not come in. I have to see the Earl before I catch the Manchester flight. I have brought a copy of my final report.'

He held out a thick buff envelope. Its address panel read: ESTATE OFFICE AND AUTHORISED PERSONS ONLY. Sir Charles gave me a stern look. 'I think you will find its comments interesting.' For a moment, what appeared half a scowl and half a smile flickered on his face. Then he was gone.

I shut the door slowly and shambled to the table. 'Get me a large coffee. I can't face a hearty breakfast.'

The others looked on sympathetically as I opened the envelope and slid out a sheaf of typescript and maps, all on creamy paper with a quality feel to it.

'Here. I think this - yes, *Conclusions and Recommendations*. When Keith Potts reads this I shall be out of a job…'

I ran my finger reluctantly down the page. *'High quality farming potential… high economic return… excellent possibilities… expansion of intensively cultivated zone…* Oh, here: it mentions the Reserve at last: *Useful income from tourism… Nevertheless, the character of some of the visitors attracted to the island verges on the unsavoury…* Oh, no!… *Negative factors countered by the magnificent wildlife…* That's better!… *deserves far better management…*What?… *areas where wildlife value have been grossly exaggerated or misunderstood… would be prepared to recommend major transfer of land use in some areas… place under a more knowledgeable supervision regime… KNOWLEDGEABLE?* That is it. Damn! That is absolutely it! We've LOST.'

Bob reached across and took the papers from my nerveless grasp. He glanced at them angrily. 'They can't do this.' He slammed them onto the table and turned to me. Neither of us had anything to say.

Angus picked them up curiously. 'There's another page. You've missed the final paragraph.'

We ignored him. I glowered into my coffee while Bob walked to the window and stared out. Slowly Angus's words as he read on began to penetrate.

'...a final decision required only the approval of the House Farm management. Unexpectedly, this was not forthcoming. I have to report that the proposed transfer has been declined by House Farm management; the reasons given appear frankly remarkable.'

Bob turned. 'Eh? what's he talking about?'

'...only possible recommendation is therefore that the Lifandoy Reserve BE RETAINED INTACT.'

Bob got there before I did. He snatched the paper and examined it as I tried to climb over his shoulder. He tossed it into the air and whooped as if he had put half the US Cavalry to flight.

'Yahaay! You did it. You've saved the Reserve! Tim, you're a genius. You won!'

'Have I? But how... I mean, Sir Charles wouldn't change his mind. He's joking.'

Bob retrieved the page and waved it under my eyes. 'Impressive joke.'

'I don't believe this. How can the House Farm management have declined the offer? Has Graham Fytts turned green, or has Wilfred gone mad?'

Angus laughed. 'Who cares?'

'I do. I don't trust my uncle.'

'What can he possibly do now?'

'I don't know,' I said firmly. 'But I shall find out right now.'

With the report in my hand I strode out of the cottage, onto the pavement and up Wilfred's path.

The front door was closed. I marched around through the garden and in through the back door. At the kitchen table Martha was sitting alone. She was listening to Wilfred's voice, which was faintly audible from the direction of the hall. Evidently he was on the telephone. The cast of Martha's features was, for her, unusually stern.

An identical copy of Sir Charles's report already lay on the table. I placed mine beside it with a flourish.

'Well? What's this all about?'

She motioned me gently to silence. I became aware that Wilfred was having a rather loud conversation on the telephone - and it was getting louder. He was having a hard time. We listened.

'I do know all that,' he said. 'With respect, you don't need to remind me of our case. I did as much to put it forward as you. Yes, I know... yes, but... if you would kindly let me...?'

A door shut abruptly in the hall. Wilfred's voice dropped to an unintelligible angry tone.

I looked at Martha. 'Sour grapes from Graham Fytts?'

'Graham is on the telephone, yes.' She was cautious.

'I've never heard Wilfred argue with him before.'

'This is the second time in two days. They were arguing about the sprays yesterday.'

'Sprays? They're an abomination. No spray is a good spray.'

Martha frowned. 'How well do you know what you're talking about, Timothy?'

I was scornful. 'Everyone knows that spraying poisons and spreading chemical fertilizers around the countryside is bad. It's obvious. It's plainly avoidable.'

'Is it? You know all the facts, do you?'

She eyed me until my gaze fell from hers. 'I'm not here to present Wilfred's point of view, nephew,' said Martha quietly. 'But I do believe he knows at least as much about the subject as you do, and is probably much more up to date. He has spent a lot of time just recently, reading about the safety of the sprays which the House Farm uses. You should respect him at least for that.'

'So I'm not only a blinkered green but an uneducated one to boot? All right: so what was the sprays argument about?'

She was surprised. 'You know very well. Wilfred told you here that he had banned spraying of weedkillers around field edges and along the Reserve boundary.'

'Did he mean all that? I thought he was just staging a diversion.'

'He meant it.'

I grimaced. 'And Graham Fytts...?'

'Objected.'

'I'll bet. I'll bet he didn't like Wilfred's decision. You have a gift for understatement, Martha.' Beyond the kitchen door Wilfred's protesting voice continued. 'Well, I suppose it's a start.' I gave a scowl of grudging condescension.

Martha scowled in her turn. 'There's no cause to be so high and mighty, nephew. If only you knew, your uncle has started a lot more than you think. He's too embarrassed to tell you, that's all.'

'What do you mean?'

'Well, I shouldn't - oh, I don't really understand it all.' Martha shook her head.

I eyed her warmly. 'Don't deprecate yourself, Martha. You're as sharp as he is, and more. Whatever he has been doing, I think you know a lot about it, and have had at least a finger in pushing it forward yourself.'

She nodded. 'Wilfred has been on the phone arranging things with all sorts of people over the last few days.'

'Arranging things? Why?'

'Wilfred has never had responsibility for taking decisions like this before. But I'm not just talking about field edges. While Graham Fytts is away, Wilfred has started a scientific revolution on the whole farm. Oh, he's not going to ban all chemicals tomorrow. The House Farm is not going organic. Even you must realize the world could never be fed without chemical farming at the moment, if ever. And he has started a review on whether oilseed, for example, is actually as profitable as they think, or whether they should grow more food crops. He is changing much - both chemicals and crops. And he is making a new start in ways you have probably never dreamt of.'

'A new start? On what?'

She sat back. 'He tells me it is called precision farming.'

'*Precision* farming? What does that involve?'

'Wilfred is arranging for an extremely detailed survey of the field soils and measurements of the crops they produce, to find which parts of the House Farm can be farmed with little or no fertilizer. He says the fields can be mapped to within one metre by satellite. A satellite can also pinpoint disease patches, so that whole fields need not be sprayed.'

'A satellite? Now I've heard everything. Surely that costs money?'

'Less than you think.'

'Chemical insecticides are evil,' I protested.

She frowned. 'As you very well know, *all* insecticides are made of chemicals. How could they be anything else? And insecticides are not unnatural, either. I've read that much for myself. The cabbages growing in your vegetable patch contain fifty natural insecticides. Mind you, I agree that too much use of sprays is evil.'

'I expect he's doing it because he thinks he will recoup his costs by saving the farm a fortune in wasted chemicals,' I said suspiciously.

'Of course. But he is also doing things that will make no money. Some of the silage will be left for hay, to help your corncrakes. And he has given instructions that autumn ploughing after harvest is to be stopped this year. He plans to drill next year's seed directly into the old stubble–'

'Leaving the small birds food all winter?' I frowned. 'If that works, it's a great idea–'

'And he has asked the environment officer from the island council to advise him on how to create a proper farm pond. And he has ordered hundreds of young hawthorns–'

'To replant some of the hedges Graham ripped out?' I stared. 'And he did all this off his own bat? *Why?*'

Martha looked puzzled. 'For some reason, not connected with the farm, Wilfred has spent a lot of time out and about this last week. He has been all over your Reserve. He says it has really changed his outlook, seeing all the wildlife in a way he hasn't done for many years. That is part of what he is presently trying to communicate to Graham Fytts…'

We listened to the distant voice, which had risen to new heights.

'So Graham doesn't like Wilfred's decision on the sprays?' I nodded.

'Well, no, he doesn't. But I told you, the sprays were yesterday's argument. Today's is worse.'

I raised an eyebrow. 'Fytts is angry because Wilfred's wider recommendations about extending the farm were overturned? That's hardly his fault.'

Martha gave me another of her appraising stares. 'No, Graham is not angry because Wilfred's recommendations were not accepted. He is angry because they *were.*'

25. - Surprises

I was still staring at Martha when the door opened and Wilfred entered the kitchen. When he saw me, he gave me a look I hope I shall remember all my life. It was a bleak one; but it was not a regretful one. It was that of a chap who has chosen his course in life and has paid a very high price for the freedom to live it.

His voice was hoarse. 'I thought you would appear soon.'

Even in victory I was not disposed to be kind. However, after his recent grilling it seemed over the top to add another dent to Wilfred's armour immediately. I chose a lesser irritation first. 'Martha tells me you still insist using some chemicals.'

Wilfred gazed at me. 'I do insist that the Farm's work is important. If you don't accept that it has *any* value, we will have to differ. I respect your principles - I certainly hold to mine; but I do see the sense in yours also - and I think I have changed enough to show I have pragmatism. I can do no more to save the wildlife from damage for now.'

'Well, you should!' Still unwilling to offer him any comfort, I snapped back. 'It needs defending. Someone has to make it plain that there is a limit that should not be crossed.'

Wilfred sat down heavily on a kitchen chair. 'As it happens, nephew, that is exactly what I said myself.'

■   ■   ■   ■

Jessica stared. 'Wilfred has been dismissed as deputy manager? Do you mean he's out of a job?'

'Not entirely. But being demoted to looking after the shepherds is a big fall from managing the whole estate farm.' I shook my head. 'Fytts hasn't spared him. I still can't understand what made Wilfred do it.'

Jessica turned her face away and stared up the valley. We were sitting in our favourite trysting-place, on the grass near the smooth-flowing West Burn. I gazed up the valley too: it was the only view not dominated by the painfully scarlet expanse of Mrs. Bull's fence behind us. 'Do what?'

I went on. 'He's always preaching his thing on denying oneself and taking up one's cross. But I never expected him to live it. He's allowed himself to be crucified!'

'Oh, the poor man. But what exactly did he do?'

'He changed all his recommendations. He told Sir Charles he didn't want to plough up the Reserve.'

What? Timothy, why not?'

'He has spent a lot of time looking round the Reserve recently. He had the cheek to say it was that, rather than my unconstructive comments, which had seriously changed his outlook.'

Jessica was amused. 'What about you? Has it changed your view of Wilfred?'

'What?'

'Haven't you a lot to thank him for?'

I snorted. 'He's still up to something. My dear Uncle Wilfred is being more devious now, not less. I can't imagine what else he can be up to, but I still wouldn't trust him further than the length of his sledgehammer; or at the end of it, for that matter. I feel sorry for him; but I don't trust him a step.'

'Oh, well; that's up to you.' Jess lay comfortably on the grass. 'Isn't it a glorious day? That rain last night cleared the air wonderfully. It will be hot soon.'

'Just what the Summer Fair needs.'

'Will you get to the Fair? Who's on sentinel duty?'

'I shall have to get to it. Alice will crucify me if the Cabal don't get their pesky little ice creams. No, Bob is at the ternery and will go up to relieve Jamie on the ridge at noon. I'll take over this evening in case things get exciting again. And Angus is kite-watching from the Pandys' cottage until William can take over there.'

'But you will still have your Reserve visitors to look after?'

'There won't be any new ones until the ferry arrives. This is my morning off. I've only one visitor to look after at the moment.'

'Me?'

'In one, darling.'

We lay back in each other's arms for a little while. Then I began to get twitchy.

'What's the matter, Timothy?'

'That fence gives me the creeps. For one thing Alice will be off school for Fair day, won't she? The whole Cabal could be peeping through the cracks at us.'

'Do you want to walk up the Burn a little way?'

'I'll find a quiet place to show you some orchids.'

'As long as that's all you show me...'

We made our way along the stream, threading our way along the driest paths and jumping marsh ditches with much laughter when there was no alternative. Most of the marsh was at its driest for the year, or else our progress would have been impossible. Soon we reached the pool where I had rebuked Wilfred for spear fishing. We passed the stepping stones and came to the edge of a large, much deeper pool, one of the broadest in the valley. A little way around its edge was one of the rare dry islands in the fen, a rocky hummock the area of a small house, shielded by curtains of royal fern and reed and fringed with miniature lollipop forests of marsh orchids.

After admiring the flowers we found a grassy slope rising from the pool and lay down, luxuriating in the now hot sunshine. We held hands. Then we kissed. Gradually we cuddled closer, and closer.

Jessica's voice was soft and hypnotic in my ear. 'I love you, Tim... I love you, Timothy Corn... I love you... *mmmm*... that tickles.' I nuzzled her neck in turn, sliding my lips along her smooth skin until she could stand it no longer. My lips reached her ear. After a while, my right hand developed a mind of its own. She chuckled. 'That tickles. Ohhh!... just there... that'll do... that's enough. Oooh... that's enough, now... no further, Tim... no further, please... *Hey!*'

She sat up, pushing me aside with a warning grin. 'That's enough, lover boy. If you go any further I shall give you a shove and roll you right off this slope into the water. And don't think I wouldn't: I'd just love to see your face when I did it–'

'And I know you would. All right. Actually, I would have stopped by myself. From weariness, not least.'

Suitably and unsurprisingly rebuffed, I lay back with Jess snuggled at my side. The hot sun beat down, dazing me; I was not unthankful for the chance to absorb its energy. My late night had left me with a thick head and I closed my eyes to ease the throbbing sensation. Without meaning to, I drifted into semi-sleep as the throbbing continued into a repeat of my previous night's dream. The memory of Angus's rhythmic snoring returned to disturb me as the pulse changed and grew in my imagination to a reptilian, gurgling wheeze.

Abruptly the pulse ceased. I opened my eyes slightly, trying to decide whether I was really awake. Jessica, on her side by me, was comatose. Slowly, it occurred to me that the sound I had been hearing had terminated in the real world as well as in my dream. I lifted my head and peered toward the water, from which direction I thought the noise had come.

For a few seconds there was merely the deep, smooth pool. Then I became aware of small waves lapping at the foot of the bank below us. A ring of ripples spread from nowhere as something large stirred beneath the surface. The something broke surface beyond and below our feet.

I decided I must be dreaming and wished hard that I could wake up. Tales from my island childhood came back unpleasantly, tales of Celtic legends of water-horses and bog creatures that were reputed to eat naughty boys. I stared in fascination, then horror, as the thing emerged. It was globular and huge, festooned with weed and coated with slime which fell from it in splashing gobbets.

I gave myself a sharp pinch. The pinch was painful, but I scarcely noticed. The marsh monster of my nightmare bad arrived, coming to haunt me with boyhood terrors and worse.

I screamed. 'No! *Aaah!*'

The thing in the pool turned its head. Instead of a pair of eyes it had one huge, glassy orb; in its grey depths there stirred a horrible red mass.

I gave it all I had. *'AAAAAH!'* The yell must have been one of the loudest on Lifandoy since the eruption of Jack Dooley's famous boiler.

I realized that Jessica had woken and had rolled away from me around the grassy mound. Doubtless she was already in swift retreat. I scrabbled up round the other side of the hummock. But my wits were addled and I slipped on the steep slope. I had all the co-ordination of an intoxicated crab. I whimpered.

Then from behind me I heard a wild cry. It was Jessica's voice. She had not escaped. She remained where she had halted, frozen on the bank by the water. I turned to look, my manhood battling with my dribbling terror.

At the sight which met me my heart thudded. The thing from the pool was confronting Jessica. She was emitting pitiful mewing noises, obviously hysterical. I braced myself for a lunge to save her.

I started to slither down again. Dismay was replaced by fury. My self-resolve had just about raised me to my most heroic, or more likely lunatic, frame of mind when I noticed something odd.

Jessica's face, turned towards mine, was nearly as dark and wrinkled as a dried plum. This seemed apt to her terror. What were not so apt were the sounds which she was making. She was in the grip of a profound emotion. But it was not fear. Although noisy, her cries were not despairing. In fact, they had grown to what was now a gale of uncontrollable laughter.

She levelled a shaking finger. 'Timothy? HEE-hee - oh, have you ever seen the like? Oooh! *Heee!'*

I looked at the thing from the lake. Its arms were raised. But it ignored me. Its attentions lay elsewhere. To my complete discomfiture, I saw that the slimy creature was urgently and efficiently unscrewing its head. With an audible pop, the head bounced off. From beneath it there emerged into fresh air something which was strawberry-red, wet and gasping. It was a human face.

Jessica roared. 'Ha - ha - HEEE! Oh, Wilfred! What on *earth* are you doing exploring the West Burn in a deep-sea *diving* suit?'

The face of my un-esteemed uncle began to assume a more accustomed hue. As his lungs drew in slightly less huge draughts of air he attempted a reply.

'Second-hand from Jack Dooley - *hooo!* - always fancied trying it - *hooo!* - air compressor stopped pumping - had to get helmet off - *hooo!* - sorry to disturb you...'

It was now my turn to gurgle. *'Wilfred?* You - you - *you...'* For once I was lost for insults. Jessica offered comment for me.

'Why are you deep-sea diving on the Reserve, Wilfred?' she inquired curiously.

A look of anxiety came over his face. Uncle Wilfred glanced about him, taking stock of his whereabouts. Then he snatched up his helmet and waddled hurriedly along the shore trailing his air hoses until he reached the tail of the pool. Where the stream flowed out of the pool he waded in. Just past the middle of the burn, he turned and smiled graciously across at us.

'This side of the burn is House Farm property, my dear. We have no specific ban on deep-sea diving on the farm. Nor,' he added ingenuously, 'on spear-fishing, either.'

I stood up and gave Wilfred a gaze which should have boiled him alive in the stream.

'Dearest Uncle, I don't know what you are up to, but you have all the innocence of a stationary bulldozer. You may not be legally *in flagrante delicto,* but your potential for crime is so great that unless you sink back into the depths at once I shall trespass on House Farm property to personally extract your secrets from you by force!'

Wilfred blanched. Then, defiantly, he grinned. 'In that case I should have to–'

'Wilfred!' I shouted, 'Get back to your sheep!'

There was a pungent silence. Then Jessica spoke. 'Tim,' she said, 'that was below the belt.'

I grimaced. 'I know. Sorry, Wilfred.' My uncle's face was pale. I stared at him uneasily. 'So why did you do it, after all?'

He knew I was not referring to his pond exploits. 'I understood you were accusing me of being unable to change.'

'So?'

'The accusation did not trouble me: but the possibility did.'

'Oh yeah?'

He nodded. 'In short I decided I was at least half wrong. I stand by the right, but I apologize for the wrong. And I have taken steps to cancel its effect.'

'Wilfred? Are you *real?'*

'The fact I am not all I could be neither diminishes nor increases what I am.'

I frowned down at the water flowing between Wilfred's legs. For reasons I didn't even want to think about I was finding it hard not to admire the man.

When I lifted my head he was not in the stream. Along the far side of the pool he was making his slow way in his heavy diver's boots, a solid, gnome-like figure following a path through life which was his, and very much his, alone.

· · · ·

As Wilfred retreated to his base on the House Farm side of the pool, Jessica glanced at her watch. 'Twelve o'clock? How could we have been asleep that long? I must get back.'

We kept up a sharp pace and soon reached the Bulls' cottage. Jess headed inside to change into a smart dress while I ambled past the chapel and up the street. When I reached Little Cottage I paused on the pavement to collect my wallet from the glove compartment of my car. I had my head in the vehicle when Martha's voice spoke acerbically behind me.

'You're surely not going to drive to the Summer Fair, Timothy Corn?'

I emerged smiling. 'No, Martha. I'm no fool. Are you walking down to the field now? Are you going alone?'

'I've done enough sewing for today. But Wilfred is busy: he may not get to the Fair at all.'

'I know he's busy. Did he tell you he was going swimming in the West Burn?'

'In that old diving suit?' Martha frowned. 'I told him he was too old for such things. It took him an hour to get into the rusty old thing. The Fair will probably be over by the time he's out of it, I should imagine.'

'But isn't his choir supposed to be performing at the Fair?'

'They'll have to do it alone. He wants to finish an urgent job for Graham Fytts.'

'Really? In a diving suit? What on earth can it be? And if you don't mind me saying so, I wouldn't have thought he owes Fytts any favours now.'

'My very words. But my husband wouldn't see it that way. Wilfred is firm on keeping to his responsibilities.'

'Does he think he can still redeem himself with Fytts, Martha?'

'It's too late for that, I'm sure. I think he just wants to show Graham how good a deputy he is losing - to rub in the fact that he has been hard done by.'

'But *what* is Wilfred doing?'

'I think that's his business. But I can tell you it has been occupying his every spare minute out of doors since he heard of Graham's accident.'

The sound of approaching steps interrupted Martha. 'Hello, Jessica dear. Shall we walk down to the Fair field together?'

The lane was empty of traffic. We ambled down it, enjoying the silence and the sense of holiday. Martha glanced at Jessica. 'You have rings around your eyes, dear. Are you feeling all right?'

'I *was* tired. But I had a lovely sleep this morning.'

'Have you been staying up late?'

Jess glanced at me. 'You won't be surprised to know I've been reading Daddy's Bible.'

Her eyes warned me against sarcasm. I thought of a question. 'Is it reminding you of things you learnt from him?'

'Unfortunately, yes.'

'Unfortunately?' Jess gazed across the fields. 'Daddy was very different from me. He changed a lot when he suddenly became religious. That was when I was quite young, you know.'

'Different?'

'I'd forgotten just how unusual a person he was. Things that were just interesting history to a lot of people became life itself to him. But it wasn't just that. I remember how uncomfortable he used to make me feel.'

'That sounds rather cruel.'

'Oh, he never meant to be cruel. He was a very sensitive person, always going out of his way to make people feel at ease. He would never have dreamt of embarrassing someone on purpose. But he was - well, different. Mummy and I always went to church, but it wasn't the same for us as for Daddy. Not that he shut us out: he wasn't unfriendly or unloving; he was the best father I can imagine a teenage girl having. He wasn't like Mummy - not a creature of habit like she is. Oh, the way she keeps painting that fence of hers! But Daddy and I would do the maddest things together, at only a moment's warning.

'But if you didn't see eye to eye with him about religion, if you didn't share his values, if you didn't put Jesus at the centre of everything, then there was always an inner part of his life that was closed to you. A beautiful part, I suppose. I never knew anyone who seemed to find so much fun and fulfilment just out of my sight. It was as if he waited until you had gone out of the room before telling his best joke. You couldn't feel angry, but you always felt how sad he was that he couldn't share his best times with you. Uncomfortable is the wrong word. I should have said disappointed.'

'You sound as though he disturbed you,' said Martha.

'The way he lived disturbed me. I could have ignored the fact that he was different if it only extended to Sundays. But it didn't. His Bible never had a day off. He chose to take on strong principles, and he had them all week.'

I laughed. 'Here's the pot calling the kettle black!'

Jessica shook her head vigorously. 'No. My principles are strong too, but that's merely because I have the opinion they should be. For instance, if I have children I shall pass onto them a moral code, but when they grow up I suspect they may ignore it. One day *I* might ignore it. What Daddy passed onto me was a living code, if that's not a paradox. I couldn't move him by argument any more than I could alter the way the tide comes in.'

I scowled. 'Christianity is only a moral code with superstition added.'

'No, I disagree. Daddy was in love with Jesus Christ. It was that strong a pull to him.'

'OK, so Christ was an impressive person. What about other religions? Aren't their leaders equally impressive?'

'Not in the same way.'

Martha was surprised. 'You sound sure of that. I mean, I agree but I'm surprised to hear you saying it.'

Jess gave a wry smile. 'I should know. I've studied most of them.'

'What?' Now it was my turn to raise my eyebrows. 'When?'

'I grew so angry with Daddy that I started to study them seriously just to spite him.'

'And you're now an expert on Mohammed and Buddha?'

'No, but I can appreciate why they were different. They believed they were signposts, pointing to their own ideas of God - or, in Buddha's case, the lack of one.'

'Which Jesus didn't?' asked Martha.

'His idea of God included Himself He pointed to God; but He put Himself at the end of His own finger.'

I guffawed. 'Sounds painful.'

'And different,' smiled Martha.

Jessica nodded. 'What interests me most in the gospels is peoples' reactions to Him. On my reading of it, most people followed Jesus at first out of surprise! I was reading in Daddy's Bible last night the part where it says that the crowds were amazed at his teaching, because he taught them as someone who had *authority*, not like their ordinary teachers.'

Jessica paused. Martha nodded again. 'But, of course,' said Martha, 'when the surprise wore off they expected Him to lead them to revolution like all the other messiahs of the time did. When He appeared to be stepping into a volcano they changed their minds and decided to push Him in instead. They never realized that they were all part of His plans. When we get it wrong it doesn't wreck Jesus's plans - in fact, it may lead us into being part of them.'

Jess grinned. 'So you say, Martha. But I'm certainly not a penitent, or remotely on the road to being one. All I agree on is that Jesus is unique - just as Daddy was different. Christ is the one rock that the tide of history has never moved. I don't love Him for that; quite the opposite, in fact. He reminds me of the South Rock, and I hate that more than anything else in the sea.'

I glanced at her. 'But at least you can look at it now?'

'I can.' She returned the glance, her eyes bright but not untroubled. 'I have changed a little. Not as much as Wilfred, but more than you, Tim.'

'Me? I haven't changed at all.'

'I know. But I have, a little. And it is *possible* I might change further, especially if I–'

'Go on reading?' I muttered. 'So you will go on reading the Bible?'

'I will.'

'Then you'll do it when you're on your own.'

▪ ▪ ▪ ▪

The Lifandoy Summer Fair is held on a site by the Doy Burn just opposite Doytown churchyard. Always a pretty event, it has become in recent years something of a showpiece - and, most importantly, a money sink for the many holidaymakers on the island. The majority of the island's population nevertheless puts in an appearance, although most have the sense to avoid the always overcrowded car park with its maelstrom of the massed vehicles of the tourists.

The ladies and I strolled down the valley road. We were just approaching the entrance to the Fair site when there was a chugging sound in the lane. I stared.

'I take it back. There is one islander foolish enough to drive to the Summer Fair.'

The oncoming vehicle showed a strange silhouette. But a familiar, moon-like face peered through the oddly shaped windscreen.

Jessica laughed. 'Isn't it incredible? Where did Jack get that car? What sort is it?'

I frowned. 'I don't know. It's not any make I can recognize. I think he built it up with scraps from his yard. It has the body of an old Austin, the back end of a bus, and the driver's cab - well, it looks more like the wheelhouse of an old fishing boat than anything else...'

Jack Dooley gave us a mournful smile as he turned off the lane through a field gateway in a tall hedge. We followed onto a field chock-a-block with people, stalls, marquees and off-island cars.

We scanned the crowd for known faces. 'There's Alice. I'll avoid her - she'll find me soon enough,' I said. 'There's the Earl and his wife. There's Sergeant Farquhar, standing by the school bus talking to the driver. And isn't that...?'

My voice tailed away. Walking towards us with smiles on their faces were three large men in black. Behind them, beside a hedge in the field corner, was parked a black Volkswagen. The first of the three, a head taller than me, gazed down warmly at me and stuck a hand to one side.

'Hello, Mrs. Corn.' He clasped my aunt's worn hand in his own huge one. His voice had an East Coast American accent and was worryingly familiar. 'You will be glad to hear we can let you have your husband back at last.'

227

Martha returned the smile. She turned to me. 'Timothy, I don't think you have been introduced. This is Mr. Wayne, a visitor whom the Estate Office asked Wilfred to look after. He tells me that he and his friends are military historians, looking for a crashed German wartime bomber.'

26. - The Real Raid

Jessica and I froze. 'You're what?' I gasped to Wayne. 'But weren't you in the fen yesterday...?'

Martha continued. 'My nephew Timothy is a warden on the Lifandoy Reserve. He works day and night on behalf of our wildlife.'

Wayne's face assumed a dusky hue. 'Yes, I am aware of your nephew's - ah - diligence.' He fixed me with a peculiar stare. Returning it, I became aware that his face had a fresh complexion, as of one recently well scrubbed. Wayne turned to Martha.

'However,' he said, 'I am aware that I owe *you* an apology. Until now, with everyone but Wilfred and a couple of others we have had to indulge in a small deception. My associates and I are not historians. We are actually serving officers - I am Colonel Wayne - from the US Air Force, Military Intelligence branch.'

I gave a choked yelp. Colonel Wayne ignored me and went on. 'To shorten a long account,' he said, 'the wreckage we are looking for is from a much more recent air accident. It wasn't a whole plane that came down, actually, just a small part of the cargo - a part that is of much more than academic interest to us! It is in fact top secret - and so, until today, was the news that we had lost it.'

Martha was bewildered. 'Why are you telling us now?'

Wayne's face fell. 'We can't find it; or more precisely, since it is in two parts, we can't find even half of it. We had zero detection in the supposed drop zone.'

'Pardon?'

'It didn't fall where we thought. Our information is wrong - we shall have to widen the search area considerably.'

'Do you think you will ever find it?'

'I can't tell. But since we've found nothing we can stop worrying that an unfriendly party might get to it first. Our best film detectors have drawn a blank and our radiation sensors haven't even given a signal as loud as a chickadee.'

I laughed, hysterically. 'I think you mean a dickey-bird.'

'Do I?' The Colonel wrinkled his brow. 'Anyway, as of tomorrow there will be a public appeal for help from everyone on Lifandoy.'

Jessica was interested. 'Are you going to be on island radio?'

'Not me. I'm not in charge any more.'

'Will they be sending more search parties?'

'I can't say. But the search must go on. I think they plan to use helicopters. For all your sakes, I hope they don't send the army in. Anyway, have a nice day…'

Wayne and his men walked away. At the same moment Martha spotted a distant friend and, excusing herself sweetly, followed suit. Jess and I were left to our own devices - until our peace was interrupted by a horrible sound.

From behind us came an unmistakable titter. We turned, to find the entire Cabal watching us. Led by Alice, they burst into shrieks of ridiculous laughter. Alice had an expression of unmitigated scorn.

'So you've found out at last? Carmen told us last night that they weren't crooks, but we thought we'd leave you to sweat. What are you going to tell that sexy young copper?'

I gave Alice a scowl that made her step back a full pace. 'Watch it, Alice. Here, take three quid. Buy your ices and hand over the tape, pronto. Then scram!'

Alice smiled. 'Three pounds? There are nine of us. You'll have to do better than that.'

'There was nothing in the contract about how cheap the ice creams could be. You'll get the cheapest on sale at the Fair.'

She smiled again. 'Wouldn't dream otherwise, dear boy. There: see for yourself.' She levelled a finger at a large tent nearby. We read the signboard outside. It said:

LIFANDOY SUMMER FAIR - EXCLUSIVE ICE CREAM
SELECTION.
NO OTHERS SOLD TODAY! ONLY TWO POUNDS EACH.
DON'T MISS ONE!

'*Two pounds?*' I rounded on the Cabal. 'You've set me up! Now, see here…!'

Alice's face was so hard it could have been carved. 'Eighteen pounds.' Then she stepped close to whisper. 'And don't forget the picture.'

I exploded. 'Get knotted! Three quid or nothing.'

At the back of the Cabal, leggy Patricia held up a small music player. 'Alice? I do believe that's Sergeant Farquhar over there. Ailsa could hand the player straight to her Dad now…'

Alice held up her hand. 'Well? Bankruptcy or prison?' She met me eye to eye.

'You wouldn't dare.'

'We would. After all, you haven't even the defence that you were after criminals, any more.'

I moaned and looked round for support. The only solid objects near were parked cars, the nearest being Jack Dooley's amazing vehicle. I leant on it heavily. Jack, who was standing by, looked askance at me.

'I can't understand it,' I said. 'Keith Potts was so certain the eggers were on the island. If Wayne and his friends at the Doy Hotel are innocent, then…?'

My ruminations were interrupted by a distant shout. We turned. Running across the field from the gate were the large forms of Jamie and Angus.

'Tim,' Jamie gasped, 'Thank goodness we've found you. Where's Sergeant Farquhar? William has rung to say Bob has just signalled with the kite. They're having another go.'

'They?' I stared. 'Who are *they?*'

Jamie was astounded. 'The three eggers, of course!'

I laughed gently. 'Look over there.' I directed his gaze toward Colonel Wayne and his men, standing near their car.

The lads' eyes nearly came out on stalks. Wayne noticed us and strolled over. 'Is there a problem?' he drawled friendlily. 'Can I help?'

I grinned. 'Jamie and Angus, here, thought you were on the Reserve. They're obviously mistaken.'

Wayne scratched his head. 'It's a funny thing,' he said, 'there *were* three other chaps in a car just like ours. But they were rough-looking characters, up to no good in my opinion. The biggest of the three came across one of our film detectors in the marsh. He nearly went psycho - if we hadn't been around he could have walked off with it.'

Jamie was on hot coals. 'That's them! The big one is armed. And William says Bob is about to tackle them on his own!'

My head was spinning. 'Came across one of your detectors? What do they look like?'

'They're disguised as large white eggs,' offered the colonel. 'We have two still to recover. But we know where they are.' He gave me a sideways glance. 'Anyone who held on to one would have the US Air Force breathing down his neck.'

'Ah - I think those two are about to be the subject of an armed robbery.'

■　■　■　■

Things moved fast from there. The fastest was Colonel Wayne's deceivingly bulky form. In seconds he was at his car, talking urgently into a transmitter of a sophistication that made Wilfred's car-phone seem like an Aldis lamp.

The next centre of action was the quartet of Jamie, Angus, Jessica and me. It was plain that we needed transport and we all came to the same conclusion. Only one nearby islander's vehicle still had its owner with his keys to hand. Jack Dooley, to his wonder, found himself thundering across the field with Jamie, Jessica and myself squashed into his cramped cab, and Angus clinging outside on the running boards bellowing encouragement.

A brief stop near the school bus where he was talking to the driver sufficed to add the ponderous and astonished form of Sergeant Farquhar to our other running board; then we were in the lane and screeching through the nearly deserted streets of Doytown, scattering solitary urchins and dogs. As the valley road began to roll by, I explained the long tale to Jack. He began to get excited and by the time we had passed the House Farm his Irish temperament had reached boiling point.

By Liffen Farm he was so fey that he failed entirely to stop as I directed. 'Over there, Jack. Yes, that's the track. Park on the track. No, don't drive down it... NOT down it... the burn bridge won't... stop, please... *stop,* Jack... Look out! *STOP!'*

Remarkably, the stream bridge survived. What did not escape was the stile. It flew to pieces as Jack's juggernaut crashed through it and thundered to a halt on the Reserve marsh. In a cloud of debris we tumbled out, shaken but stirred.

The kite was flying high. Even from this side of the marsh we had no need of binoculars to read the situation. The real raiders had struck with sudden and successful force. All three were running across the valley from the Mud Path toward us. Bob was in pursuit, whilst in the path of the escaping eggers stood only the figure of young William.

It was fortunate for our young constable that we appeared when we did. The eggers were as stunned as all of us by the avalanche that had brought Jack's car onto the scene. In alarm they halted, then changed their tactics. They split; the biggest and one of the smaller crooks moved separately to escape down the valley, while the third turned on his heels back toward the West Ridge.

Bob tackled the latter, who was more or less his own size. We heard Bob's angry challenge across the marsh. But his opponent was a wily match for my assistant. Bob's attempt at feeling the egger's collar resulted in him being toppled with a yell, the result of a sharp kick to the knee. The fugitive raced away, heading for the gap in the West Ridge that led to the coast.

William chased the other of the smaller eggers. This one was a rapid runner. Noting that our party had set off into the marsh to help Bob, he doubled round through the bushes. Jessica and I turned back as we realized he could well get unseen to the shattered stile and the lane behind us.

In the distance we could see that Bob's attacker was already near the foot of the West Ridge, pursued hotly by Angus and Jamie and the limping Bob. His start was substantial and it appeared that if he was fit he had the best chance of escape. Only the long crest of the West Ridge now lay between him and the chance of vanishing into the countryside.

The silhouette of the ridge was a smooth line. Then it seemed to change. All at once, bumps started to appear against the skyline, bumps that became heads. A dull noise came from the ridge crest, as the heads rose up with bodies and running legs attached. Like the long-awaited cavalry in some ancient Western, a whole line of strange figures came galloping over the hill.

I paused to focus on them in wonder, then in recognition. 'It's Mike,' I shouted. 'The twitchers are still here...!'

Down the face of the ridge streamed Mike's army. Still carrying their flailing pairs of binoculars, telescopes and tripods they ran as if a whole flock of yew sparrows had just alighted upon their dismayed quarry's shoulders.

The twitchers were the hammer. Jamie and Angus were the anvil. Into a deep bog hole between them there fell the astonished egger. Shortly he was buried under shouting and tripod-wielding figures. Shortly, Sergeant Farquhar panted into their midst to make the arrest official.

Jessica and I had a different prey in mind. The second egger had found a way around William, through the bushes. Now he made a run across the last open space to the stile. Suddenly, Jack Dooley stood before him. The old engineer was wielding a lump of stile as a makeshift shillelagh. The egger ignored Jack's warning and snatched up another shard of timber. They exchanged blows. Both suffered and, to our dismay, Jack reeled back, shouting in Irish.

Jessica was there before me. She approached the egger as he clambered through the wreckage. Red-faced, he swung at her. I gave a cry of wrath, racing forward. But I was not needed. As Jess dodged, she gave a shrill yell of command.

All at once, a flood of small figures sprang up around the egger. In the distance, the bulky form of the school bus in the lane by the farm explained the stampede; the crook gaped as he was confronted with a mob of small girls, Alice and the Cabal and many more besides. They were an appalling sight as they all waved rackets and bats, screeching at him.

He had no chance. Apart from the girls, he had also to cope with the avenging form of William; and with two new assailants, Thomas Pandy's dogs, which followed the posse and leapt baying upon him.

The man yelled in fury. Shaking off the dogs, he charged at the girls: but at another sharp word from Jessica the group parted like a curtain before his charge. He stumbled in surprise. Then two well-placed hockey sticks brought about his complete downfall. He fell headlong. All that could be seen thereafter was a dark heap writhing beneath two hounds and a flailing forest of sticks and bats.

· · · ·

I was probably the first to realize that our forces had been badly divided. Some way down the West Burn from the stile a huge figure arose from some reeds. The biggest egger had chosen a slow but well concealed route. Now he made his way straight for the stream. A binocular case around his neck, carefully held in one hand, showed that his escape had a special purpose to it.

William, who had just stood up, saw where I was heading. 'Don't, Tim,' he shouted. 'You mustn't take the risk with *him.*'

I slowed obediently. As if in answer, the big egger reached into his jacket pocket. In his hand there appeared what was unmistakably a small revolver.

He pointed it at me. *'Git away!'* he shouted, waving his arm in case his meaning could possibly be unclear. To add to his defiance, he reached into his binocular case and produced two large white eggs, clutched in one huge hand. Unwilling to retreat, I dropped behind a bush to see what he would do. There was a distant roaring sound in my ears, which seemed to be getting louder.

He continued to the burn. He was only a few strides from the water and the empty fields beyond it when something unexpected happened.

The burn at this point was fringed with tall vegetation. Out of the greenery there stepped a weird figure. It was Uncle Wilfred, still wearing his diver's suit, minus helmet. Plodding into the path of the bear-like egger, he held up a hand, an amphibious caricature of a traffic policeman.

The crook stopped, dumbfounded. There was a sudden silence. As if it were a slow motion film, I saw the hand of the egger come up. He levelled his weapon. The gun kicked back with a small flash and a loud bang.

Wilfred recoiled as if hit by a rock. He fell, his arms flying up. Inside me, a light seemed to go out. In my inner darkness, I went berserk.

This time I was not about to flee from my monster. Long ago I had been good at rugby: dodging through the bushes I got within range of the egger and launched into a classic tackle. On the sports field I would have flattened most opponents. But the egger merely swayed as I hit his thighs, then slid down onto me, crushing me into the mud.

He stared down, then brought his gun hand round, reversing the pistol to make the barrel a club. There was a roaring sound in my ears and something shadowed my vision. 'I hate wardens. First I crush your eggs,' he said pleasantly, 'then your skull. Say your prayers.'

'Say yours,' I replied. 'But don't forget to lift your eyes to heaven.'

He sniggered. Then he looked puzzled. Finally he looked up and saw what I had seen.

Above us, descending so fast it might nearly have been in free-fall, was the source of the growing roar. It was the biggest helicopter I had ever seen. Bristling with weapons, it seemed as big as an airship.

The egger, half crazed, reversed his weapon, pointed it, and fired. The bullet ricocheted harmlessly from the chopper's armour. The crook might as usefully have thrown a tomato.

I had never seen anyone fire a revolver at the US Air Force; it did not strike me as a wise thing to do. On this occasion it was the equivalent of starting a war. In moments, hatches all over the craft had opened, ropes had snaked down, and something like a whole platoon of uniformed bodies was descending so fast their owners might almost as well have jumped. Within seconds, both my antagonist and I had been crushed under a mountain of the military.

Several large hands grabbed me and dragged me out of the *mêlée*. I was dumped gently on the bank of the stream. As I rolled over, I turned my head. On the opposite bank three solid figures in black were standing dead still, each with a sleek-looking firearm levelled with both hands, marksman-style. The centre one was Colonel Wayne: he nodded to me.

'You needn't have worried. He'd have had three bullets through his arm if that pistol had gone any lower. Sorry we weren't a trifle sooner. Quick - how's your uncle?'

Still too crushed to stand, I crawled over to Wilfred. He lay on his back, his face pale. I closed my eyes and, for the first time since I was a kid, said a prayer.

When I opened my eyes Wilfred was looking up at me. He was grinning. 'These suits have so much metal in them, they make one feel like a walking tank,' he said. 'But armour plating does come in useful now and then.'

We stood up slowly together, clinging to each other for support as we looked around. Most of the Americans were re-embarking on the now landed chopper, while a small detachment was watching their captive. The battered form of the egger lay pulverized in the grass as if a tank had rolled over him. As we eyed him wordlessly, Bob and Jamie came hastening up. Bob bent and retrieved from the grass two large, white eggs.

'I'd better get these back to the nest on the knoll right away,' he said.

I took them gently from him and inspected them carefully. 'I have a better suggestion.'

'What?'

'I think we'd better return them to the US Air Force.'

'Return them to *whom?*'

We turned at a splashing sound. Colonel Wayne was wading across the burn. He smiled. 'Easier in daylight, I think.'

As I handed the eggs to Colonel Wayne, Bob gaped. 'What about the snowy owls?'

Before I could reply, a loud shout in a wild tongue came from behind us. We turned.

Across the fen, a large, pure white bird was flying towards us. It gave a shrill, piercing scream. We stared. But a bloodstained Jack Dooley gave another whoop of delight. As the bird flew to him and landed on his shoulder he crooned to it, caressing it and smiling across at us with bright eyes.

'It's my Cocky! Cocky has come home again. Where have you been hiding him all this time?'

27. - Truth Will Out

We were waiting expectantly on the pavement outside Big Cottage when the doctor emerged. To our surprise, Wilfred walked down the path with him.

There was a mild cheer from the bystanders as Wilfred emerged. He accepted the adulation with a shy grin, but said nothing.

'Hey, doc! That was fast work,' I said. 'Shouldn't he be in bed?'

The doctor, an islander known to all of us, shook his head sadly. 'No, I'm sorry. Wilfred is free to wreak good works on you all again.'

'Can't you even cure his grin?'

'Not without plastic surgery.'

'What happened to the bullet hole?'

'There's a fine dent in the brass collar of his diving suit. But the only medical effect, apart from a nasty bruise, was overheating from being in the suit for too long. I nearly had to operate to get him out of it.'

The doctor stepped into his car and drove away. Wilfred came over to me. 'Are you all right, Timothy?'

'I still feel like the helicopter landed on me, but that's all. Er - Wilfred?'

He waited expectantly. 'Yes?'

'I owe you an apology. Colonel Wayne has explained the conversation I overheard. Perhaps you *are* turning a shade of green, after all, even if you still believe in using a few chemicals.'

He frowned. 'We need them used with wisdom and precision, and in much smaller quantities. But we cannot stop using chemicals entirely, Timothy. Quite simply, feeding us all without them would take far more land than we have.'

'Organic farming would *preserve* the world around us.'

'It would not. It would mean we should have to plough up every last scrap of it.'

'We must try. It's immoral not to.'

'It's immoral to let people starve. If intensive farming was abandoned, half the world would go hungry.'

I spluttered. 'That's outrageous!'

'By the time you were my age, it would be far worse. Without even the bare minimum of chemicals, we should have to drain and plough up not only your nature reserve, but most others also, and fell all our woodlands, in Third World fashion.'

'I'd like to see you try!'

Jessica, at my side, gave a whimsical smile. 'Darling, you and your uncle sound like the two halves of a totally split personality.'

Wilfred eyed her pensively. 'Say, rather, that our points of view may be the two the world has to reconcile... But there are many other factors, I know, like making our diets less wasteful - have you ever tried dandelion coffee? - and making distribution more fair. But I do not believe God created chemistry for it to be a tool only of evil. Nevertheless, I am as sorry as you are, that I will not now be allowed to bring about a serious reduction in the House Farm's chemical use.'

I snarled. 'Dandelion coffee? Ugh! But abolition is what you mean, not reduction.'

My uncle fixed me with a steely eye. 'I may have become more environmentally conscious, nephew, but I have no intention of joining you in becoming scientifically unconscious. Economic reality, lad - we can't eat weeds.'

I sulked. 'Unconscious? Hah. My mind is as logical and open as yours.'

'Good. Then it won't be long before you become acquainted with the Creator as well as the Creation.'

'I said open, not gullible.' I waited for Wilfred to react and take the bait. To my surprise, he declined.

'As the Bible puts it, Timothy, I am a *fool for Christ*. That's my life. And it is nothing to do with my agricultural views - our places on that could easily be reversed. But it happens to be my life. Your life is your own - you must be a fool for whoever or whatever you will.'

'I make my own mind up. No-one influences me.'

'Even if that were really true, of you or anyone, you would still have the seeds of ruin in you. I see now that there are many ways in which we mistreat the earth, and that there are practices that even Christians - perhaps especially Christians - need to change. But no green movement can save the earth, let alone the human soul. Only in Jesus is there a future and a hope for us - and, most importantly, for you.'

I shook my head. 'You'll never give up, will you?'

He was about to answer when there came a sudden hail of greeting. We turned. Mike and his twitchers, packed up, were clearly en route for the ferry at last. I waved them to a halt immediately.

'Thanks, lads. What changed your minds? We thought you'd gone.'

'Couldn't leave you in the lurch.' Mike grinned. 'We checked the ferry bookings and found the eggers were booked to leave on the same ferry as ourselves. We were sat on the quay waiting when we saw them drive away from the Harbour Inn and head inland. We guessed something was up - that they were planning a raid and a quick getaway. We ran all the way up the West Ridge to find them.'

'And we're glad you did!' I shook hands with all the twitchers within reach. 'Thanks, all of you.'

'What will happen to the eggers?' asked someone. 'Will they get off with a tiny fine like they usually do?'

I laughed. 'They won't even be charged with egging. As Sergeant Farquhar pointed out, that's the one thing they didn't do. But we won't be seeing them for a long time. Our police will throw the book at them and if it misses, the USAF will be probably extradite them.'

Wilfred shook Mike's hand too. 'Thanks from me. But what's next for you? Is it time to go for the belted kingfisher and the yellow-bellied sapsucker?'

'No. They're both busted. The kingfisher has belted off again and the sapsucker was just a dirty woodpecker.'

'So what will you all do now?'

'There's always something out there.' Mike pulled out his electronic pager. 'The griff is that there is a big peep at Dungeness, and an odd *Acro* on Tresco. Some of the lads are off to Dunge to clean up on the peep and the rest are after the *Acro.*'

Wilfred smiled thoughtfully. 'Really. And what about you?'

'I don't need either.'

'Do you have any plans?'

'Possibly. I've had an offer to work my passage to Tristan da Cunha or else to Costa Rica. Or again, I might do neither. I've been in the bird race a long time: perhaps I should drop out.' He turned to me with a grimace. 'I could go back to quiet old Cheshire and flog my local patch for a bit. Get a job, if I can. Maybe even become a warden. Perhaps my wife might have me back. I miss her a lot and she still sends me texts all the time. There comes a time when you see how little your life has achieved. It makes a birder think...

Then Mike turned back to Wilfred, an inquiring look on his face. 'Say, while I think about it, what was that saying you quoted me the other day again? The one about eagles - you said it was very old?'

Wilfred smiled again. 'It is old. In fact, it's from the Bible:

'They that wait upon the Lord shall renew their strength;
they shall mount up with wings as eagles; they shall run, and
not be weary; and they shall walk, and not faint.'

'I like that.' Mike smiled. '"*Like eagles,*" eh? There's nothing soars as well as an eagle in a thermal. Perhaps I should start reading the Bible, too. Anyway, cheers again.'

Mike gave Wilfred a crunching handshake, then turned to me.

'Mike?' I said, 'I've been meaning to ask you. I've been right through the bird field guide and I still can't guess. What sort of rare bird is an LBJ?'

He chuckled. 'In Twitcherspeak? I thought you would have known that. LBJs aren't rare - we see them all the time. If the bird looks interesting but we have no idea what it is - it might be just a sparrow - then we call it a Little Brown Job.'

I laughed. Mike started down the street. Then he turned his head. 'By the way, Mr. Warden? Are you aware you have an escaped–'

'Sulphur-crested cockatoo on the Reserve? Yes, we knew!'

He chuckled again and was gone. As he disappeared, a familiar black Volkswagen rolled up the street. A couple of carloads of muscular uniformed types followed. We strolled a few yards to meet the convoy. Colonel Wayne jumped out of the Volkswagen by Little Cottage and greeted us warmly.

'How are the heroes?'

I grinned. 'There's nothing wrong with us that we would admit to; except for a lack of snowy owl eggs.'

He laughed. 'Can't do anything about that, I'm afraid. But at least we have all our detectors back. That gets us back to square one, at least. And it might get you both medals if I can swing it for you. But I wish I knew where our missing secret cargo has hidden itself.'

Wilfred nodded. 'I found every sort of litter on the Reserve,' he said, 'except for what we wanted. It's amazing what there is lying around the island - and the uses it can be put to. Islanders are natural scavengers. We can make all sorts of things from rubbish. Take Timothy's new gateposts, for example…'

Wilfred stepped across the pavement and gave one of my posts a casual prod with his toe. A small piece of black paint flaked off, revealing the original orange. We both smiled at Colonel Wayne, waiting for him to concur. But he did not.

The intelligence officer gazed at the orange scar. Then he took in the whole of the post. Then he switched to the other post. He looked back and forwards three or four times, his face darkening at each new comparison. He bent forward, reaching out with one trembling finger to touch the dent left by Wilfred's sledgehammer. When he raised his eyes, they were wide and still getting wider.

'These *aren't* - I mean, I don't *believe* you - ah, you *couldn't* have…?'

His voice tailed away. Wilfred and I looked at each other. Rather rapidly, we became aware that we were ourselves under observation. In fact, we had become objects of great interest to enough bulky, irate young Americans to make us feel very observed indeed.

■   ■   ■   ■

Half an hour later we were both in very much lower spirits. We still stood together on the pavement, now surveying two large mounds of soil and a heap of wooden wreckage where once my gate had stood. Gathered around in sympathetic silence were Jessica, Bob, Jamie and Angus.

Across the street came the sound of a snigger. Alice and the Cabal stood there. 'Pity about the medals you were to get, wasn't it? And don't forget, you still owe us the ice creams and we still have that recording…'

I strode over to the girls. At the expression on my face they shrank back, with only Alice holding her ground. I fished in my pocket and held out five pound coins. *'The music player,'* I ground out.

Rosalind took the coins, counted and bit them, and looked at Alice. Alice scowled, sighed and nodded. The player appeared, passing from Cynthia to Rosalind to Alice to me. Before it reached me the coins had long vanished. Bob took it from my hand, tapped a number of keys, then handed it back.

Alice took a couple of steps forward. 'That's not all!' she hissed anxiously.

I fished in my other pocket. Down at the bottom I found a soft, crumbling lump.

A solitary comforting thought struck me. 'These were the trousers I was wearing when I fell in the West Burn,' I said conversationally. I held out my hand and Alice cupped hers expectantly. The dough-like lump fell into them. She stared down at it. I grinned. 'The autograph wasn't very legible anyway.'

Alice was still reeling when there came a gentle call down the street. 'Timothy? Have you a moment?' It was Martha. 'I was just taking some fresh flowers to the chapel when I saw two little birds like that one I saw before. They're very pretty, whatever they are. They hardly seem afraid of me, at all.'

'There aren't many sorts of birds that would come that close to people. And most that would are common, or else very unusual. But yes, I've plenty of time, Martha.' I plodded up the street after her. The others followed curiously.

■　■　■　■

As we walked round the chapel to the marsh side, a stench of fresh paint assailed us. When we reached the low wall overlooking the marsh the smell became almost overpowering. Our eyes followed our noses. To our right, the wall gave way to a tall wooden fence. The long stretch of fence overlooking the marsh had all been scarlet; but the first part of it had already changed colour. Wielding a paintbrush eagerly was a wiry, active-looking lady whose hair, done up in a bun, was exactly the same hue as Jessica's.

Jessica waved. 'Hello, Mummy,' she said.

'Hello, dear,' cried the lady. 'I know the fence has only been scarlet for a fortnight, but I couldn't resist changing it back again. I *did* so like that lovely shade of yellow it was before.'

We turned our eyes from the ghastly sight and examined the marsh below the wall. On a little pool, only a stone's throw from the busy Mrs. Bull, a tiny creature the length of my hand commanded our attention. It had a needle-like bill, slate-grey upper-parts, a white throat with bright orange-red sides and a repertoire of little twittering sounds. The incredibly dainty little bird paddled round in circles.

As we watched, a second bird, less brightly coloured, joined it. The fairy-like creatures spun round in circles like clockwork toys. They looked up at us, twittered to each other, then lifted and flickered to another, even nearer pool. Then as though by magic they vanished: for minutes we were left with only our memories as we searched the green shade of rush and weed. Then the first bird appeared again, elfin and mysterious as ever.

Bob glanced across to the chameleon-effect fence. 'How *yellow* the place is,' he murmured. 'We've been walking past it the whole time.'

I nodded. Jessica squeezed my hand. I gave her a tired smile. 'Yes. They are very unusual little creatures. Those are the *other* rare birds from Fetlar. It wasn't snowy owls we should have been looking for, but Lifandoy's first red-necked phalaropes. Keith's secret was safe all the time.'

Jess and I exchanged a kiss. We both knew it was a moment we would remember for a long time. We were not alone in our knowledge. On my other side Wilfred and Martha were standing together, arm in arm. Wilfred had an entranced expression. He met my eyes. 'Timothy, I think this completes my little change of heart at least, even if we have to wait for *your* conversion.'

I snorted and glanced at Martha. She also was gazing at Jessica and me. But Martha said nothing. Her eyes were hard to meet. For a moment, I felt Martha was smiling less at us than at two people she could not see - that she was seeing two very different people she believed this young couple would one day become. I frowned. Fond as I was of Martha, I was not at all sure I liked the future she seemed to see.

Wilfred turned back to the phalaropes. 'Have you ever seen anything more beautiful?'

I agreed. 'No. Not even my new gateposts were as good as this.'

Wilfred laughed and put his other arm around my shoulders. 'It's a pity about your gateposts. But you can be grateful for one thing. In my new job, I shall be much less busy. When you repair your gate, you will find I shall have plenty of time to come and help.'

And he grinned, broadly.

THE END

The next in the Lifandoy series:

An Orchid on Lifandoy

Another story in the lives of Tim and Jessica begins with a mysterious tragedy and a spectacular accident.

The tragedy involves an exceptionally rare flower. The location of a beautiful wild Lady's Slipper Orchid, found growing on the island, is hidden in a coded message. But what dark event has silenced its sender; and who is racing in an expensive powerboat toward Lifandoy?

By chance, a different ORCHID, an experimental rescue rocket, is due to be tested at sea that day. A dramatic accident leads to urgent searches for both "orchids" across the small island. Tim and Jessica become involved in both, while Tim's dangerously helpful Uncle Wilfred, Jessica's scheming young sisters Alice and Rosalind, plus some of Tim's former drinking cronies and the invasion of Lifandoy by the Press, all add complications. More serious problems for Tim are a clash with ruthless farmer Graham Fytts, and the arrival of murky international politics on quiet Lifandoy.

Tim struggles to explain the evil behind such threats. Meanwhile Jessica, reading her lost old Bible, her only memento of him, discovers a series of women in its pages whose lives seem to have a strange echo in her own. What do they have to do with the loss of her father's lifeboat, and her relationship with the new lifeboat's crew?

Finally, will the desperate searches locate either of the "orchids" in time? Will Jessica's sharp brains lead to a great discovery and defeat their enemy? Could Alice's mischief, Uncle Wilfred's good deed and Jessica's bravery combine to save the day? And where *is* that rocket, after all?

From Lulu or more details from www.hillintheway.co.uk